EXILES AND CITIZENS
Spanish Republicans in Mexico

Latin American Monographs, No. 29
Institute of Latin American Studies
The University of Texas at Austin

EXILES AND CITIZENS

Spanish Republicans in Mexico

By PATRICIA W. FAGEN

PUBLISHED FOR THE *Institute of Latin American Studies*
BY THE UNIVERSITY OF TEXAS PRESS · AUSTIN AND LONDON

Library of Congress Cataloging in Publication Data

Fagen, Patricia W   1940–
   Exiles and citizens

   (Latin American monographs, no. 29)
   Bibliography: p.
   1. Spaniards in Mexico. 2. Spain—History—Civil
War, 1936–1939—Refugees. I. Title. II. Series:
Latin American monographs (Austin, Tex.) no. 29.
F1392.S7F3   301.45′16′1072   72-3781
ISBN 0-292-72002-5

Composition by G&S Typesetters, Austin
Printing by Capital Printing Company, Austin
Binding by Universal Bookbindery, Inc., San Antonio

Preface

The creation of the Second Spanish Republic in 1931 marked the culmination of the hopes of generations of Spain's most enlightened sectors. The vanguard of Spanish liberalism and republicanism, the leaders, and the ideas for nearly all the reformist movements of the nineteenth and twentieth centuries were centered in the nation's cultural elite. The intellectual sectors not only developed the theories upon which the Republic eventually was based, but a large portion of the intellectuals were active in the forefront of opposition movements against the Church, the Monarchy, and, finally, the dictatorship of Miguel Primo de Rivera in the 1920's. Believing in the social commitment of the educated classes, they founded and supported liberal and reformist political parties, established regional nationalist parties, and often joined the Spanish Socialist party.

Despite the high level of political consciousness among Spanish intellectual and professional groups, however, most were inadequately prepared to deal with the social and political crises which emerged during the Republic and the Civil War. Because they were a cultural elite, they tended to rely a great deal on education and reform to solve problems which some in Spain wished to solve through social revolution, and others were determined not to change at all.

With the outbreak of the Civil War, in 1936, intellectual and cultural life and academic organization were disrupted. A significant portion of the intellectual and generally well-educated sectors of Spanish society were able to escape into exile, nearly destroying intellectual life in Spain for a century thereafter. The country to which most of them came was Mexico. Thus, when Spanish cultural life first revived again after the Civil War, it was no longer centered in Madrid, but rather in Mexico City.

The Spanish exiles of 1939, without ceasing to be a part of Spanish history, became also a factor in Mexican history. For Spain they remained part of a long, liberal, and at times radical tradition, a tradition which died only temporarily upon their defeat and flight. The dilemma for the Spanish exiles was that, having once fought for their political and social ideals in Spain, they left and thus ceased to play an active role in Spanish events. In Mexico they found a political and social system that seemed to incorporate many of the same ideals that had inspired the Republic in Spain. Because they were not native-born citizens, however, they had little or no creative part to play in Mexican political development.

The Republican refugees were able to work in Mexico, and their skills contributed significantly to Mexican economic and intellectual progress. But outside the economic and professional realms, Mexico was only partly effective as a "melting pot" for the Republicans. Over the years the exiles, especially in the older groups, have continued to be psychologically torn by the intensity of their loyalty to Spain, both as their homeland and as the political ideal for which they went into exile, and their loyalty to Mexico, which for so long has been their adopted country. While they look back to Spain in terms of subjective identification, they have strong economic, professional, and familial ties which are Mexican.

As suggested above, this book will deal primarily with the intellectuals and the professionals in the Spanish migration. In referring to intellectuals, I am applying the term fairly broadly to include both those who characterize themselves as "intellectual" and, in general, those who have earned all or part of their livelihood by writing, teaching, or working in related cultural fields. At times reference is made to "prominent intellectuals," a term intended to apply to the few dozen individuals who acquired international reputations in their fields before emigrating to Mexico. Many of these individuals were specifically invited to come to Mexico in 1938 to participate in the Casa de España. Persons termed "professionals" include those working in medicine, law, journalism, publishing, banking and finance, administration, and other such occupations. The intellectuals and professionals have been singled out for attention because, as a group, they have profoundly affected academic and cultural life in Mexico, and because they have organized and supported the wide variety of Spanish associations through which Republican Spain has survived institutionally in exile. Furthermore, the general problem of an educated elite in political exile is of increasing interest and relevance in today's politically tumultuous world.

It is inadequate in this case merely to extend thanks to the Spanish exiles and Mexican informants who aided me in this project.[1] The story is, after all, essentially theirs. As the author I have at times done little more than supply a format for the presentation of their attitudes and ideas. I thus feel a far greater sense of responsibility and concern for the individuals about whom I have written in this monograph than a historian normally feels toward projects based primarily on research in libraries and archives. The people whose story I have told participated in its writing to the extent of taking considerable time to respond to my many questions, helping me to understand the dynamics of their situation, inviting me into their homes, and allowing me to share in their community activities. I only hope that I have repaid them for their participation by treating the subject matter in an accurate and a sensitive manner.

My thanks also go to El Colegio de México for having extended to me the use of their facilities as a visiting scholar. Finally, I would like to express my gratitude to Professor John J. Johnson and

---

[1] A list of Spaniards and Mexicans interviewed appears in the Appendix. They are mentioned individually in footnotes when the text specifically depends on their information and impressions. (In repeating statements and reviewing Spanish criticism of Mexico, I do not include the names of interviewees who have asked to remain anonymous.)

to my husband, Professor Richard R. Fagen, who read and criticized this manuscript in various stages of its development and whose comments and suggestions enabled me to carry on with my work.

PATRICIA W. FAGEN

Contents

EXILES AND CITIZENS

Spanish Republicans in Mexico

1. THE SPANISH REPUBLIC

There was singing in the streets and great exultation when King Alfonso XIII abandoned his throne and the Second Spanish Republic was proclaimed. Spaniards celebrated the end of what they considered to be a decadent monarchy, supported by a top-heavy military and a reactionary church hierarchy. The liberals and Socialists, syndical leaders, and intellectuals who assumed the governance of Spain in April, 1931, were confident that their rule would prove better and more just than that of any previous government. The aim of Spain's new, popularly elected leaders was no less than a "peaceful revolution," one which would turn the country into a modern democracy and raise the economic, social, and cultural standard of living for all the people.[1] Five years later,

[1] For various views in English treating the period immediately preceding the declaration of the Republic, see Gabriel Jackson, *The Spanish Republic and the Civil War, 1931–1939*, pp. 1–7, 24–25; Gerald Brenan, *Spanish Labyrinth: An*

as a result of political naiveté, international events, and substantial bad luck, the Second Spanish Republic was plunged into a civil war which ended in its permanent defeat.

The initial enthusiasm which greeted the Spanish Republic of 1931 only temporarily masked the widely divergent and sometimes incompatible goals of its supporters and participants. During the Republic, as often before in Spanish history, political, social, regional, and religious differences made effective government extremely difficult. Precisely because the new government, more than any previous regime, opened the political arena to broad popular participation, it suffered the direct consequences of the historic and conflicting aspirations and demonstrations of discontent from all sectors of Spanish society.

The Republic was handicapped both by its composition and by the urgency and complexity of the problems with which it had to cope. First, as a government composed predominantly of middle-class elements in a country where the middle class was always small and isolated, the Republican leaders could not easily retain the loyalty of a variegated population. Second, because the government was liberal rather than revolutionary, it chose to work slowly for limited objectives in the face of problems which many Spaniards believed called for extreme solutions. Also because of its liberalism, the new leadership was reluctant to restrict the civil liberties even of those who refused to accept the legitimacy of Republican institutions.

The three major problems which stood in the way of Republican unity were regional nationalism, popular radicalism, and the continued influence (and opposition) of church, military, and aristocracy. With the first of these the government dealt relatively effectively and generously; cultural and even political autonomy for Catalans and Basques was duly recognized and these provinces were incorporated into the Republic largely on their own terms. In response to the second problem, the government broadened its political base, but still never submitted to the revolutionary social demands of the working classes; failure to solve the third problem, or

Account of the Social and Political Background of the Civil War, chap. 5; Hugh Thomas, *The Spanish Civil War*, pp. 17–18; Salvador de Madariaga, *Spain: A Modern History*, pp. 361–377; Rafael de Altamira, *A History of Spain: From the Beginning to the Present Day*, translated by Muna Lee, chap. 14.

set of problems, brought about the Civil War, and in the end destroyed the Republic. During the Civil War, a fourth problem arose which further divided the Republican defense: the internationalization of the Spanish struggle, and the consequent intervention of the Soviet Union and the Spanish Communist party on the Republican side.

Despite the fact that the masses rallied to the defense of the Republic when it was attacked in 1936, disunity and dissatisfaction with the government persisted and even increased during the Civil War (1936–1939). Among the Republican leaders, virtually all of whom believed in democratic principles, in progress, and in reform, there were, nonetheless, unresolvable differences on issues of military organization and wartime strategy. Among the popular classes who fought for, but in large part were unrepresented in, the Republican government, there was even less consensus. Ideological conflicts and bitter personal competition among partisans of the Republic had reached crisis proportions before the end of the Civil War and, after defeat, they contributed to the complexity, the disunity, but also the idealism which characterized exile life in Mexico, France, and the other countries to which the defeated Spaniards fled.

The thousands of Spaniards who fled the country in 1939 shared the sorrows and bitterness of lost idealism and defeat. The events which had uprooted them physically affected their world view and gave them a common though partial political identity. Nevertheless, there was little agreement among them as to the cause of their tragedy or the course to follow in defeat. In exile the refugees continued to argue political issues not yet resolved, hoping that the Franco government would fall, and they would have a second chance. The issues which had divided them before and during the war emerged over and over again in exile, constantly debated, but never resolved.

Regional nationalism, which had increased in vitality during the Republic, was preserved in exile, sometimes more strongly held than Republican loyalties. Working-class Anarchists and Socialists, whose revolutionary aims had never been acceptable to Republican liberals, continued in exile to criticize the former government's failure to enact meaningful social change. They further censured the Republican leaders for having "sold out" the Civil War to the Com-

munist party and the Soviet Union. The church, the military, and
the aristocracy managed more successfully than the Republicans to
unite under the banner of their Spanish Falange and Francisco
Franco, and, with a little help from their German and Italian
friends, they won the war Civil War. Thereafter, the Franco regime persecuted the remaining Republicans in Spain, almost totally
destroyed existing political parties and syndicates, and severely re-
stricted regional-cultural activity. The associations purged in Spain
were kept alive in exile, but rivalries among Republican groups
served to divide the refugees. Further hostility and division among
the refugees over the issue of the role of the Communist party made
united exile action against Franco's government impossible.

The story told in the following chapters is not about Spain, nor
specifically about the Second Spanish Republic or the Civil War. It
is concerned with the group of exiles, forced to leave their homeland because they—or persons close to them—fought in the name
of the Spanish Republic and lost. The story begins after defeat, but
it cannot be told without reference to, and understanding of, its
historical origins. Thus we shall briefly review in the Republican
past the series of events and confrontations which so dramatically
shaped the lives of these Spaniards and forced them to live out their
lives as political exiles.

The Character of the Government: Problems and Accomplishments

The 1931 elections to the Spanish Cortes were undoubtedly the
most honest elections in Spanish history, but the situation of the
Republican government was at all times precarious. Its leaders
were the politically moderate and leftist sectors of the middle class,
including prominent Reformist intellectuals, Socialist theoreticians,
and advocates of limited regional autonomy. Manuel Azaña, the
first prime minister of the Republic, represented perfectly the character of the new government. An intellectual, a writer and lawyer,
he had for years supported the Reform party,[2] a group which was
middle class in its constituency and which had espoused constitutional monarchy, more democratic elections, social, administrative,

[2] Juan J. Linz, "The Party System of Spain, Past and Future," in *Party Systems and Voter Alignments: Cross National Perspectives*, edited by S. M. Lipset
and S. Rokkan, pp. 217–218.

and especially educational reforms. The liberals, moderate Socialists, and independents composing the First Constituent Cortes were, like Azaña, predominantly members of the middle class. They took seriously their responsibility for attacking the major problems of the country, and, from the first, they devoted their energies to creating conditions for progress and reform in Spain. They did not, however, consider moving in the direction of revolutionary social change, which was the goal of important sectors of the Spanish populace not participating in the government.[3] The prime minister and his deputies, many of whom had little or no previous legislative experience, had to effect a political platform that would appease the lower-class radicals and satisfy regional nationalists without unduly offending the pro-Monarchist factions who were in the opposition from the beginning.

In its first two years, the Republican government moved toward the accomplishment of much of the legislation the reformers had been advocating for more than two centuries. After long debate, Azaña was able to push through a statute granting Catalonia the status of an autonomous state within the Spanish Republic. Although only partially fulfilling the aspirations of the Catalan separatists and criticized by unitary centralist Republicans, the compromise statute did sufficiently reconcile Catalan cultural nationalists to gain for the Madrid government the loyalty of this wealthy and and modern province.[4]

The most serious economic issue facing the Republic was the need for land reform, a problem recognized since the eighteenth century, but with which no government had effectively dealt.[5] The

[3] This is attested by José Ortega y Gasset, in *Rectificación de la República: Artículos y discursos*, and by De Madariaga, in *Spain*. Both writers were enthusiastic supporters of the original Republic but grew increasingly disillusioned as the radical demands of the masses forced the government from its mildly reformist orientation. See also José Gaos, *Confesiones profesionales*, p. 112.

[4] Brenan, *Spanish Labyrinth*, p. vii, and Jackson, *Spanish Republic*, pp. 27, 72–76. Basque nationalism was less satisfactorily resolved and became a serious issue later in 1934 (Jackson, *Spanish Republic*, pp. 140–143).

[5] For a discussion of the history of the Spanish agrarian situation, see Brenan, *Spanish Labyrinth*, chap. 4; Raymond Carr, *Spain, 1808–1939*, pp. 417–419. Spanish liberals in the nineteenth century had decided that the way to combat the feudalistic aspects of land tenure was to sell village land and Church common lands. This policy had the unfortunate consequences of depriving village agriculture of its sustenance and enlarging the rural proletariat. The land situation in the twentieth century was considerably worse than it had been in the eight-

Republican minister of labor, Socialist Francisco Largo Caballero, attempted to organize the growing numbers of landless peasants, and some legislation which would improve the position of small holders vis-à-vis the large landed estates was passed by the Cortes. For the first time in anyone's memory, the politicians in Madrid paid sincere attention to village needs. Nevertheless, when the comprehensive agrarian law finally was passed in September, 1932, it was overly legalistic and inadequate to the problem.[6] The law succeeded mainly in demonstrating the government's good will, but in the meantime agrarian conflict and dissatisfaction persisted.

In the area of educational reform, Republican enthusiasm was unbounded, and a vast program of new school building was initiated at once. In its educational policy, the government enjoyed the widest popular support. Free public secular education had been a long-time goal of both middle-class liberals and working-class radicals.[7] Although financial pressures eventually curtailed school construction projects, the expansion and improvement of educational facilities remained a major Republican goal.

In order to guarantee the predominant role of the state in education, and effectively to transform Spain into a modern democratic republic, the government judged it essential to reduce the strength and influence of the bulwarks of tradition, the church and the military. Article No. 26 of the 1931 Constitution declared the church separate from the state, eliminated it from public education, and limited the clergy in a variety of their activities. Official anticlerical legislation, coupled with a rash of church burnings by mobs shortly after the proclamation of the Republic, won for the new government the condemnation of the church hierarchy. Thus the largest

---

eenth and nineteenth centuries. The new government, however, feared the effects of a truly radical land-reform program (Jackson, *Spanish Republic*, pp. 85, 169–170; Carr, *Spain*, pp. 611–613).

[6] Jackson, *Spanish Republic*, pp. 78–84.

[7] The middle-class liberals already in Madrid and Barcelona had established a few progressive schools, independent of and contrary to the wishes of the Church. The working classes within both the Anarchist and Socialist syndicates operated special programs for literacy and general education for the benefit of their members (Brenan, *Spanish Labyrinth*, pp. 165–166, 219–220). Free public secular education was perhaps much too basic a goal, according to Spanish poet Dionisio Ridruejo, looking on the accomplishments of the Republic. He criticizes the intellectual and liberal leaders for having placed nearly all their hopes for progress on educational reform (*Escrito en España*, p. 54).

and most influential institution in Spain moved from distrust to open opposition.[8] In 1932 certain structural changes were made in the army, the navy, and the civil guard in order to re-form the top-heavy military establishments. The military had been the major bulwark of the Monarchy, and only a minority of the officers had publicly declared their full allegiance to the Republic. Even they bitterly resented the efforts to limit military size and influence. As the church had, the military blamed official government policies for instances of popular violence against officers. Declaring that the country was descending into anarchy, a small group of generals in the summer of 1932 attempted a coup d'état against Azaña's ministry. The first attempt was easily defeated, but the next time the generals rose, in 1936, they succeeded in bringing the country to civil war.

Economic difficulties, stemming both from Republican policies and from the effects of the international depression, plus increasing political polarization and violence from aroused factions of both the Left and the Right, urban and rural, countered the effectiveness of government reforms and diminished popular confidence in Republican rule. The deputies of the Cortes and the cabinet ministers, who were not as a rule professional politicians, tended to respond too slowly or too timidly to crisis situations, and Prime Minister Azaña, despite his intellectual gifts and idealism, did not function well as a popular leader.[9] In the elections of 1933 the ruling center-left lost its majority to political groups which, although not opposed to the republican form of government, were considerably to the right of the Azaña ministry. The defeat of the moderate and progressive Republican elements was brought about by the electoral

[8] A noted Spanish historian, also a refugee, António Ramos Oliveira, considers the failure of the Republic to have been due to Article 26 more than to any other single cause; he regards as totally unrealistic the liberal tradition of interpreting all Spanish problems in terms of anticlericalism (Ramos Oliveira, *Historia de España*). A great number of refugees, most of whom are anticlerical themselves, feel that the Republican government should have allowed the church to retain more of its privileges, or, alternatively, should have been ready to defend the provisions of the constitution with force, as did the Mexicans in their revolution. Jackson, on the other hand, considers the legislation altogether reasonable and states that its effects were greatly exaggerated, both inside and outside Spain (*Spanish Republic*, pp. 60–62).

[9] Juan Marichal, "Prefacio general," in *Obras completas*, by Manuel Azaña, edited by Juan Marichal.

abstention and disaffection of Anarchists and other radical groups, and by the increased voting strength of Catholic and conservative elements.[10] The newly elected Cortes was intent on curbing and controlling radical working-class and peasant groups whose activities, many Spaniards felt, threatened national security.

POLARIZATION

Prior to the Civil War the working classes were represented by two trade unions, the Socialist Unión General de Trabajo (UGT) and the larger Anarchist Confederación Nacional de Trabajo (CNT), both of which had developed their ideological position and expanded their influence in the late nineteenth century. Each was divided into moderate and more revolutionary factions, with the latter tending to dominate in times of crisis. Both groups reluctantly lent their support to the establishment of the Republic, but continued to agitate for revolutionary rather than purely reformist change.

The Anarchists, in particular, neither participated in, nor saw any of their aspirations realized by, the bourgeois Republican government, and within a short time they were working to undermine its authority. The peasants in southern Spain, especially in Andalusia, had a long history of Anarchist uprisings, beginning almost a century before the Republic; since the libertarian ideal for which these peasants fought was far from what was offered them by the new government, the uprisings continued.[11] By the early twentieth century, anarchism was also the strongest force in the urban syndicates, especially in Catalonia.

Although there were Socialists who supported and participated in the Republican government, these tended to be intellectuals and members of the bourgeoisie. The Socialists who were members of the Socialist workers' syndicate, the UGT, favored far more radical objectives than did their leaders in the Cortes. Such middle-class party moderates as Professor Julián Besteiro and Indalecio Prieto, who led the party, were frequently at odds with the revolutionary

---

[10] Women, who tended to be more vulnerable to the advice of Catholic priests, voted for the first time in 1933, often for conservative candidates.

[11] Ridruejo, *Escrito en España*, pp. 178–182; E. J. Hobsbawm, *Primitive Rebels: Studies in the Forms of Social Movements in the Nineteenth and Twentieth Centuries*, pp. 89ff.

aims of the UGT, which represented the mass of Socialist voters. Francisco Largo Caballero, the leader of the UGT and the first minister of labor for the Republic, was a man of working-class origin who was radical and sometimes revolutionary in his aims. Like the Anarchists, he and the UGT workers were more concerned with direct action than with political theories of government.

Neither the peasant uprisings nor the syndicalist strikes which had plagued the Monarchy and the dictatorship disappeared during the Republic. Both workers and peasants distrusted the mild reformism of the government and rejected the slow and legalistic methods of parliamentary politics. Therefore, from the outset, the Republican government had to use a certain amount of force in order to maintain its authority, although it was evident from the first that too much force would deprive the government of the support of the masses. This was precisely the effect of the policies of the government elected in 1933.

The upper classes, much of the church hierarchy, and most of the military, who would not accept the Republic as the legitimate government of Spain, found in every indication of its weakness greater reason to organize themselves to bring it down. Disaffection among rightist sectors culminated in the formation in October, 1933, of the Spanish Fascist party, the Falange, which attracted devout Catholics who were drawn to its traditionalist, religious ideology, as well as rightists who admired Italian and German fascism and wished to establish a corporate state in Spain. Disillusionment on the Left reached its peak with an October, 1934, revolt of Socialists, Anarchists, and separatists throughout Spain. In the mining area of Asturias, the revolt almost succeeded, and the brutal manner in which the conservative government (elected in 1933) put down the workers and revolutionaries there swung public opinion toward the more radical parties. Popular reaction against the repression of the Asturians led to the election of a number of younger, radical candidates, who united in a popular front government in February, 1936.[12]

---

[12] See descriptions of the October Asturian Revolution in Jackson, *Spanish Republic*, pp. 144–161; Thomas, *Spanish Civil War*, pp. 79–85; Carr, *Spain*, pp. 232–235; Brenan, *Spanish Labyrinth*, pp. 284–289. Manuel Azaña feared the effect of government by the leftists elected to the Popular Front; although presi-

The Popular Front, although more broadly based than any previous government had been, could not halt the polarization to the Right and Left within the general population and more especially among the youth. Nor was the new government any more successful than the old in defining its social and economic policy, or in dealing consistently with opposition groups. In 1936 nobody knew which of the dozens of factions and interest groups could be counted on to remain loyal to the Republic, and few in Spain conceived of a future without violence.

THE CIVIL WAR AND POPULAR REACTION

The Civil War in Spain was initiated by a military uprising in Morocco, followed by garrison revolts throughout the rest of the Republic and the invasion of southern Spain by the rebellious Moroccan troops on July 18, 1936. Initially, the dissident officers knew they could count on substantial support from Monarchists, Fascists, and most of the conservative, Catholic Right, groups which either had never accepted the Republic or had grown distrustful of it soon after its inception. The uprising of the officers won for the rebels about a third of Spain, but, throughout most of the country, common soldiers, local civilian authorities, and citizens generally resisted the attack. Republican defense was most successful where trade-union organization and leadership supported established civil authority and led the popular resistance to the military coup.[13]

The Republic did not fall in a few days, as the generals had hoped, and in the places where rebel forces, concentrated under

---

dent of the Republic during the Popular Front, his political significance declined thereafter (Marichal, "Los Designios españoles de Manuel Azaña," in Azaña, *Obras completas*, p. xxxviii).

[13] The political parties of the Left and the trade unions, or syndicates, resisted most strongly and were responsible for the failure of the military uprisings in the areas where the syndicates were a significant force. The resistance might have been successful had not the central government been hesitant about arming the leftists and revolutionaries, fearing that the same arms would be next used against the government itself. The government still feared, with good reason, a proletarian revolution on the left almost as much as a military rebellion on the right (Thomas, *The Spanish Civil War*, pp. 131–144). According to Julio Alvarez del Vayo, the people had formed their militias and were prepared to fight long before the government was capable of instructing them (*Freedom's Battle*, pp. 24ff). Alvarez del Vayo held a number of posts in the Republic and was an especially close associate of Juan Negrín, later the Republican prime minister.

the leadership of Francisco Franco,[14] were not immediately successful, popular militias were organized to defend the government. Although the proletariat, radical youth, regional nationalists, and civil authorities almost unanimously opposed the military uprisings,[15] these groups could not all be expected to remain loyal and fully obedient to the central authorities in Madrid.

Anarchists in the rural villages of Andalusia and Aragon or in the urban factories of Catalonia did not fight to save the Republic. They saw in the outbreak of the Civil War the opportunity to create their own long-awaited revolution. Private land was seized and run communally by various villages; factories were wrested from their owners and run by committees of workers.[16] Anarchist-CNT militias would accept direction only from their local leaders, not from anyone connected with the central authorities. The Catalan-based Trotskyite POUM (Partido Obrero de Unificación Marxista), like the Anarchists, organized and retained the loyalty of its own workers. The Socialists, although well-represented in the Popular Front government, could not easily control the actions of the revolutionary sectors of the UGT. Some groups within the UGT followed the example of the CNT in taking over factories and running them by committees of workers. Central authority, never highly respected in most of Spain, was almost ignored in the early months of the Civil War.[17]

Moreover, the war quickly was internationalized. A few weeks after the July uprising, the military rebels under General Franco

[14] Franco was elected commander in chief of the military leaders in September, 1936 (George Hills, *Franco: The Man and His Nation*, especially pp. 256–257, 279).

[15] An interesting fictionalized treatment of the early days of the war describes how the youth, as well as older men and women of Madrid, left jobs, families, and the normal round of life to rush to Sierra, north of Madrid, to defend their city from attack by the forces of General Mola. Those in the city who did not belong to one of the political parties or to any of the worker-militia groups were sometimes harshly treated (Paulino Masip, *El Diario de Hamlet García*). The novel is interesting also for its account of the involvement of some intellectuals and the gradual politicization of others who had never considered politics worthy of their attention.

[16] See the observations of George Orwell on the Anarchists of Catalonia (*Homage to Catalonia*, pp. 4–5, and chapter 9).

[17] "The workers, through their party and trade-union organizations, became the real rulers of the country and the organizers of the War," asserts Brenan (*Spanish Labyrinth*, p. 317).

were receiving arms, troops, and equipment from the Fascist powers. Britain and France for their own reasons were determined not to become involved, and, as a result, their governments embargoed military equipment badly needed by the Republic. The Soviet Union began to exhibit an interest in Spain, and, during the summer of 1936, sent military equipment and advisers to the Loyalist Azaña government. However, no democratic government save Mexico, whose resources were small, aided the Republican side.

Although the original Republic of 1931 was an example of moderation and liberal democracy, it became fully dependent for its survival in 1936 upon the defense efforts of Anarchists and Socialists within Spain, and upon Soviet aid from outside. Neither the image of Republican liberalism nor the liberals themselves could easily withstand the counterpressures of their own supporters, and the government's plight was worsened with the growing strength of the Soviet-encouraged Spanish Communist party. The next three years saw a civil war within the Civil War as the diverse factions within the Spanish Republic all struggled to assert their political influence and to dictate the direction of policies. Meanwhile all of them were outnumbered in men and supplies in a war to the death against their common enemies.

REPUBLICANS AND THE SOVIET CONTRIBUTION

The Soviet Union sent few organized fighting units to Spain, but it did send a considerable amount of war matériel and, through the Communist party (Comintern) apparatus, it helped to organize and recruit the International Brigade. A number of Russian advisers also went to Spain and attempted to reorganize the Republican military efforts. Before the arrival of these Soviet advisers, the Communist party in Spain had been an insignificant political force, but because of the Russian contribution during the war, the party was quite successful in rallying considerable support from radical Socialists and Spanish youth. The Communists, correctly forecasting the outbreak of a general anti-Fascist war after the Spanish struggle, were intent on forming the broadest possible alliance of democratic and Socialist factions in Spain and throughout Europe. For this reason they were opposed to social revolution in Spain and supported the more conservative bourgeois sectors of the Republican government against the popular revolutionary movements.[18]

Socialists and Republican moderates began to complain shortly after the outset of the war that the youth within their parties were being "corrupted' by Communist influence.[19] In April, 1936, politically active youth in Spain united in a Junta Socialista Unificado (JSU), supposedly a union of the Socialist and Communist groups. The association expanded rapidly during the war, its activities increasingly controlled by the Communists. The members of the JSU, in fact, were not necessarily or even usually doctrinaire Socialists or Communists. Rather, they were radical young people who had little tolerance for what they considered to be the absurdly cautious course being taken by the "bourgeois" leadership of the Republic. The aid and organizational skills of the Soviets, on the other hand, appealed to young activists as the only force dynamic enough to win the war.

The crisis of pre-war violence and polarization, followed by wartime terror, revolution, and the growth in Communist influence, seemed to prove to many that Spain, after all, was not republican, at least not as had been envisioned in 1931. Realizing that the most active and passionate fighters in the Republican defense were not liberal, but radical, not democratic, constitutional reformers, but social revolutionaries, many Spaniards who had been fully committed to the young Republic became disaffected during the war. Intellectuals and liberal politicians (especially where the two groups overlapped) found themselves ignored by the masses they had expected to lead. Disillusioned and unable to adapt to the exigencies of wartime politics, many abandoned the Republic both emotionally and physically.[20]

Those who supported the Communists' influence on the Spanish Republic have claimed that it was primarily their reorganization of the military which made the many Republican victories possible.

[18] See Noam Chomsky, "Objectivity and Liberal Scholarship," in *American Power and the New Mandarins*, p. 81, for a critique of Communist objectives.

[19] Interviews, with Enrique López Sevilla, February 23, 1967, and with Victor Salazar and Dr. Jacinto Segovia, March 4, 1967.

[20] For some who wished to leave, Mexico offered an honorable alternative to remaining. Not all those who left Spain before the end of the war, however, shared the sentiments described above. See chap. 2, below.

The reorganization, however, caused bitterness and division within
the Republican forces, because it threatened Republican integrity
and ran counter to the original bases of resistance. At the time of
the 1936 uprising, popular militias arose to fight the invaders.
These militias were more responsive to their own leadership than
to the central government. Precisely for this reason, in the subsequent Communist-directed reorganization, the centralization of
power, arms distribution, and administrative direction was given
primary importance. The Communist suppression of the dissident
Anarchist and Trotskyite POUM militias was, at times, as brutal
as the suppression of the popular forces by the Fascists themselves.
The CNT resisted the Communists but was defeated; many of its
leaders were punished and deprived of any further role in the war.
Such stern action further alienated a large sector of the population,
severely damaged morale, and made any meaningful popular cooperative effort almost impossible.[21]

By May, 1937, serious cleavages had developed between groups
in Spain supporting the Communist activities on behalf of the Republic and those opposed to all Communist participation. Anarchists, Trotskyists, and regional nationalists consistently opposed the
Communist influence, while Republican and Socialist opinion was
divided. The division was most bitter within the Socialist party,
and the outcome of the Socialist split proved critical for the future
of the Republic as a whole.

The Socialists were in power in Republican Spain from September, 1936, to the end of the war, but in May, 1937, the government
of UGT leader Francisco Largo Caballero was replaced with that
of a physician and intellectual, Juan Negrín. Prior to the war,
Caballero had been known as a radical and had been dubbed the
"Spanish Lenin." Because he was ideologically opposed to the Communist military reorganization and the consequent subordination
of workers' militia, however, the party found him relatively un-

---

[21] The most vivid description of the Communist-Anarchist struggle is to be
found in George Orwell's *Homage to Catalonia*. With a sympathetic view toward the Anarchists and Trotskyists, he describes the punishment they received
from the Communist-controlled regular military whenever they tried to assert
their will. (See especially chap. 11.) Orwell and Chomsky (*American Power
and the New Mandarins*) both blame the Communists for subverting the col-
lectivist measures taken in Anarchist areas and for depriving these areas of
needed military and civilian supplies.

cooperative.[22] Negrín, hitherto associated with the moderate branch of the Socialist party, considered Soviet military aid to the Republic to be vital and therefore was willing to surrender a measure of political independence in order to assure the continuation of that aid. Among Negrín's most controversial acts in this respect was the transfer of a large portion of the gold in the Republican treasury to Russia, as advance payment for Russian help.[23]

Spanish politics thereafter focused on two men: Prime Minister Juan Negrín and the leader of the Socialist party, Indalecio Prieto, both of whom had formally opposed the revolutionary Caballero branch of the Socialist party. When Negrín became prime minister, conditions in the Republic were rapidly worsening, and certain of his ministers grew increasingly pessimistic regarding the chances for victory. Negrín's minister of defense, Socialist leader Indalecio Prieto, was most outspoken in his defeatism. Prieto became unofficial leader of an important group of Socialists and Republicans who favored peace negotiations with Franco over continued resistance and who wished to reduce the presence of the Communist party in the government.

The Communists, watching Prieto's influence grow, were determined to oust him from his important military post. Soviet material aid was suddenly drastically reduced. Negrín understood what was required, and Prieto was removed. Negrín, however, had his own reasons for wishing to relieve Prieto of his post. Defeatism in the minister of defense hardly seemed appropriate, and its effect on the war effort was demoralizing. Negrín already had attempted to initiate peace negotiations with Franco, but Franco was unwilling to grant any political guarantees to the Loyalists. Fearing the severity

[22] In order to unite the Left, Largo Caballero had been named prime minister in September, 1936.

[23] The worth of the gold was estimated by Alfonso Ayensa, an economist and then vice president of the Ateneo español, as $500 million (at the exchange rate before the 1934 devaluation of the dollar) ("Foro de Excelsior," *Excelsior*, Jan. 23, 1972). The gold transfer, justified on the basis of Republican fears that, should the funds remain in Madrid, they might fall into enemy hands, was nevertheless considered a national betrayal by Negrín's opponents. Prominent Socialist Luis Araquistaín bitterly suggested that perhaps Stalin did not really want a Republican victory after all, because he wished also to stay in Hitler's favor, but at the same time considered aid to Spain to be politically useful, temporarily. Araquistaín wrote this in the second of three articles on "El comunismo y la guerra de España," in *El Universal*, May 18, 1939, pp. 1, 4.

of Franco's reprisals should he surrender, Negrín continued his resistance.[24]

Before the end of the war, Negrín lost the support of most of the parties in the Popular Front. He had not only alienated his own Socialist party,[25] but had antagonized moderate Republicans and had quarreled bitterly with regional leaders.[26] The Anarchists, of course, blamed Negrín for permitting the Communists to treat them so harshly. To his advantage, Negrín still had a large personal following of dedicated leftists, many of whom were fellow intellectuals; most of the army still agreed with his policy of resistance; and, finally, despite the difficulties they caused him, the Communists stood by Negrín.

In January, 1939, the nationalist armies began a massive attack on Catalonia, hitherto solidly within the Republican camp and the scene of a recent and impressive Republican victory on the Ebro River. This time the exhausted population saw no hope of resistance and, instead, began to retreat toward the French border. By February 9 all of Catalonia was in nationalist hands. Between January 28 and February 10, nearly a half-million refugees fled from Catalonia into France.[27]

Many of those who fled died en route, either from enemy fire, or, more often, from hunger and cold. The French border was opened

---

[24] The story of the differences between Negrín and Prieto, only sketchily drawn here, can be traced through the correspondence between the two men during the early summer of 1939 in which each defended his actions and blamed the other for what had taken place (Indalecio Prieto and Juan Negrín, "Epistolario"). The debate as to whether Prieto was dismissed solely because of Negrín's acquiescence to Communist domination, or whether the prime minister felt that Prieto was no longer useful because of his defeatism, persisted in exile.

[25] Although Negrín himself was a prominent Socialist, Prieto became the strongest leader in the party after the Caballero faction had been weakened thanks to the joint efforts of Prieto, Negrín, and the Communist party.

[26] The quarrels dealt mostly with the degree of centralization which regional leaders were willing to tolerate and the greater degree Negrín wished to impose on them for the purposes of the war.

[27] *Excelsior*, March 10, 1939, p. 1, reported that 400,000 refugees were still in France, having fled from Catalonia. Isabel O. de Palencia, in *Smouldering Freedom: The Story of the Spanish Republicans in Exile*, pp. 34–39, describes the flight. Although she did not participate herself, she reports the stories of a number of friends and relatives who did. The desperate conditions she describes have been corroborated in various interviews, with stories even more tragic and fantastic than those she relates. It is important to note that a large number of those

to admit the fleeing Republicans, at first to permit only civilians to cross, but opened later to unarmed soldiers as well. Once in France the refugees met with disappointment. They were forced into French concentration camps, herded together, as they later reported, more like prisoners of war than political refugees.[28]

After the fall of Catalonia, the Republic virtually collapsed. In Madrid, still nominally Republican, morale was extremely low and physical conditions were intolerable. President Azaña, considering the war to be over, had already fled to France. He refused all pleas to return to lead the Republic.[29] Azaña resigned the presidency on February 27, and the man next in line, the president of the Cortes, Diego Martínez Barrio, refused to succeed him. The presidents of the Basque and Catalan states were of the same mind, and Negrín's government, for all practical purposes, ceased to function.

The political groups which, with Prieto, advocated immediate peace negotiations, and those which opposed the prime minister on anti-Communist or other bases, began to work on their own to bring an end to the war. A junta, which included most of the non-Communist members of the Popular Front, was organized under Colonel Segismundo Casado. The junta carried out a successful coup against the Negrín government on March 5, 1939. The coup, however, was the junta's only success. As Negrín had, the men of the new Junta found Franco totally unwilling to agree to any po-

---

who fled to France were not political refugees, but persons fleeing before the advancing armies in fear of the violence which was to follow. Most of those who were simply displaced persons and not political refugees returned to Spain shortly after the war.

[28] De Palencia, *Smouldering Freedom*, pp. 45–52, 60–74. For a detailed description of the camps see Silvia Mistral, *Exodo: Diario de una refugiada española*, pp. 1–4. The French separated the men from the women and children, placing all the refugees they could find into camps which for months lacked even the most primitive facilities for shelter or health. Moreover, Franco's agents were permitted to enter the camps, either to threaten the exiles or to attempt to persuade them to return to Spain. Those who did return were people who had fled, as noted above, from simple fear, rather than for political reasons.

[29] See Constancia de la Mora, *In Place of Splendor*, p. 414. The author was married to one of the most important of the Republican generals, Ignacio Hidalgo de Cisneros, a Communist and a strong supporter of Negrín. She concluded that President Azaña's cowardice had rendered him useless to the Republic for the duration of the war. She considered his refusal to return to Spain a major cause of the quick international recognition which was extended to Franco.

litical guarantees once peace was restored. Faced with this situation, the junta, representing the Spanish Republic, unconditionally surrendered to Franco's forces on April 1.

The war had been longer and more terrible than anyone could have foreseen. After so much destruction and internal division, the original issues on which people had staked their lives had become clouded. The hopes and idealism which for three years spurred the war effort had disintegrated dramatically by 1939, and most Spaniards welcomed peace. Unfortunately for the partisans of the Republic, it was not peace but capitulation. Franco claimed total victory, assumed political power in Spain, and prepared to take revenge on his enemies.

Virtually all of the activists and officials of the government, the military, and the syndicates who were able to escape from Spain had left by the middle of March. Once the nationalists controlled Catalonia, the French border was closed, and thereafter only quite limited numbers could escape by plane or boat from Alicante and Valencia on the eastern coast. Those who did flee from Spain— who were not interned in the concentration camps of southern France—scattered to the various cities of France and throughout Europe and the Americas, wherever their resources in money, friends, or fortune took them. In Europe they did their best to live, work, and avoid internment by the French, capture by the agents of Franco (and forcible return to Spain), or, later, arrest by the Germans (and return to Spain).

Those who were able to escape from Spain most easily were the men of means and influence, including those who had achieved status in the trade-union movement. The masses, the rank and file who had fought for the Republic, suffered more in defeat and subsequent reprisals than the bourgeoisie who had governed.[30] The Spanish working classes, the peasantry in particular, had distrusted the bourgeois Republicans almost as much as they had distrusted the aristocrats of the Monarchy. They had been drawn in far greater numbers to the Anarchist ideal of a total anticapitalist revolution and a libertarian society than they had been attracted by the Republican and Socialist alternative of working through progressive legislative process for increased reform.

[30] Stanley G. Payne, *Franco's Spain*, pp. 110–112.

Not only did the Republic fail to recognize the revolutionary aspirations of the masses, but the Civil War required that the Anarchists, Trotskyites, and orthodox Socialists submit to the dominance of "professional" revolutionaries, modeled on the Soviet example. After the defeat, Franco's repressive measures virtually annihilated the syndicalist structure of the working class.[31] By the mid–twentieth century it existed only in skeleton form, and officially among only a few exile groups who had little reason to hope that their old syndicates would again be relevant to the future of Spain.

The legacy of the Civil War, both inside Spain and among those in exile, was one of division, bitterness, and mutual distrust. Yet nearly all those who left Spain as political exiles, whatever their political affiliation or class, believed that a Spanish Republic in some form would again replace the dictatorship which had defeated it and that they would eventually return, the final victors.

[31] Ibid.

2. DEFEAT AND RESCUE

THE CIVIL WAR AND INTERNATIONAL RESPONSE

Democratic governments in Europe and America welcomed the peaceful Spanish "revolution" which replaced the arbitrary and ineffective Monarchy with a liberal Republican government in 1931. Yet, when the Spanish Republic was attacked from within and without, in 1936, only Mexico and the Soviet Union officially came to its support. The war in Spain began as a civil conflict in which political groups loyal to the Republic and wishing to preserve the liberal parliamentary form of government attempted to put down an insurrection initiated by factions within the military, the clergy, and the conservative sectors. Soon, however, the war expanded into a conflict involving Germans, Italians, Russians, and contingents of soldiers from nearly every country in Europe and the Americas. Between 1936 and 1939, Spain was an international battlefield, and the armies opposing each other in that "civil war" represented essentially the same ideological and political forces which fought each other in World War II, a few years later.

From the first, the governments of Italy and Germany considered it in their interest to send military aid and troops to the national-ists,[1] under the leadership of Francisco Franco. The majority of governments in Europe and America, however, were not so certain where their interests lay. Despite their sympathies with the Span-ish Republic, many politicians and diplomats deemed it ill-advised to support what appeared to be an increasingly unstable, leftist, anticlerical government fighting its own conservatives, military, and clergy. More important, European leaders feared that military support of the Spanish Republic would risk armed conflict with Italy and Germany. The government in Spain at first seemed able to contain the military rising in July, 1936. But before the end of July, Italy and Germany began supplying the rebels with funds, arms, and men. Thereafter, the Republican government, without external aid, started to lose ground.[2] Initially, France, under Léon Blum, was sympathetic to the plight of the Republic and considered granting assistance. However, the British government, with which the French regularly consulted, feared the consequences of any military involvement, and was not disposed to intervene. In mid-August the British convinced the French to join them instead in a committee against intervention in Spain. By early September, nine European countries had signed a nonintervention declaration. Of the signatories, two, Germany and Italy, violated the agreement by continuing to aid the nationalists, and one, the Soviet Union, broke its pledge by supporting the Republic.[3] The Italian and German aid, for a variety of reasons, was more effective and important than that supplied by the Soviet Union.[4] Only Mexico, not a signatory

[1] The Spanish Falange, by the outbreak of the war, had emerged as the single most important political faction in the nationalist combination. Much of its ideological content came from Italian Fascist thought.

[2] David T. Cattell, *Soviet Diplomacy and the Spanish Civil War*, V, 14.

[3] Hugh Thomas, *The Spanish Civil War*, pp. 257–260; Julio Alvarez del Vayo, *Freedom's Battle*, pp. 66–70; Gabriel Jackson, *The Spanish Republic and the Civil War, 1931–1939*, pp. 314–317.

[4] The Soviet Union, as described in the previous chapter, sent advisors rather than soldiers. The equipment which it supplied the Republic was paid for in ad-vance with a substantial portion of the Republic treasury. At times, as noted previously, the Russians withheld war equipment in order to obtain specific political objectives. Whether the Soviet aid was essential or ultimately damaging

to the nonintervention pact, provided arms and matériel to the Republic throughout the conflict.[5]

Mexico was a constant critic of the Nonintervention Committee formed by the signatories of the London pact, on the grounds that the committee failed to achieve the single aim which accounted for its existence, the exclusion of all foreign involvement in Spanish affairs.[6] Both of the Mexican representatives to the League of Nations, Narciso Bassols and, after 1937, Isidro Fabela, argued that the assumption made by the Nonintervention Committee that the war was a civil conflict was untenable in view of the aid that Franco was receiving from Italy and Germany. Further, they argued, the nonintervention pact was actually aimed against the Republican cause. If arms or munitions were not sold by the signatories of the pact to the Republican side and steps were not taken to halt the military aid extended by Italy and Germany to the nationalists, then "nonintervention" was tantamount to intervention on behalf of the nationalist rebels. The London agreement, according to Bassols, delayed the aid which the League of Nations, by its charter, actually owed to the freely elected and legitimate government of Spain. Bassols and later Fabela contended that the war in Spain was a case of the legitimate government of a League member being attacked by another country, and that, therefore, the League itself was bound by its charter provisions to aid that government. Even the Spanish representative himself, Julio Alvarez del Vayo, grudgingly agreed to respect the policy of nonintervention, thereby tacitly upholding the thesis that the war in Spain was exclusively a civil war without cause for international involvement. The Mexican delegates, however, continued to uphold what Mexico considered to be Spain's rights, especially the right of protection against foreign aggression.[7]

_____
to the Republican cause has long been a subject of bitter debate. For example, compare Madariaga's condemnation (*Spain*, pp. 511–514) with the laudatory evaluation of Alvarez del Vayo (*Freedom's Battle*, pp. 127–129).

[5] Marcelino Domingo, *El mundo ante España, México ejemplo*, p. 252.

[6] Omar Martínez Legorreta, *Actuación de México en la Liga de las Naciones: El caso de España*, pp. 67ff.

[7] Ibid., p. 176; Isidro Fabela, *Cartas al presidente Cárdenas*, pp. 14, 19. The Nonintervention Committee accomplished only one concrete action: when the Soviet Union began to feel that it was more in its interest to cooperate with the Western powers with regard to Spain, its government agreed to comply with the

Mexican aid went well beyond the verbal commitments made in the League of Nations. Spain was desperately short of war matériel and necessities of all kinds. France had sold only a few planes to the Republic before joining Great Britain in the nonintervention agreement, and, until Russia began selling arms to Spain in late September, 1936,[8] Mexico was the only country from which the Republican government could purchase needed military equipment. But Mexico had only a small armaments industry and, while Cárdenas sold the Republican government what he felt he could, Mexico did not possess war matériel in quantities comparable to those of the major Western powers that were committed to the nonintervention pact.[9] Therefore, besides sending arms from its limited stock, Mexico attempted to acquire arms of foreign manufacture for shipment to Spain. Although Mexican officials insisted that they always received permission from the manufacturing country before reselling these arms to Spain, there were governments which refused to sell any arms to Mexico, fearing that the material would be reexported to Spain without permission.[10]

AID TO THE DEFEATED REPUBLIC

The great moral and psychological value of Mexico's military aid and its support of the Spanish Republic in the League of Nations should not be underestimated, but Mexican policy in the last months of the Civil War and following the Republican defeat was

---

committee's demands that Russia withdraw the men of the International Brigade from Spain, in November, 1937. These men had not fought in Spain as representatives of their countries of origin. Rather, they had joined the special brigades sponsored by the Soviet Union either from motives of idealism or because they were politically unwelcome in their home counties. Many could not return home after leaving Spain, and it was the Mexican government, again, which allowed individual members of the brigades to settle there (Lois Elwyn Smith, *Mexico and the Spanish Republicans*, pp. 219–220).

[8] The arms were used first in November, 1936, five months after Franco first began to receive German and Italian arms (David Cattell, *Communism and the Spanish Civil War*, IV, 73).

[9] Cárdenas reported to the Mexican Congress in September, 1936, that the Spanish ambassador, Félix Gordón Ordaz, had asked for and received twenty thousand seven-millimeter rifles, and 20 million cartridges ("Segundo informe del presidente Lázaro Cárdenas al Congreso de la Unión, rendido 1 de septiembre de 1936" [México, Secretaría de Relaciones Exteriores, *Relaciones internacionales de México, 1935–1955 a través de los mensajes presidenciales*, p. 21]).

[10] Martínez Legorreta, *Actuación de México*, pp. 100–101.

of far greater historical significance. Step by step, President Cárdenas committed Mexico to a deep and lasting responsibility for
the liberal Spain which eventually surrendered to Franco but never
quite resigned itself to defeat. Mexico became a major haven for
Republican exiles. The exodus began considerably before the final
battles and reached its peak in the early months of the Second
World War. First came a few hundred children, next an important
group of Spanish intellectuals; and finally the Spanish Republican
refugees came en masse.

A large number of parents in Spain found that the conditions of
war made it impossible for them to care for their children properly.
Furthermore, the war created many orphans who because of general conditions were uncared for. Beginning in 1937, a number of
these children were evacuated by Spanish authorities to other countries. About fifteen hundred went to Russia, and many of them
remained there.[11] Approximately five hundred children went to
Mexico,[12] and smaller groups went to Belgium and to France.

The children sent to Mexico received a great deal of public attention. Many Mexican families who favored the Republican cause
volunteered to adopt them. Even some wealthy Spanish families
living in Mexico who were not favorably disposed toward the Republic also expressed interest in them. The Mexican government,
however, decided that these children should not be brought up in
the homes of wealthy families, but rather should be kept as a group,
educated in the leftist ideas for which their parents had fought or
were fighting, and brought up in a completely Mexican environment.

The governor of Michoacán offered to provide living accommoda-
tions and educational facilities in Morelia, and his offer was accepted by President Cárdenas.[13] The children arrived in June, 1937.
They were installed in the dormitories of the Escuela "España-
México," which had been established for them. The Spanish teachers who had accompanied them were sent to Mexico City, and their

[11] Vera Foulkes, Los "Niños de Morelia" y la escuela "España-México": Consideraciones analíticas sobre un experimento social, p. 18; "Spanish Emigrés
Seek Return," New York Times, April 9, 1967, p. 28. This article deals with the
Spanish community in Russia and its continued loyalty to Spain.
[12] Foulkes, Los "Niños de Morelia," pp. 18–19.
[13] Salvador Novo, La vida en México en el período presidencial de Lázaro
Cárdenas, pp. 27–28.

teachers, subsequently, were usually Mexicans who also lived in the school.[14]

The success or failure of the environment created for the "Children of Morelia" has been much debated. The children were almost entirely from homes of low socioeconomic levels. Before leaving Spain they had suffered substantially from the confusion, chaos, and material shortages of the war. Living in Mexico, without relatives and without the presence even of the original Spanish teachers upon whom they had come to rely before they were settled in Morelia, the children experienced difficulty in adapting to their new environment. There were many problems with the school, which operated between 1937 and 1943, in terms of finances, discipline, and the propaganda content of the curriculum. As a rule, the children did not become an integral part of the Spanish Republican communities which developed after the bulk of the emigration to Mexico. Nor were all of them integrated fully into Mexican society. Nonetheless, most of them today are economically self-sufficient and working at middle-class occupations. Given the socioeconomic background from which most came, and the limited upward social mobility in Spain, it is unlikely that they would have entered these occupations had they stayed there.[15]

For the Mexicans, these five hundred children were living symbols of the first concrete Mexican commitment to the care and adoption of Spanish Republican refugees. Far more significant for the future of Mexico than the care of these children, however, was the Mexican invitation early in 1938 to Spain's best-known intellectuals to participate in the Mexican-created Casa de España. Mexican officials took steps to enable a limited number of Spain's most prominent intellectuals to come to Mexico so that they might work more productively than was possible at that time in Spain.

Many of the older intellectuals in Spain were not contributing directly to the war effort and instead were being housed and protected at government expense in Valencia, where they were in less physical danger than in Madrid.[16] Virtually all Spanish intellectuals

[14] Foulkes, Los "Niños de Morelia," pp. 24–25. For a more recent discussion of the children of Morelia, see Siempre, June 4, 1968, p. 4.

[15] Foulkes, Los "Niños de Morelia," pp. 24–25.

[16] See the description of intellectual life in wartime Spain in José Moreno Villa, Vida en claro, p. 223.

were initially committed to the Republican ideal, but many became disillusioned with the trends toward political extremism during the war and wished to divorce themselves from wartime politics. The Mexican government offered a desirable alternative. It proposed to bring the Spanish cultural elite to Mexico and to provide the facilities and the income which would permit them to continue working in the arts, humanities, sciences, and other fields. Those who accepted the Mexican invitation, it was thought, would not have to feel that they were abandoning their country spiritually, because from Mexico they could write and speak freely and effectively in favor of the Spanish cause. At the same time, they could contribute to Mexican intellectual life by lecturing, writing, and directing students in scholarly pursuits.

Conversations which opened the way to bringing the intellectuals to Mexico began in 1937. Daniel Cosío Villegas, then ambassador to Portugal, had many friends in Spain who kept him informed of the difficulties of intellectual life and the damage that had been done to universities, libraries, and publishing houses. Given Portugal's support for Franco, there was little that could be done by the pro-Republican Mexican ambassador to help his Spanish friends. Instead, he wrote to an influential Mexican acquaintance, Luis Montes de Oca, director of the Bank of Mexico, indirectly suggesting to President Cárdenas that Mexico should consider inviting twenty-five or thirty Spanish intellectuals to come to Mexico.[17]

Other prominent Mexican intellectuals supported Cosío Villegas's plan, including Alfonso Reyes, Genaro Estrada, Manuel Martínez Báez, and Eduardo Villaseñor; as the originators of the plan, these men had studied or traveled at one time or another in Spain and felt personally involved in the misfortunes of their former companions and mentors.[18] The Mexicans who sponsored the invitation to the Spaniards eventually were appointed by President Cárdenas to serve as directors of the Casa de España. Alfonso Reyes, diplomat, lawyer, and essayist, became its first president; Daniel Cosío Ville-

[17] José Miranda, "La Casa de España," p. 3; Interview, with Daniel Cosío Villegas, March 21, 1967.

[18] Miranda, "Casa de España," p. 3; Philip Taylor, "The Spanish Intellectuals in Mexico, 1936–1955," p. 6; Alfonso Reyes, "La Casa de España en México," *Boletín al servicio de la República Española*, August 15, 1939, p. 2.

gas, diplomat, historian, and writer, was its first secretary; Eduardo Villaseñor, minister of the interior, served on the board of directors. The Casa de España was initially intended as a center in which the refugee intellectuals were to work until they might find teaching or research posts in other Mexican institutions. The original members were expected to present lectures sponsored by the Casa and to visit some of the Mexican provincial universities, offering series of lectures or classes; at times their visits were paid for by the host universities, while at other times the expenses were covered by the Casa. Once the Spaniards obtained other academic positions, they were expected to support themselves. For the most part, they became financially independent within a short time.[19]

Those who were invited to the Casa de España accounted for only a small percentage of the Spanish intellectuals who eventually came to Mexico. The Casa could accept only a few of these newcomers, although it did expand its staff to over forty before the end of its first year of existence.[20] After the arrival of the first professors from Spain, the National University and various academic and technical institutions directly invited other prominent Spaniards to serve on their staffs, but most intellectuals who eventually reached Mexico were not specifically invited by any Mexican authority at all. Rather they came after the war with the major

[19] Interview with Daniel Cosío Villegas, March 21, 1967; Miranda, "Casa de España," p. 3.

[20] Most of the invited membership in the Casa was selected by Daniel Cosío Villegas and Alfonso Reyes, both of whom were well acquainted with the Spanish intellectual community: Interviews with Daniel Cosío Villegas, March 21, 1967; Dr. Manuel Martínez Báez, April 27, 1967; and Eduardo Villaseñor, May 3, 1967. The original members included: Ignacio Bolivar (honorary member); José Carner, Pedro Carrasco, Roberto Castrovido, Alvaro de Albornoz, "Juan de la Encina," Enrique Diez-Canedo, Juan José Domenchina, León Felipe Camino Galicia, José Gaos, José Giral, Benjamín Jarnés, Gonzalo R. Lafora, Manuel Márquez, José Medina Echavarría, Agustín Millares Carlo, José Moreno Villa, Francisco Pascual de Roncal, Manuel Pedroso, Jaime Pí y Suñer, Luis Recasens Siches, Aurelio Romero Lozano, Juan Roura Parella, Adolfo Salazar, Rafael Sánchez Ocaña, Juan Solares Encina, José Torre Blanco, Jesús Bal y Gay, Joaquín Xirau (resident members); Urbano Barnes, Cándido Bolívar, Rosendo Carrasco, Isaac Costero, Fernando de Buen, Francisco Giral, Juan López Dura, Antonio Madinaveitia, Manuel Rivas Cherif, Juan Xirau, María Zambrano (special members); Germán García, Ramón Iglesia, Otto Mayer Sierra, José María Miguel i Vergés, Mariano Rodríguez Orgáz, Leopoldo Zea (scholarship students). This list comes from Miranda, "Casa de España," pp. 8–9.

wave of refugees, financed by either funds of the Spanish Republican government or their own resources.

The Casa de España was supported by funds from the Secretary of Education of the Mexican government, from the Fondo de Cultura Económica, from the Banco Nacional de México, and from the National University.[21] One of the immediate consequences of the generous levels of support was that the Spaniards invited to the Casa received academic salaries substantially higher than those generally paid to Mexican university professors. Moreover, they were paid, not by class hours, as was the custom in most Mexican universities, but as full-time faculty. Until their arrival, there had been no such positions in Mexico. Professors of the various departments of the National University and the state universities, unless independently wealthy, had been accustomed to teaching only part-time, earning a major share of their income through practicing another profession. When they wrote or did research, it was done, in effect, on their own time. Soon after the establishment of the Casa de España, prominent Mexican intellectuals were incorporated into its staff.[22] At this point, they, too, received for the first time a full salary for their academic work, including teaching, writing, research, or other creative activities. Following the example of the Casa, the National University also took the important step of offering a few full-time posts to its most academically important faculty members.[23]

After the defeat of the Spanish Republic and the outbreak of the Second World War, it appeared clear to the Mexicans that their Spanish guests would remain in Mexico for an indefinite period. The hope was expressed that they would become increasingly involved in Mexican life. At the end of 1940 the Casa de España was renamed El Colegio de México, becoming at that time a fairly well structured teaching and research facility with a staff of Spanish and Mexican professors and mostly Mexican students. On the insistence of Cosío Villegas and Spanish philosopher José Gaos, students were chosen on the basis of high academic merit and were

[21] Fondo de Cultura Económica, *Catálogo general, 1955*, p. 402.
[22] Miranda, "Casa de España," p. 5.
[23] Interview with Arturo Arnaiz y Freg, professor of history at the National University, April 2, 1967. Full-time faculty positions still are the exception rather than the rule in Mexican universities.

awarded scholarships to enable them to devote themselves full-time to their studies.[24]

The Casa de España–Colegio de México proved a success, as great a success as any of its founders had hoped. Professionals brought from Spain to Mexico under its auspices, especially the medical doctors and scientists, were from the first active in their own fields and within a short time became economically self-sufficient. All of the members of the Casa were engaged in an active schedule of courses and lectures, and, even during the early months after their arrival, they were producing an extraordinary number of publications. Over the years the Casa de España–Colegio de México has founded a large number of important periodicals, of which the best known today are *Foro Internacional, Nuevo Revista de Filología Hispánica*, and *Historia Mexicana*. Many of those who have worked in the Casa-Colegio have participated as well in the activities of the Fondo de Cultura Económica, one of the largest publishing houses in Latin America.

THE MEXICAN COMMITMENT

The invitation to a limited number of intellectuals and the provisions made for a group of war orphans represented only the beginning of Mexico's important political commitment to the Spanish Republicans. In early 1939, the Mexican government turned its attention to the thousands of Spaniards who had fled Spain to France ahead of Franco's armies. Since the revolution of 1910 Mexico has prided herself on being a country open to political exiles, especially those fleeing rightist dictatorships. There was no precedent in 1939, however, for the mass immigration and settlement of any large group of people. On the contrary, Mexican law was, and remains, quite strict on admission of immigrants, and even stricter with regard to those who qualify for citizenship. In recent Mexican history, only the Spanish refugees have been offered the rights of unlimited immigration and almost automatic citizenship subsequent to immigration. Despite the lack of precedent, the Mexican government, and especially President Cárdenas, determined that Mexico should welcome thousands of Spanish refugees and allow them to make Mexico their second homeland.

24 Miranda, "Casa de España," pp. 4, 7; José Gaos, *Confesiones profesionales*, pp. 80–81.

As the mass of Republican refugees escaped across the Pyrenees and reached the safety of France, French officials deemed it expedient and necessary to intern all known Spanish Civil War refugees, and only a few of the exiles, notably those of wealth and influence, were able to elude them and avoid internment. Even fewer refugees were able to flee from Spain by plane or boat directly to countries where they might hope to avoid internment. Most, whether they escaped the French camps or not, left Spain without adequate funds to survive for more than a few months, without their personal papers and documents, and with no prospects for the future.

Those interned suffered the discomforts and privations as well as the indignities of virtual arrest. Those who escaped the camps frequently faced the challenge of survival in countries in which they were illegal entrants and in which it was difficult to find work.[25]

Mexican aid to the Spanish refugees took two forms. First, attempts were made to provide reasonably comfortable living quarters for about 25,000 of those in France. Second, Mexican government officials carried out successful negotiations with the French government and with officials of the Spanish Republic-in-exile to remove thousands of exiles of all ages and classes from France and provide for their resettlement in Mexico.[26]

On February 10, 1939, before the war in Spain had ended officially, the Mexican minister to the League of Nations, Isidro Fabela, made a tour of the refugee camps in France to examine the possibilities of extending Mexican aid to those interned there.[27] In a dispatch to President Cárdenas, he reported that among those interned were a number of men of considerable prestige, skill, and

[25] Estimates of the number of Spanish refugees in France vary from 400,000 to 500,000 (See Mauricio Fresco, *La emigración republicana española*, p. 40). Fresco was a Mexican consular official in France who was responsible for much of the initial aid which Mexico extended to the refugees. He estimated that there were more than 300,000 in the camps alone. See also Isidro Fabela, *Cartas al presidente*, "Carta No. 10," February 24, 1939, p. 119; Smith, *Mexico and the Spanish Republicans*, p. 207; Salvador de Madariaga, *Spain*, p. 581. On March 10, 1939, *Excelsior* reported that 400,000 refugees fled from Catalonia to France after the fall of Catalonia to Franco's armies (pp. 1, 8). Before Mexican aid was available, according to Jacques Vernant (*The Refugees in the Post-War World*, p. 279), there were some 400,000 Spanish exiles in France, costing the French government an estimated 7 million francs daily.

[26] Fresco, *La emigración republicana*, pp. 33–44.

[27] Fabela, *Cartas al presidente*, "Carta No. 9," February 9, 1939.

intelligence, and that most of those with whom he had spoken had expressed a strong desire to go to Mexico.[28] He noted that if Mexico were to help the refugees, action would have to be swift, since there was danger that within a short time both France and Great Britain would recognize Franco as the legal head of the Spanish government. Should recognition occur, those governments would be likely to comply with Franco's demands that all Spanish political exiles be extradited to Spain.[29]

In late 1938, President Cárdenas had made it known through his ambassador to Spain, Colonel Adalberto Tejada, that Mexico would be willing to receive sixty thousand refugees; since the Civil War was not yet over, Cárdenas had asked that his offer not be made public until conditions required, in order not to weaken Republican morale during the continued fighting.[30] The Mexican president had been kept fully informed of the situation of the Republican partisans in the last months of the war by Narciso Bassols, who, before his appointment as Mexican ambassador to France at the end of 1938, had worked actively in Spain on behalf of the Negrín government. In April, 1939, Bassols publicly announced that Mexico would accept an unlimited number of refugees if the Republican authorities would arrange to finance their transportation and settlement in Mexico.[31] Cárdenas had been enthusiastic about the idea, especially after reading Fabela's letters concerning the conditions under which the refugees were living. Once the reports from Fabela and Bassols had been presented to the Mexican cabinet, its members gave the president their full support.[32]

Cárdenas's motives were practical as well as altruistic. In his report to Congress in September, 1939, he publicly elaborated the advantages he hoped to gain by inviting the refugees: Mexico would receive the contributions of a group closely related by race

28 Ibid., "Carta No. 10," February 24, 1939, pp. 124–125.
29 Ibid., p. 125; Smith, *Mexico and the Spanish Republicans*, p. 209. In the end the French did surrender Catalan leader Luis Companys, Socialist Julian Zugazagoitia, Anarchist ex-minister Juan Peiró, and other important leaders (Thomas, *Spanish Civil War*, p. 619). Franco's request for the return of all political exiles, however, was officially ignored both in England and in France.
30 Domingo, *El mundo ante España*, p. 254; *Excelsior*, April 2, 1939, p. 1.
31 Félix F. Palavicini, *México: Historia de su evolución constructiva*, IV, 272; Smith, *Mexico and the Spanish Republicans*, p. 223.
32 Interview with Jesús Silva Herzog, May 4, 1967. Silva Herzog supported Bassols's suggestion to the cabinet.

and spirit to the Mexicans themselves, a group which included men of high abilities and energy who could play a role in the development of Mexico. The Spanish Republicans, or so the president hoped, would integrate themselves more easily than most foreign groups. Their contributions would come at a minimum cost because the Republican government had agreed to underwrite the entire cost of transportation and settlement.[33]

Once the decision had been made to welcome the exiles, Narciso Bassols was instructed to work with the Spanish Republican officials to oversee the selection of the refugees, to arrange transportation, and to administer their evacuation from France.[34] The Mexican officials working under Bassols in France in cooperation with the Republican exile leaders were able to transport thousands of refugees from France to Mexico between 1939 and 1943, when the whole of France was occupied by Germany.

The Republican exiles in France, however, were politically and financially divided throughout the operation and carried their differences to Mexico. It proved impossible for them to coordinate their efforts in order to establish a single organization which would oversee the selection of emigrants and provide refugee aid. As it developed, the two major Republican leaders, the last prime minister, Juan Negrín, and the Socialist leader Indalecio Prieto, each founded his own refugee aid association, each one separately funded and claiming to be the sole legitimate agency. Although Negrín was left in control of all the funds of the defeated Republic, Prieto was able to establish his financial independence by acquiring a substantial portion of the Spanish treasure. He accomplished this surprising feat through a timely intervention in the affair of the ship *Vita*.

The *Vita*, a pleasure yacht, was selected by Prime Minister

[33] "Quinto informe del presidente Lázaro Cárdenas al Congreso de la Unión," in *Relaciones internacionales*, pp. 36–37. This issue is discussed further in chap. 3, below.

[34] Bassols's instructions with regard to the choice of refugees to come to Mexico were to give priority to skilled agricultural workers and to fishermen, who would aid in the development of rural Mexico. Otherwise the selection and the manner of selecting was to be left mostly to the Republicans themselves. The Mexican policy with regard to desirable and undesirable Spanish refugees is discussed in chap. 3.

Negrín to carry part of the Spanish treasure from Spain to Mexico. Cárdenas previously had agreed to accept the *Vita* cargo and to hold it in Mexico for safekeeping until either Negrín or his representative could receive it. The cargo, consisting mainly of jewels and art objects, arrived in Tampico on March 28, 1939.[35] It was received in Mexico not by Negrín's designated representative, Dr. José Puche, ex-rector of the University of Valencia, but by Indalecio Prieto, Negrín's political enemy. Prieto happened to be in Mexico at the time, touring Latin America after having attended the inauguration of the president of Chile.[36]

Exactly how Prieto was alerted to the presence of the *Vita* in Veracruz, how much the cargo was actually worth, and what motivated President Cárdenas to turn it over to a man he must have known to be a rival of the prime minister, have been topics of controversy for years.[37] The importance of the matter lies in the fact that Prieto acquired a considerable sum of money from the liquidation of the *Vita* treasure, which in turn enhanced his political position and power in the exile community.

In order to legitimize the funds and his own role in their acquisition, Prieto put the money at the disposition of the Permanent Committee of the Spanish Cortes. The Cortes committee represented a large portion of the members of the Spanish Republican legislative body who had survived the war and had gone into exile. The Cortes committee, meeting in Paris, accepted the *Vita* funds, and created under its own auspices the Junta de Auxilio a los Refugia-

[35] The Spanish treasure sent to Mexico on the *Vita* consisted of confiscated jewels, and stocks and bonds, with an estimated value of $50 million (Salvador de Madariaga, *Spain*, p. 589). This treasure should not be confused with the portion of the Spanish treasure shipped to the Soviet Union, which was never returned. See also Smith, *Mexico and the Spanish Republicans*, pp. 229–230; *Excelsior*, March 31, p. 1.

[36] Negrín had appointed Prieto his personal minister after ousting him from the far more important post of minister of defense.

[37] Various points of view concerning the treasure are found in the "Epistolario" of Indalecio Prieto and Juan Negrín; Smith, *Mexico and the Spanish Republicans*, pp. 229–237; Thomas, *Spanish Civil War*, pp. 604–605; Madariaga, *Spain*, pp. 590–591. Additional information came from interviews with Mariano Granados, former justice of the Spanish supreme court, who was involved in various aspects of the transactions, September 7, 1966, and Dr. José Puche, November 15, 1966.

dos Españoles (JARE). Prieto was placed in charge of the administration of JARE funds, which were to be used to aid refugees.[38]

Juan Negrín considered himself betrayed by his fellow Republicans when the JARE was formed. He himself had organized what
he considered the sole official refugee aid and evacuation committee
with the funds remaining to the Republic in the form of stocks and
bonds. Negrín's committee, the Servicio de Emigración para Republicanos Españoles, the SERE,[39] was already in operation and working with Narciso Bassols, before the JARE was officially formed.
After 1940 the JARE took over the major responsibility for transporting and caring for the refugees,[40] but initially the SERE worked
closely and intensively with Mexican officials in the matter of
refugee evacuation. Within the SERE were representatives of every
political party and major syndicate of the Republic; each was given
a quota and told to prepare lists of proposed emigrants. The SERE
itself then compiled lists of all prospective refugees, which included
information on their occupations, the number of family members,
their war service, their political affiliations, and the countries to
which they hoped to be evacuated.[41] These lists, in turn, were given
to the Mexican officials for final decisions on selection or elimina-
tion by means of interviews and additional investigation.

Mexican officials who were in France at that time have insisted
that the selection procedure was just,[42] but many of the Spanish
refugees protested that it was not. There was considerable criticism
regarding the operation of the SERE, which some insisted was only
nominally representative of all parties and syndicates of the Republic and in fact was a tool of the dominant Communist elements
in Negrín's government. Refugees also expressed doubts regarding
the impartiality of the Mexican officials in charge of the operation,

[38] "Acuerdo adoptado por la Diputación Permanente de los Cortes, reunida en
Paris el 31 de julio de 1939," published by the JARE, p. 99.
[39] The committee of the SERE was founded in Paris in March, 1939, and was
in immediate contact with a representative of the Mexican government in order
to make the necessary arrangements for the transport of the refugees (Interview
with Dr. José Puche, November 15, 1966).
[40] For a more complete discussion of the political implications of the SERE and
the JARE and the activities of each, see chap. 6.
[41] Patricio G. Quintanilla, "Comité Técnico de Ayuda a los Españoles en
México: Memoria." These are the official records of the SERE.
[42] Fresco, La emigración republicana, pp. 9–10.

Narciso Bassols and Federico and Susana Gamboa, all of whom
were at that time held to be Communists or Communist sympathizers. Many refugees claimed that members of the political groups
who had supported the Prieto-Casado coup against Negrín and
members of the Anarcho-syndical groups were discriminated
against in favor of Negrín's political allies.[43] There are sound
grounds for believing some of the charges, but it is also true that
persons representing the complete range of Spanish political ideology came to Mexico within the first few years of exile. It is unlikely, therefore, that the selection procedures were effectively exclusive. Furthermore, once the JARE assumed the burden of the
transport of refugees to Mexico, of course, whatever political
favoritism existed went to the benefit of the pro-Prieto factions.

With funds provided by SERE's Comité Técnico de Ayuda a los
Españoles en México[44] and various private groups, about twenty
thousand refugees were evacuated from France within a period of
approximately fifteen months in 1939 and early 1940.[45] A large
portion of the emigrants who were brought to Mexico during those
months came on one of four ships chartered by the SERE: the first,
the *Sinaia*, arrived on June 13, 1939 with 1,599 passengers; the
next, the *Ipanema*, arrived on July 7 with 994 passengers; they

---

[43] See further discussion of Mexican and Spanish partiality in chap. 3. A
number of the refugees interviewed supported the contention that the selection
procedures were biased in favor of supporters of Negrín and the Communists.
Anarchists and members of the CNT were particularly critical. A description
of the manner in which Mexican officials purportedly conducted their interviews
with refugees appears in the memoirs of a former member of the CNT who
came to Mexico as a young woman. She contended in her writing that some of
her compatriots were rejected by Mexican officials for having criticized Negrín
(Silvia Mistral, *Exodo: Diario de una refugiada española*, pp. 148–158).

[44] See *Cultural Creations of the Comité Técnico de Ayuda a Los Españoles en
México* [The Technical Committee of Help to Spaniards in Mexico] (pamphlet), p. 9.

[45] "La emigración, el SERE y el Comité Técnico," *Boletín al servicio*, vol. 2,
chap. 45 (July 6, 1940), p. 1. According to Philip Taylor, agencies of the Spanish Republican government-in-exile paid for the travel and resettlement of about
ten thousand refugees of all political affiliations. Of these, about seven thousand
went to Mexico, two thousand to Chile, and smaller groups to other countries
(Taylor, "Myth and Reality: How Red Were the Spanish Reds?" p. 122). These
figures, of course, do not include refugees who were self-financed or who were
funded by private agencies. Among the private agencies the Quaker groups were
especially active and important.

were followed by the *Mexique*, which arrived on July 27 with 2,091 passengers;[46] and, finally, the *De Grasse*, which carried 206 refugees to New York to be transported to Mexico by train.[47] No refugee ships were chartered during most of 1940, but large numbers of refugees continued to arrive individually or in small groups, self-financed or aided by private groups. Meanwhile, in the first months of 1940, the SERE claimed to have exhausted all its funds,[48] and the JARE prepared to take over the responsibility for transport and care of Spanish exiles. By 1941, due to precarious conditions in France under German occupation, the evacuation of refugees was increasingly difficult to arrange. In 1941, three ships, the *Cuba* (renamed the *St. Dominique*), the *Quanza*, and the *Serapinta* were able to reach Mexico under the auspices of the JARE.[49]

Estimates vary widely on the total number of Spanish refugees to reach Mexico. Passenger counts made on the SERE and the JARE ships are known to have been inaccurate, and in any case only a portion of the refugees arrived on these ships. Evidently, there was no accurate count made of the thousands of refugees who came to Mexico individually or who came after having spent some time in another country. The Dirección General de Estadística does list 6,234 Spaniards as having arrived in 1939; 1,746 in 1940; 1,611 in 1941, and 2,534 in 1942, but the accuracy of these figures cannot be assumed.[50]

[46] These notes were taken from Patricio G. Quintanilla, "Comité Técnico de Ayuda." This "Memoria" was the official record compiled by the SERE at the time the SERE-chartered ships were arriving in Mexico. The record contains photographs, mementos, and a variety of information about the refugees: their background, their skills, and their immediate destination in Mexico. The "Memoria" was made available to me by Dr. José Puche, who was Negrín's representative in Mexico for the SERE.

[47] Information taken from data compiled by Smith in *Mexico and the Spanish Republicans*, pp. 237–238. Smith lists 1,800 passengers for the *Sinaia*, and 2,085 for the *Mexique*.

[48] "La emigración, el SERE y el Comité Técnico," *Boletín al servicio*, p. 1; also editorial in the *Boletín al servicio*, July 20, 1940, pp. 1–2. See chap. 6.

[49] Smith, *Mexico and the Spanish Republicans*, pp. 253–354.

[50] Ibid., p. 305. These figures probably err on the conservative side. According to Taylor ("Spanish Intellectuals"), such figures are totally untrustworthy, because the government was not systematic in its method of counting: sometimes only heads of families were counted, sometimes family groups, including cousins and other relatives. Palavicini counts the total refugees arriving in groups, by boat or train, as 7,393, but he concluded that the total number of those who actually came to Mexico before the end of the Second World War was at least

Spanish exiles sought refuge in most countries of the Americas other than Mexico and emigrated in substantial numbers to Cuba, the Dominican Republic, Argentina, Chile, and Venezuela. However, only Mexico was willing to accept them in virtually unlimited numbers. Given Mexico's unwavering policy of friendship for the Spanish Republic and its open door to the Republican refugees, it is not surprising that it should have become the major center of Spanish exile life and culture.[51] Given the number and quality of the refugees who settled in Mexico, it is not surprising either that their impact should have been felt by the country as a whole. In the following chapters the nature of this impact will be described, and the life styles, commitments, and attitudes of the Spanish exiles living in Mexico will be examined and analyzed.

15,000 (Palavicini, *México: Historia*, p. 272); Fresco estimates about 16,000 (*La emigración republicana*, p. 53); other estimates are higher, usually ranging between 20,000 and 40,000. The Spaniards did not keep official records, since the embassy in Mexico was closed between 1939 and 1945. (See Vernant, *Refugees in the Post-War World*, p. 662.)

[51] Quantitatively, more of the refugees settled in France than in any other country, but Mexico received by far the greatest number of educated and trained individuals. In France, due to language problems and barriers against foreigners in many professions, it was difficult for professionals to find employment. There was considerable demand at that time, however, for unskilled and semi-skilled labor, and many Spanish workers were employed in French factories.

3. EARLY CONFRONTATIONS AND ACCOMMODATIONS

UNWELCOME GUESTS

Most Mexican intellectuals, with the exception of a few opposed to President Cárdenas on ideological or personal grounds, supported him in his pro-Republican policy and subsequently encouraged him to open Mexico to the refugees. As soon as it became obvious that the Republic would lose the war and that thousands of refugees would be seeking new homes in Europe and the Americas, such men as Isidro Fabela, Jesús Silva Herzog, Eduardo Villaseñor, Antonio and Manuel Martínez Báez—all of them respected in both academic and government circles—began to advocate bringing the exiles to Mexico. In letters and conversations they stressed the humanitarian aspects of an open-door policy and, further, the substantial number of highly skilled and accomplished individuals who had escaped from Spain as the war was ending and from whose presence Mexico might benefit greatly.[1]

[1] See Isidro Fabela, "La emigración de los refugiados a México," *Cartas al*

By the time the matter of a general Republican refugee invitation was being debated, the initial small group of Spanish intellectuals invited to Mexico in 1937 and 1938 was already successfully working in the Casa de España and in various Mexican universities. They were highly regarded by almost all the Mexicans with whom they worked. In fact, many Mexicans expressed both pleasure and surprise at the ease with which the Spanish intellectuals were absorbed into the Mexican academic structure.[2] The large group of postwar refugees was by no means composed entirely of intellectuals or professionals. Nevertheless, the positive experience of that first group of Spanish Republicans who came to the Casa de España did help to create a favorable view among the Mexican elite toward the possibility of including the thousands of exiles still in France.

Yet, when Cárdenas publicly declared his intention to permit the postwar Spanish refugees to enter Mexico, his decision in general was not a popular one. The Mexican press and many of its readers, especially Mexicans of conservative Catholic tendencies, strongly objected to the prospect of thousands of leftist anticlerical Spaniards settling in their country. The individuals and groups who had opposed Mexico's strong support of Spain in the League of Nations and who considered Franco not as a traitor but as the leader of the forces that had liberated Spain from communism,[3] began an active campaign in early March, 1939, against the increased Mexican commitment to the Republican refugees. There had been little real protest when the Spanish orphans, the "Children of Morelia," arrived and little active opposition to the invitation extended to the intellectuals of the Casa de España. The former were too young and too few to be dangerous; the latter were not only few in number but also considered politically moderate. A general invitation to unspecified thousands of refugees of all political shadings was an-

---

Presidente Cárdenas, pp. 124–132; interviews with Daniel Cosío Villegas, Arturo Arnaiz y Freg, April 4, 1967; Jesús Silva Herzog, May 4, 1967.

2 Interviews with Daniel Cosío Villegas, Antonio Martínez Báez, and Manuel Martínez Báez, March 22, April 26, April 27, 1967, respectively. All three stressed that Spaniards accepted Mexican hospitality with tact and gratitude, and that, although many of the Spaniards were internationally prominent in their fields, few behaved in a patronizing manner toward their hosts. The problem of competition from Spanish intellectuals, apparently, was not a serious one.

3 Alfonso Junco, in *El difícil paraíso*, outlined the ideological content of this point of view.

other matter, and the popular press vigorously protested what it called an invitation by the Mexican government to foreign extremists and revolutionaries.[4]

Cárdenas's policy of land expropriation and reform and his close working relations with such known leftists as labor leader Vicente Lombardo Toledano had earned him considerable opposition from the sectors adversely affected by his reforms. The Mexican press, apparently responsive to the feeling of these elements and searching for opportunities to embarrass the president, found an issue in his sympathy and concern for the refugees. Cárdenas himself complained of the press campaign against his friendly posture toward the Republican exiles and publicly expressed the hope that it would end once they arrived.[5] The adverse propaganda, however, did arouse public opinion, and, by the time the refugees reached Mexico, hostility to their presence had been stirred up in many sectors of the population.

As Franco's position in Spain improved, Fascist propaganda grew apace and evoked considerable response in Mexico in the same sectors which opposed the leftist tendencies of the government. A number of Mexicans who found no appeal in either Hitler or Mussolini were attracted by the hispanism, the social content, and the traditional values supposedly upheld by Spanish fascism and represented by such idealistic statements as those of José Primo de Rivera.[6] The Spanish Republic, on the other hand, even to those

[4] So hostile was a large sector of the press to the Republican cause that Mexican hispanist Félix Palavicini believed that the Mexican press must have been to some extent at the disposition of Franco's Fascist agents. (See Félix F. Palavicini, *México: Historia de su evolución constructiva*, IV, 273.) Catalan refugee historian Pere Foix, in a laudatory biography of Cárdenas, described the bitter press attacks on the Republicans in which they were called "assassins, incendiaries, and violators of nuns" (Foix, *Cárdenas*, p. 259). Salvador Novo, not a great admirer of the refugees, remarked that many Mexicans who mistakenly believed what they read in the press thought that the Casa de España was a luxurious hideaway in which Spanish Leftists were involved in revolutionary conspiracies, and that the Republicans who would follow the intellectuals would come armed and shooting (Novo, *La vida en México en el periódo presidencial de Lázaro Cárdenas*, p. 355).

[5] "Quinto informe del Presidente Lázaro Cárdenas al Congreso de la Unión, rendido el 1 de septiembre de 1939" (*Relaciones internacionales de México, 1935–1955 a través de los mensajes presidenciales*, p. 36).

[6] Junco's *Difícil paraíso* is a work dedicated to the inspiration of José Primo de Rivera. It stresses the social content of Spanish Fascist thought and the need to oppose the social and political chaos caused by the Communist influence on

who did not oppose its liberal democratic principles, seemed an experiment which had failed.

Even a number of Mexicans who agreed with their country's pro-Republican policy in the League of Nations and who supported Mexican aid to the Civil War refugees in France, nonetheless objected to the invitation to the refugees to emigrate to Mexico en masse. Their opposition stemmed from four concerns: First, convinced as so many were that the extremist elements had taken over in Spain during the war, moderate and conservative Mexicans feared that the arrival of the refugees would fortify the extreme Left in their country. The Left, they believed, was already too strongly encouraged by the favorable attitude of the Cárdenas government toward it. Since there was no doubt that Narciso Bassols, whom Cárdenas had named to participate in the selection of those refugees who would be admitted, was a Left sympathizer, there appeared good reason to suppose that he would favor leftists in general. If, thanks to Cárdenas and Bassols, the same revolutionaries and Communists who had wrested control of the Spanish Republic from its founders were to come to Mexico, they might well involve themselves in Mexican politics, hoping to accomplish similar goals.[7]

Second, opponents of the refugees predicted that even if the latter did not interfere in Mexican domestic politics, they would attempt to continue the Spanish Civil War from Mexican soil, thereby placing Mexico in a very embarrassing international situation.[8]

---

the Spanish Republic. See also Albert L. Michaels, "El nacionalismo conservador mexicano desde la Revolución hasta 1940," *Historia Mexicana* 16 (October–December, 1966): 226.

[7] The Mexican press gave much publicity to moderate and conservative dissidents from the Negrín government, who, from exile, made public the disputes within the Spanish government, thereby confirming the suspicions of conservative Mexicans. See, for example, the articles of Luis Araquistaín, moderate Socialist intellectual; the three articles on "El comunismo y la guerra de España" were published on May 17, 18, 19, 1939, in *El Universal. Excelsior*, June 2, 1939, p. 9, printed an editorial in the regular section "Gotas de amargo," in which the writer declared that Mexico no more wanted extremists, thieves, and political criminals than did France. If wishing to avoid admitting these undesirables meant that he was a *franquisto*, then he could only hope that Bassols also would be a *franquisto*.

[8] Novo, "¿Que fizo el tesor?" in *La vida en México*, pp. 272–276. The article, written originally on July 8, 1939, criticizes the supporters of Negrín already in

To admit the refugees would be a humanitarian gesture, but, given the number of political activists among them, the gesture was considered likely to involve Mexico in Spanish politics.

Third, fear that the Spaniards would compete with Mexicans economically was the most frequent cause of alarm. The labor leadership under Confederación de Trabajadores Mexicanos (CTM) chief Vicente Lombardo Toledano was solidly pro-Republican, and the CTM paper, El Popular, consistently praised Cárdenas's invitation, criticized the Mexican press for not doing so, and attempted to convince readers that the Spanish workers were brothers, not competitors.[9] The rank and file, however, apparently were not easily convinced by the labor leaders. The CTM on several occasions found it necessary to send representatives to various parts of the country to reassure local syndicates that there was nothing to fear. The very energy with which El Popular attacked the pro-Franco, anti-Republican propaganda implied the widespread attractiveness of the latter's message. By early July the instances of local worker hostility were so frequent that the CTM held special sessions to consider the problem and to develop measures which might counteract the influence of those who opposed the Republicans.[10] Even in such professional groups as the medical associations and the teachers' syndicates there was concern that professionally competent individuals among the exiles would compete successfully for Mexican positions.[11]

The peasants were more hostile than the city dwellers, and they were determined to keep the Spaniards off the land whatever the government plans to the contrary. There were protests from Vera-

---

Mexico for having come with the intention of continuing the war and recovering the Spanish government for themselves.

[9] A very large number of pro-Republican, anti-Franco articles can be found in El Popular throughout the spring of 1939. Articles of warm welcome and high praise appeared in June and July as the refugee ships arrived.

[10] Lois Smith, Mexico and the Spanish Republicans, pp. 225–226; Excelsior, June 16, 1939, p. 3. The special meeting of the CTM is discussed in Excelsior (July 6, 1939, pp. 1–2: "Tomará dispositivos la CTM a fin de contrarrestar la labor contra los emigrados").

[11] The syndicate of medical surgeons agreed that the Spanish doctors should avoid major population centers and should not work in private consultation (Excelsior, April 30, 1939, pp. 1, 6). The syndicate of workers in the field of teaching agreed to help organize Spanish teachers, with the object of finding positions for them in outlying areas (Excelsior, June 7, 1939, p. 3).

cruz, Jalisco, and México, all regions which were expected to incorporate substantial numbers of refugee farmers.[12] Among much of the Mexican peasantry, the Catholic church was strong, and throughout the central and western states the anti-Revolutionary, clerical *Sinarquista* movement had gained substantial rural support. The *Sinarquistas* were believed to have been influenced directly by Spanish Falangist ideology, and they were known to uphold traditional Spanish values and religion against what they considered to be the corruption and damage of United States and Bolshevist ideas. Having been told that "to defend Spain and to defend Mexico is to fight against the degrading influence of both the Anglo-Saxon and the Communist,"[13] these peasants hardly could have been expected to offer a warm welcome to the anticlerical, "red"-tainted, and relatively cosmopolitan Republicans.

Fourth, many Mexican citizens were displeased at the prospect of a large-scale Spanish emigration because, since the colonial period, Spaniards had not been regarded warmly in much of Mexico. Most Mexicans knew about Spain only what they had been taught in primary and secondary schools, and Mexican educators considered that the major function of education was to instill a sense of "Mexicanidad," a separate Mexican identity. The Spaniards were thus treated historically as the conquerors, not as the patriotic founding fathers of the Mexican nation.[14] The Spaniards

[12] Special police protection was planned for those refugees who would go to parts of Veracruz state, because of fears of murder and banditry there (*Excelsior*, June 17, p. 3). Another article in *Excelsior* on the same date, on p. 13, reported that trouble was expected in the Guadalajara region of Jalisco, where peasants feared that the land for which they had struggled was to be taken from them. On July 14, on p. 1, *Excelsior* reported that officials were unable to convince *ejiditarios* in Veracruz to accept the refugees, and therefore the newcomers would become small-plot owners instead. There were reports of violence in Huasteca (*Excelsior*, July 5, 1939, p. 11), and strong complaints from Mexico state that the *ejido* land might be given to refugees (*Excelsior*, June 23, 1939, pp. 1, 12).

[13] Quote from Nathan L. Whetten, *Rural Mexico*, p. 496. (See also Michaels, "El nacionalismo conservador mexicano," pp. 223–225.)

[14] See Josefina Vázquez de Knauth, *Nacionalismo y educación en México*. This is a detailed treatment of the manner in which Mexican nationalism has been buttressed and defined in its educational system. In describing the official textbooks in use during the 1930's and 1940's, the author noted that the emphasis placed on the contributions and culture of the Mexican Indian resulted in a strong anti-Spanish bias. (See esp. pp. 165, 180, 193.) Various textbooks are individually described (pp. 170–198).

with whom the Mexicans were best acquainted were the immigrants who had come to Mexico in the nineteenth and twentieth centuries to make their fortunes and who rarely mixed with the Mexicans. Historically, they have been referred to as *gachupines*. The term, used pejoratively, at one time included all Peninsula-born residents of colonial Mexico, but it was extended during the nineteenth century to refer to all Spaniards who lived in Mexico, even those who had been there for generations but who maintained their separate identity. The image of the *gachupines* was of a people who worked tirelessly for their own reward, saved their money, and usually exploited those Mexicans who worked with or under them.

THE GOVERNMENT JUSTIFICATION

The Mexican government did what it could to dispel the misinformation and anxieties of its citizens regarding the Spanish refugees. Less than a month before the *Sinaia* arrived with the first large group of refugees from the French camps, the minister of the interior, Ignacio García Tellez, called a press conference to protest the strongly critical articles appearing in certain dailies.[15] The issues, however, continued to be debated extensively in the press from early March, 1939, until long after the refugees had settled in Mexico. Government officials fed this debate with a quantity of articles elaborating the reasons why the Spanish presence in Mexico would be of great benefit to the Mexican people.

When the government first reported that it had authorized Narciso Bassols to help select refugees for admission to Mexico, official notices to the press emphasized that all Spaniards who applied were required to promise that, should they come to Mexico, they would refrain altogether from any participation in Mexican politics.[16] There would be no restrictions placed on the admission of persons who had held military or political positions in Spain, but they, like all refugees, would have to assure the Mexican officials that their energies would be directed toward leading productive, useful lives in Mexico, not toward altering Mexico's political

---

[15] *Excelsior*, May 24, 1949, pp. 1, 4.
[16] See *Excelsior*, March 15, 1939, p. 1; March 20, p. 1; April 2, p. 1. The political restrictions were based on Article 33 of the Mexican Constitution which forbids foreigners from interference in Mexican politics.

forms, nor toward using the country as a temporary base of political action directed elsewhere.[17] The government refused to predict how many leftists would be admitted, since all parties and movements of the Popular Front were to be represented proportionally among those persons chosen for the ships bound for Mexico and the only priorities to be given were to certain occupations. Bassols's instructions, however, supposedly were to refuse asylum to all "agitators."[18]

Another reassurance offered in official reports to the press was the reminder that these skilled Spaniards would cost Mexico nothing, since the Republican exile agencies would pay all costs of transportation. Upon arrival, moreover, the refugees were to be screened and sent to those regions and areas where their services and skills would be most needed, areas which did not include, it was made clear, the overcrowded urban centers. Farmers would be given high priority in order that the more sparsely populated states would be settled and the land cultivated; fishermen, not very numerous in Mexico, likewise were to be encouraged.[19] On April 14, Cárdenas sent notes to all the state governors asking them for help in settling the refugees and requesting that they inform him how many they would be able to accept and in what capacities they would be able to employ them productively.[20]

According to official Mexican statements, Spaniards, excepting the intellectuals, would qualify for emigration only under strict limitations, to prevent them from competing with Mexican workers. Further, they were required to give assurance of their willingness to work either on agricultural cooperatives or on land granted them by the government but operated with their own resources. The exile organizations were expected to use their financial means to found new and useful industries, so that the refugees would not

[17] This theme occurred in at least five separate articles in *Excelsior* during the month of March, 1939, alone. One article, based on a government report, assured readers that if the refugees had been agitators at one time, their careers would end as soon as they reached Mexico (April 2, p. 1).

[18] *Excelsior*, March 31, 1939, p. 1; April 2, pp. 1, 11. A preference for Basques and Gallegans was noted because these people were known as good farmers and fishermen (idem, April 3, 1939, p. 1).

[19] *Excelsior*, April 3, 1939, p. 1; March 29, 1939, pp. 1, 11; *El Universal*, April 3, p. 1.

[20] *Excelsior*, April 14, 1939, pp. 1, 8. "Selección de tierras para que sean colonizadas por los republicanos españoles."

become a financial burden to the Mexican government subsequent to their arrival. All Spaniards would have to be willing to go wherever in Mexico they were assigned by their own authorities or the Mexican officials. The Mexican government assured its citizens that all applicants, no matter what their original political affiliation, would have to accept Mexico's democratic, constitutional regime. None of the refugees were to participate actively in Mexican politics.[21]

The only persons among the refugees exempt from all restrictions on place of settlement and nature of economic pursuit were prestigious Spanish intellectuals. The Mexican government assumed that individuals of such caliber would work in the professions of their choice, while living in the major urban centers.[22] The Spanish intellectuals had been arriving in Mexico City in small numbers since the foundation of the Casa de España, and periodically the press would take special note of the more prominent among them. Unlike the bulk of the emigrants, most of these men of recognized scholarship and culture would have been welcome in a variety of countries, and Mexicans were proud to receive as many as chose to come to their country.

THE REFUGEES ARRIVE

The *Sinaia*, the first organized and publicly financed refugee ship, arrived on June 13, 1939, with 1,599 passengers who had been selected jointly by Spanish officials of the SERE and by the Mexican ambassador Narciso Bassols, aided by Federico and Susana Gamboa of the Mexican legation in Paris. This first voyage was financed by the Comité de Ayuda a los Españoles, of the SERE.[23]

[21] *El Universal*, April 3, 1939, pp. 1, 3. *Excelsior* (April 2, p. 1, and April 3, p. 10) carried the reminder that Mexican unemployment was already at 300,000. (See also Smith, *Mexico and the Spanish Republicans*, p. 224.)

[22] Smith, *Mexico and the Spanish Republicans*, p. 224; *Excelsior*, April 3, 1939, p. 10. Salvador Novo, in an article written on June 24, 1939, justified the fact, disturbing to some Mexicans, that the Spanish professors at the Casa de España were better paid than the Mexican professors at the National University. Spain had given Mexico scholars of international reputation who would be happily received in any country, Novo noted. Mexico, therefore, should be honored by their presence and be willing to pay a reasonable price for their services (Novo, *La vida en México*, pp. 356–358).

[23] Smith, *Mexico and the Spanish Republicans*, pp. 231, 238–243. *Excelsior* (June 14, 1939, p. 1) announced the arrival of sixteen hundred people on the *Sinaia*.

The SERE was prepared to care for the material needs of the refugees until they were financially self-sufficient, and plans had been made before the *Sinaia*'s arrival for the placement and employment of most of its passengers. The day after the *Sinaia* docked, the government proudly announced that most of the new arrivals would be leaving almost at once for a number of different states where work was awaiting them. Of the passengers, only two hundred, all of whom were persons of intellectual or professional standing—teachers, journalists, and writers—would go directly from Veracruz to the Mexican capital.[24]

About twelve thousand spectators turned out to see the *Sinaia* dock, including Veracruz citizens of all ages and high political officials from the capital. Speeches, fanfare, and enthusiasm marked the event.[25] Yet, there were many aspects of the welcoming scene that disturbed and angered some Mexican observers. Those who had all along doubted both Cárdenas's motives for inviting the refugees and the government's sincerity in reassuring the people that no "undesirables" would be included had their suspicions confirmed when the refugees were seen marching behind banners of the Communist party. It was reported throughout the country that the Spaniards answered the Mexican welcome with the Communist sign of the clenched fist.[26] For the Republican refugees, the clenched fist, was, in fact, not a Communist symbol but rather a general salute, common to all groups in Republican Spain; this fact, however, was not widely reported.[27] While some of the report-

[24] *Excelsior*, June 15, 1939, p. 1.

[25] The arrival of the *Sinaia* occasioned headlines in all the daily press on June 14. Articles and pictures followed during the next few days. Spaniard Carlos Martínez describes the welcome of the refugees at Veracruz as having been a joyous event (*Crónica de una emigración: la de los Republicanos españoles en 1939*, p. 15). In interviews I held with others who arrived on the same day, I found that Mexican hostility and the discomforts of Veracruz were more vividly recalled.

[26] For example, in the June 15, 1939, editorial in *Excelsior* (p. 5), the writer complained that the refugees' first act had been to participate in a Communist parade. The editorial implied that the refugees had been brought to Mexico to serve the interests of such men as Vicente Lombardo Toledano, leftist head of the CTM. The refugees were regarded as ungrateful and unworthy of Mexican hospitality, and the writer feared that someday the refugees' clenched fist might be directed against the Mexicans themselves.

[27] One paper which made a special point of explaining the clenched fist was *El Popular* (editorial, June 14, 1939, p. 3). The editorial blamed the "fascists" for pretending that this symbol indicated any Communist affiliation among the

ers who interviewed the refugees took note of their suffering and exhaustion, the reports, on the whole, were not favorable, except when they dwelt on the number and quality of the Spanish scholars and professionals who had chosen to come to Mexico.

In the months that followed, the number of Spanish refugees increased as other ships docked: the *Ipanema* on July 7 and the *Mexique* on July 27, at Veracruz, and the *De Grasse* at New York on December 30, carrying, among them, a total of approximately five thousand passengers.[28] Thousands of other individuals, mostly those who had escaped internment in France, financed their own passage by whatever means they could. As the arrivals became more frequent, they also became more routine. There were no more incidents of clenched fists and there was no more evidence to the effect that leftists and extremists represented the majority or even a large minority of the refugees.

REEVALUATIONS

Just as the advocates of the Republican invitation had predicted, overall opposition to the refugees gradually declined as more and more Spaniards arrived and settled peaceably throughout Mexico. Even among conservatives long opposed to Cárdenas's policies, the realization grew that the newcomers as a whole represented no political threat to Mexico. Mexican workers and professionals, finding their jobs and positions still intact, relaxed their hostility and began to accept the Spanish presence more calmly. In the Mexican press the early emotionally charged criticism gave way to a more balanced treatment. Sympathy was expressed for the ordeal which the refugees had endured, and more optimism was voiced that the Republicans could become useful and productive citizens of Mexico.

As early as mid-June, 1939, Salvador Novo, a well-known writer who had been critical of Cárdenas's pro-Republican policy, began to

---

refugees. Mario Ojeda Gómez, professor in the international relations program at El Colegio de México, recalls that as a schoolchild in Veracruz, he was dismissed, along with all the children from local public schools, to greet the *Sinaia* and to sing the Communist "Internationale" in welcome (Interview, April 26, 1967). *Excelsior*, in an editorial (June 15, 1939, p. 5), in part forgave the refugees for staging a "Communist parade," on the grounds that they had been misinformed about Mexican politics by Mexican leftists.

[28] See chap. 2 for data on the number of passengers on each ship.

criticize the previous irresponsibility of the Mexican press. Novo, a conservative, felt that the Spaniards represented the best of past emigrants to Mexico, and considered that the Republicans would do no worse than their predecessors.[29] Acknowledging the confusion and uncertainty prior to the arrival of the *Sinaia*, Novo noted that most fears had proved unjustified, since the active politicians represented the smallest group among the refugees. The other two groups, the intellectuals and professionals on the one hand, and the workers and peasants on the other, he felt were composed of men and women committed to their work, from whose presence Mexico would benefit.

Other favorable editorials began to appear in the politically moderate daily press, reassessing past editorial conclusions. One of the most outspoken editorialists pleading for a more humane treatment of the refugees by both press and citizens was Pedro Gringoire of *Excelsior*. Gringoire claimed that the only political problem, in reality, was a misunderstanding on the part of the Spaniards who first arrived in Mexico. They had been informed that Mexico was a country of leftists and revolutionaries and had acted accordingly, thereby providing the ammunition which their enemies used against them. The disturbing aspects of the *Sinaia* welcome were not repeated, he said, because Spaniards on subsequent voyages were better informed regarding Mexico. Moreover, Gringoire declared, the economic anxieties had proven as ill-founded as the political. A few thousand Spaniards scattered throughout Mexico could not adversely affect the Mexican economy.[30]

By midsummer the press no longer uniformly accused the refugees of wishing to spread communism among the Mexicans, but directed political criticism instead toward those Mexicans who had been responsible for the selection and orientation processes. Emphasizing the fact that the Spaniards were chosen by Cárdenas, Bassols, and the Gamboas, who were held to be Communist sympathizers,

---

[29] Novo, *La vida en México*, p. 359 (story originally dated June 24, 1939).

[30] Pedro Gringoire, "El pulso de los tiempos" (*Excelsior*, June 30, 1939, pp. 5, 9). See also R. Cabré, "México, única esperanza de milares de españoles que pasan horrores en Francia" (*Excelsior*, June 24, 1939, pp. 1, 4). By the time the *Ipanema* reached Veracruz, Mexicans, for the most part, were satisfied that the Spaniards would be useful and productive in Mexico, and that most of the refugees were more interested in work than in political agitation (*Excelsior*, July 5, 1939, pp. 1, 11).

some Mexican columnists blamed these men for having given the
refugees the false impression that all Mexicans were like them. The
suspicions of moderates and conservatives on this matter were sub-
stantiated by some of the refugees who, for the benefit of the Mexican press, described the selection as thoroughly humiliating and
stated that many Republicans confronting leftist Mexican inter-
viewers had found it expedient to claim allegiance to Negrín or
adhesion to the Communist party in order to be granted passage on
one of the ships chartered for Mexico.[31]

As the general accusation of *all* Republicans for holding extreme
political views dissipated, public opinion against the newcomers
came to be concentrated on the major political figures in the immigration. Most of the refugees, it was agreed, had come to Mexico to
work and raise families, not to engage in political activities. The
politicians, on the other hand, were alleged to have come with the
intention of using Mexico as a base for conspiracy and renewed
political activity aimed at Spain. "Some men are capable of being
conquistadores," an article in *El Universal*, entitled "Líderes, no,
sólo refugiados," concluded, advocating that Mexico refuse to admit
politicians.[32]

RURAL AND URBAN IMMIGRANTS

As previously noted, the Mexican government had promised that
the refugees would be dispatched to the underpopulated regions of
Mexico and given employment in areas determined by the various
state governors. Each time one of the refugee ships arrived, there
were photographs and statistics to indicate that, in fact, most of the
refugees were settling in less populated areas. According to the
figures published by the Spanish Comité de Ayuda a los Refugiados
Españoles (of the SERE), only approximately 15 percent of the
passengers of the *Sinaia* went to Mexico City, while the remainder

[31] See statements by Spaniard Fernando Suárez (*Excelsior*, July 7, 1939, pp.
5, 9) in which he describes the miserable conditions on the *Sinaia* and the
rigorous leftist orientation which, supposedly, was the daily fare.

[32] *El Universal*, July 10, 1939, p. 3. An even stronger article in *El Universal*,
"Propaganda de España novicia" (June 19, 1939, p. 3), expressed the fear that
Spanish Communist politicians might spread their ideas to the popular classes
in Mexico, thereby causing another revolution which would destroy Mexican
democracy.

were scattered among the states; in the case of the *Ipanema* approximately 20 percent went to Mexico City, and among the passengers of the *Mexique* approximately 5 percent went to the capital.[33] The Spaniards also complied with the suggestion of the Mexican government that they establish agricultural cooperatives on government land, financed by the SERE. The largest and most sophisticated of these was Santa Clara, in the state of Chihuahua.

Within a short time, however, it was clear that the policy of scattering the refugees throughout the sparsely settled states of Mexico, of using them to develop new industry and agriculture, had failed. Despite their apparent readiness to go anywhere, the Spaniards soon declared themselves either unwilling or unable to remain in the remote regions to which many of them had been sent. The majority of those who had gone to the countryside as farmers quickly appeared in the nearest cities. Many who had settled in small provincial towns and cities were on their way to the major cities and especially to the capital within a few months. Even the well-publicized Santa Clara experiment failed within a year of its founding. The Spaniards who had been scattered throughout Mexico moved again to the urban centers, a migration which began at the end of 1939 and continued during the years which followed. By the early months of 1940, Mexico City was not only the cultural and financial center for Spanish refugees, but the population center as well.[34] The swelling of the refugee population in the city caused

[33] Figures on the number of families sent to various states come from the official records of the SERE, *Comité Técnico de Ayuda a los Españoles.* These percentages were derived by adding heads of families and the bachelors and using this sum as the base figure.

[34] I have no figures on the migration or the dates of migration to the capital, and it is doubtful that any meaningful figures exist. When the refugee ships docked in Mexico, the refugees were registered, but they were not required to carry or show identity cards, nor were they required to register again when they reached their destination in Mexico. Therefore, the Mexican government had no means of checking their whereabouts or of preventing them from moving anywhere in the country. Once most of them adopted Mexican citizenship, of course, at the beginning of 1940, there ceased to be any monitoring of their movements at all. There is no doubt that the majority of the refugees settled in Mexico City within a decade or so after their arrival. Most of those with whom I have spoken who had gone somewhere outside of the city first moved to the capital within a year. Refugees who came by other means than on one of the chartered ships could go directly to Mexico City.

administrative and financial problems for the Spanish officials of the SERE and the JARE[35] and was a source of some consternation to Mexican citizens.

The Spaniards themselves have blamed their agricultural failures on local Mexican hostility and lack of official cooperation, on their own preference for urban life, and on their tendency to band together. As early as mid-June, 1939, there were reports that the refugees were leaving the state of Puebla and moving to Mexico City because conditions in Puebla had been intolerable and local officials inhospitable.[36] Likewise, the peasants of the countryside in the Huasteca region resisted the settlement of Spanish peasants despite extensive government propaganda.[37] Spanish peasants who attempted to farm in Mexico found that the standard of living in rural Mexico was far below that of Spain, and that they could not compete with Mexican peasants, who were willing to live so poorly.[38] Moreover, it is clear that many urban Spaniards, realizing that priority for emigration was to be given to farmers, either claimed to be farmers or expressed willingness to become so in Mexico. Unaccustomed to the isolation of the countryside and with a minimum knowledge of agriculture, however, they could not easily adjust to rural living.

One of the most widely known and frequently criticized of the exile efforts to settle in rural areas was the attempted colonization

[35] The Mexican government left the administration and financing of the refugee aid entirely in the hands of officials of the SERE and JARE until late 1941. Spanish officials did not attempt to enforce Mexican residence requirements. The refugees in Mexico City, however, were more likely than those outside to request financial aid of one kind or another from the SERE and the JARE offices. Dr. José Puche, administrator of the SERE funds, took note of the problems caused by the unexpectedly large number of refugees in Mexico City and blamed the rapid drain on the SERE funds on the fact that so many of them needed financial aid ("Informe del Dr. Puche," *Boletín al Servicio*, February 22, 1940, pp. 6–7).

[36] "Dificultades de los refugiados," *El Universal*, June 22, 1939.

[37] *Excelsior*, July 5, 1939, p. 11; July 14, p. 1; Smith, *Mexico and the Spanish Republicans*, p. 262. One informant who believed his case to be typical was urged by Mexican officials to go to a rural area and become a teacher. He refused because of widespread rumors that Mexican peasants frequently cut off the ears of Spaniards attempting to settle in their areas. Instead he came directly to Mexico City (Interview, March 5, 1967).

[38] Or such was their claim. This statement was made by Socialist leader Indalecio Prieto; quoted in Smith, *Mexico and the Spanish Republicans*, p. 263.

project at Santa Clara, near Chihuahua. In 1940 the SERE purchased a ranch of approximately 150,000 hectares, built homes and irrigation dams, established a town center, purchased farm machinery and livestock, and opened the new project to about 450 colonists. Families were eventually to purchase their land and homes from the SERE through profits earned on the sale of crops. Despite apparently careful planning and early enthusiasm, however, the original 450 colonists had by 1944 dwindled to a mere 68 persons.[39] Most of the settlers retreated to urban occupations in Chihuahua or Mexico City. The Santa Clara cooperative failed not only because the settlers were inexperienced in agriculture, but also because they could not agree on the ideological or organizational basis on which the community was to be run. Although many complained that the soil was unsuited to intensive farming, the more important problems arose from the dissension caused by political rivalry among the project administrators.[40]

The center of Spanish refugee life thus was established in the Mexican capital. Not only were the SERE and JARE officers there, but also the Spanish associations and meeting places which were becoming prominent features of exile life naturally flourished in the city. In Mexico City—and really only there—a Spanish Republican could participate in a pattern of life which was similar in many of its social and cultural aspects to the life he had left behind in Madrid, Valencia, or Barcelona. As the length of exile increased and hopes for a rapid return to Spain waned, the pull of the city grew ever stronger to the homesick exiles.[41]

[39] Whetten, *Rural Mexico*, pp. 166–168.

[40] The allegedly poor quality of the land and the inexperience of the settlers obviously contributed to the difficulties at Santa Clara, but most of those interviewed who had been directly or indirectly involved in the Santa Clara project maintained that Communists, or Communist sympathizers who had had a major voice in the direction of the settlement, alienated many of the settlers; and one informant, Francisco Lurueña, claimed that Santa Clara had been run as an "armed camp" (Interview, April 22, 1967).

[41] In *Exilio*, a novel by Mexican writer Sara García Iglesias, the characters are modeled after specific Spanish refugees with whom she was acquainted. One of the major figures begins his exile determined to stay in the solitude of the countryside, away from what he considers to be the useless debates and nostalgia of his compatriots in the capital. In the end, despite the fact that he does manage to live peacefully and successfully in rural Mexico, he can conceive of marrying and settling permanently only in the capital city. (See also Carlos Martínez, *Crónica*, pp. 15–22.)

SPANISH INTELLECTUALS AND MEXICAN CULTURE

The initial government intention had been to limit residence in Mexico City to a small Republican intellectual and professional elite, but it was not long before Spanish refugees of all classes and professions had settled there. More than the earlier Spanish settlers or any other foreigners who had preceded them, the Republicans actively participated in nearly all aspects of Mexican economic and cultural life, and they were at once a conspicuous presence in the capital city.

The group, which the Spaniards themselves defined as "intellectuals," was far more extensive than the Mexicans had anticipated, and thus, even if only intellectuals and professionals had settled in Mexico City, they would have exceeded by far the number expected. Furthermore, there were important differences between the intellectuals who sought passage to Mexico after the defeat of the Republic and those who left Spain before the end of the war and came to Mexico as guests of the government. The latter, for the most part, were older men with international experience and moderate political ideas. They were few in number and were easily accepted into the Mexican intellectual milieu. Those who came later, in large part, were younger and more politically committed, often former members of the wartime Socialist party or one of the radical youth groups. Many came to Mexico after having lived in hiding in France, eking out a precarious living in French towns or cities. Their acceptance, as we shall see, was far from automatic. Because of their number and their diversity, the nature and degree of their absorption into the Mexican environment was complex.

Despite considerable differences in status, life style, and political views, however, Spanish intellectuals of all types were conscious of their own importance as the bearers of Spanish culture and were anxious to help each other, in order to maintain their collective identity. On March 13, 1939, in Paris, a group of intellectuals founded the Junta de Cultura Española, which had as its primary objective to "save the spirit of Spanish culture . . . and to maintain the Spanish intellectuals in union."[42] The Junta worked independ-

[42] "Actividades de la Junta de Cultura Española," *España Peregrina* 1 (February, 1940): 42.

ently but in cooperation with the SERE to secure as many visas as possible to the countries of America, especially Mexico, for its members. Among the exiles, the Junta determined that there were more than five thousand persons belonging to what it called the "intellectual class."[43] Since all presumably worked in some field related to Spanish culture, to unify them and to provide for them was considered vital to the preservation of that culture.[44]

Not all of the refugees who had worked in culturally related fields prior to emigration continued in these fields in Mexico. Many, unable to find work directly suited to their skills, were forced to take positions in various industrial or business and financial enterprises.[45] It was not uncommon for them then to rise rapidly to positions of executive responsibility and material success, relegating their intellectual pursuits to avocational interests. On the other hand, for working-class Spaniards in Mexico, new material success in some instances allowed them the resources and leisure to pursue literary and intellectual interests for the first time. Whatever the means by which individual exiles chose to earn their livelihood, they looked to the writers, artists, scholars, and scientists among them to maintain and preserve the values and culture of their community. Moreover, exiles of all kinds shared a considerable pride in the importance of their cultural leaders to an increasingly rich and varied Mexican intellectual and cultural scene.

Mexicans, at first, were dismayed by the influx of Spanish refugees to Mexico City. In an editorial directed to the government, one

[43] *Cultural Creations of the Comité Técnico de Ayuda a los Españoles en México*, p.43. There is no definition of "intellectual class" in the text.

[44] Ibid.

[45] The refugees themselves, through private funds and through the SERE and the JARE, founded a variety of industries and enterprises which offered jobs to newly arrived exiles. (See Mauricio Fresco, *La emigración republicana española*, pp. 168–178, for a list and a description of all the industries founded in this manner. See also Dr. Puche's report in *Boletín al Servicio* [February 22, 1940], pp. 6–7.) The Spaniards showed a remarkable ability to work their way from poverty to financial success, often in fields in which they had no previous experience. The ease with which former intellectuals and highly trained professionals entered business activities with great material success surprised and—it must be added—disturbed many observers, both Spanish and Mexican. Michael Kenny, in "The Integration of Spanish Expatriates in Ibero-America and Their Influence on Their Communities of Origin," discusses at length the nature of Spanish adaptation and integration in Mexico.

writer complained that not only were there far too many intellectuals in the emigration, but that too many of the so-called intellectuals were really "political refugees."[46] The complaint was understandable. The politico-intellectual, a common feature of Republican Spain, was more rare in Mexico. Nobody could predict, at that time, whether the hundreds of new inhabitants of Mexico City, grouped together as "intellectuals," would later prove to be intellectuals or politicians, or both (or neither).

If the Spaniards defeated the Mexican intention that only a few prominent intellectuals should be allowed to settle in the capital, the results nonetheless eventually proved mutually gratifying. Because their number so far exceeded both Mexican and Spanish expectations, it was not possible to incorporate all Spanish intellectuals into existing cultural or academic establishments. On the contrary, the presence of so many individuals involved in all aspects of culture—writing, art, theater, journalism, music, and so forth—generated energy for a variety of new cultural enterprises, sometimes initiated by the Spaniards themselves, sometimes by Mexicans, with Spanish participation.

The Mexican cultural elite, prior to the arrival of the Spaniards, had grown increasingly conscious of its contribution to the nation. These Mexicans were aware of new intellectual and artistic trends in the rest of the world, and were anxious to create a cultural milieu which would be in keeping with international trends. At the same time they reflected the peculiar conditions of their own country. The Mexican cultural elite was not large, and its impact on the general population was, perforce, limited. After 1939, however, hundreds of Spaniards suddenly appeared in the capital, anxious to work for the benefit of their host country, and requiring employment for their own survival. They came offering skills which were in short supply in Mexico: in linguistics, in the sciences, in the methodology of a number of academic disciplines, and in the bases of the major European schools of philosophic thought. The Mexicans, finally, had the critical means necessary to create in their capital a cultural, an intellectual, and an artistic center of world importance.

Spaniards in the capital were thus working toward the accom-

[46] "Preferencia a campesinos y obreros; ya no intelectuales," *El Universal*, July 30, 1939.

plishment of two separate goals. First, as representatives of the Spanish intellectual elite in exile, they sought to keep alive the spirit and continuity of Spanish cultural life. Second, in placing their skills at the service of their hosts, they contributed to the Mexican movement for national intellectual and cultural regeneration, a movement which had begun long before they arrived. When the first Republican refugees settled in Mexico, they thought of themselves as guests, repaying the favor of asylum with a commitment to work for the benefit of their host country. They maintained their own separate cultural identity, and preserved in Mexico intellectual, social, political, and cultural associations which they had transplanted from Spain. They did so initially, because they believed that these associations would soon be reestablished in Spain, upon their return from exile. Only after World War II did most of the exiles fully realize that the Republic would not be reestablished and that they had to plan for an indefinite stay in Mexico.

The Mexicans, with more accurate perception of international politics, realized as early as 1940 that the Spanish refugees were "permanent" guests. On January 23, 1940, President Cárdenas, as the last step in his commitment to the Spanish Republican cause, offered the refugees the right to Mexican citizenship. The Mexican government issued a decree which allowed the Spanish refugees to apply for citizenship with no stipulation other than the requirement that they sign their name and give their place of birth.

Cárdenas's generous offer forced the exiles individually and as a community to reevaluate their identity as loyal Spaniards and their commitments to life in Mexico. A large majority of the exiles accepted the opportunity to become Mexican citizens, since Mexican citizenship meant the end of nearly all formal restrictions placed on them with regard to work and travel.[47] Some of the more

---

[47] Dr. Puche of the SERE estimates that about 70 to 75 percent of the refugees adopted Mexican citizenship. Even if one could find figures stating what exact percentage of the exiles applied for citizenship, the figures would not be very helpful. Usually, only the men applied for citizenship, so that they could work at whatever they chose; wives and children became citizens automatically upon the naturalization of the heads of the families, so few women applied separately. Philip Taylor states that 7,470 heads of families adopted Mexican citizenship in the first five years of exile ("Myth and Reality: How Red Were the Spanish 'Reds'?").

politically active Spaniards, however, committed to the idea of returning to their homeland as soon as possible—meaning as soon as Franco fell—considered it a moral obligation to retain their Spanish passports, and not to accept the citizenship of any other country.

With or without citizenship, however, the Spaniards considered themselves, from the first, a separate cultural community in Mexico. Despite the frequently cited common Hispanic origins and shared colonial past, both Spaniards and Mexicans acknowledged the overall differences between them in values, life styles, and personalities.[48] The refugees, for their part, as they gradually came to accept the permanence of their exile, placed increasing importance on the distinctiveness of their community. Newly created Spanish intellectual, social, political, and cultural associations were no longer seen as transitional structures, but as the means by which Spanish identity and Republican loyalties could be preserved in Mexico.

The refugees have maintained a dual allegiance: professional life and some social and cultural contacts with Mexicans in a Mexican context; a great deal of cultural activity, most social interactions, and of course, all political activity, with fellow Spaniards, organized around Spanish themes. For some Mexicans, who hoped for a greater commitment on the part of their guests, this dual allegiance of the refugees is reminiscent of the attitude of the *gachupines*, and is regarded critically. For some Spaniards, too, the practical motives for a separate Spanish community have disappeared. Such Spaniards consider that those who maintain their allegiance to Spain solely for reasons of sentimentality have become *agachupinados*.[49] Sentimentality aside, individual survival has been de-

---

[48] There is considerable agreement on the part of both Spaniards and Mexicans on the differences in character, and these differences were described to me in a number of interviews. They are depicted charmingly in a story by Spanish writer Max Aub, "La verdadera historia de la muerta de Francisco Franco," in *La verdadera historia de Francisco Franco y otros cuentos*, which is the story of a Mexican waiter in a restaurant-café frequented by the refugees; the waiter hates the refugees, above all because they are "loudmouths," and he longs for the return of the dignified Mexican clientele. See also the discussions in chap. 4 and chap. 9, below.

[49] See Kenny's frequent treatment of the theme *agachupinado* in "Integration of Spanish Expatriates."

pendent on each refugee's ability to find his place within the Mexican economy. Furthermore, the overall impact of the Spanish Republicans on the Mexican environment ultimately has proved far more meaningful than has their influence on the future of Spain.

4. CONTRIBUTIONS AND IMPACT

The first concern of most of the new exiles in Mexico was to find a job. Both the SERE and the JARE sought to meet this concern by founding a number of enterprises in such fields as publishing, manufacturing, and finance, but few of these enterprises survived more than two or three years. It was not within the Spanish community, but rather in the rapidly expanding Mexican economy that the Spanish exiles found the opportunities they sought.

At first, the need for work was so great in Mexico that many of the exiles accepted menial jobs well beneath their levels of learning and experience. Even intellectuals and professionals were willing to engage in almost any kind of work in order to earn enough to feed their families.[1] In time, a number of these people, sometimes

---

[1] Extremes in good and ill fortune were typical; for instance, a former judge of the supreme court of Madrid earned his first Mexican pesos selling small bars

quite accidentally, became very successful businessmen.[2] In Mexico, neither skill in financial matters nor the monetary benefits thereby acquired were treated so disparagingly as in Spain. Spaniards later candidly admitted that in many cases the spiritual loss of their homeland was compensated for, in part, by having acquired a much higher level of material well-being than would have been possible for them at home.

Within a relatively short time after settling, however, most of the established Spanish intellectuals and professionals were able to find employment related to their fields of specialization, or at least to acquire positions in which they could make use of their training. The productivity of the refugees as a whole has been impressive, and many individuals have accomplished their most important work in exile. Nearly all the post–Civil War achievements from which the Spanish intellectuals and professionals have earned their considerable international recognition owe a great deal to their opportunity to work freely in Mexico.[3]

Of all of them, the transition was least difficult for the most prominent of the intellectuals. Their initial gathering place was the Casa de España, converted in 1940 to El Colegio de México.[4] In the Casa, the newly arrived Spaniards worked independently and with prominent Mexican intellectuals, devising new courses of study, arranging seminars, writing, and developing new ideas. The

---

of soap to houses of prostitution. Working thereafter at a variety of enterprises, he eventually acquired monetary success, and after many years was able to practice law again. Isabel de Palencia provides much anecdotal information about prominent exiles in *Smouldering Freedom: The Story of the Spanish Republicans in Exile*.

[2] In most of the interviews I asked the person interviewed to name the area or areas in which the Republicans had made the greatest contribution to Mexico. None of the Spaniards mentioned business, although most of the Mexicans interviewed did, sometimes as a compliment, sometimes not. Carlos Martínez, in his *Crónica de una emigración*, covers virtually all fields in which the Spaniards have participated in exile, and lists the names of the most prominent persons in each field. In the chapter devoted to business and finance, however, not one Spaniard is named; only the names of enterprises in which Spaniards have played important roles are given. Evidently, some ambivalence remains regarding success in business.

[3] The Mexican economy expanded significantly during World War II, making it easier than anyone had anticipated to incorporate the refugees into the economic structure.

[4] See chap. 2.

Casa, as an academic and intellectual experiment, proved so successful that Spanish participation came to be sought at other Mexican institutions, and within a short time the Colegio ceased to be
the sole or even the most important Spanish intellectual center.
Spanish intellectuals entered nearly all the important Mexican universities and scientific facilities; their impact was felt not only in
all the academic disciplines, but throughout Mexican cultural and
economic life.

ACADEMIC CONTRIBUTIONS

Philosophy was one discipline to benefit significantly from the
arrival of Spanish intellectuals. The emigration included a number
of internationally known individuals in the field, including José
Gaos, Eduardo Nicol, Juan Roura-Parella, Luis Recasens Siches, and
Juan David García Bacca. These men arrived when philosophy in
Mexico was in a state of transition. Since about 1925 the previously dominant influence of Bergsonian philosophic thought had been
declining in favor of the Germanic phenomenologic and existentialist schools. The new trend first reached Mexico through José
Ortega y Gasset, and was reinterpreted in line with Mexican nationalist ideals by Mexican philosophers, outstanding among whom
was Samuel Ramos.[5] During the 1920's and 1930's, a few Mexicans
did go to Germany to study, but the continued influence of Germanic thought and its Spanish tone was, more than any other factor, due to the German-trained Spanish philosophers who came to
Mexico as exiles.[6] Of these Spanish philosophers, and, in fact, of
all the Spanish intellectuals, none attracted so much praise and respect as José Gaos, one of the original members of the Casa de
España. Gaos's contribution was unanticipated. It was hardly expected that a Spaniard with comparatively little knowledge of
Mexico would inspire a new school of Mexican self-awareness, but
this in fact was the outcome of Gaos's work. Attracting a small
group of Mexican students to his seminars at the Casa, he founded
what he called the Grupo Hiperión. Through this group, young
Mexican scholars, including Leopoldo Zea, Octavio Paz, and Luis
González, were encouraged to use existentialist German and Span-

[5] Patrick Romanell, *The Making of the Mexican Mind: A Study in Recent
Mexican Thought*, pp. 140–145.
[6] Ibid., pp. 145–147.

ish Ortegian thought as a basis for examining the essence of Mexican identity. The well-known series of books, *El mexicano y lo mexicano*, was a direct result of Gaos's influence on this group, and Gaos himself was an important contributor to the series.[7]

Spanish academicians, in many cases, have been able to compensate for the traditional lack of attention paid by Spanish scholars to American themes, and have contributed to research on Mexican and other American materials. The group most seriously involved in *lo mexicano* has been the anthropologists. Older anthropologists, such as the distinguished Pere Bosch Gimpera, did not change their primary research interests from Spain to Mexico, and they were only marginally concerned with work on Mexican subjects. For the younger men, however, Mexico became the center of all their research. Juan Comas, for instance, helped found the Institute of Anthropology and History with Antonio Caso in 1939 and, during his first few years in Mexico, worked in the Instituto Indigenista Interoamericana. He and other Spaniards, including Santiago Genovés, whom he trained, have been involved in the discovery, classification, and description of Mexico's enormously varied Indian population and in making public the history of Mexico's past civilizations. Spaniards sometimes note with wry amusement that the Mexican nationalism, from which many consider themselves to have suffered, owes much of its inspiration to the glorification of the Indian past, a glorification which was aided by the work of Spanish anthropologists.[8]

Although Spanish historians traditionally have had little interest in topics related to the Americas, historians among the refugees have accomplished some important research in Mexican colonial

[7] Ibid.; José Gaos, *Confesiones profesionales*, p. 112, and *En torno a la filosofía mexicana*, II, 65ff.; Interviews, with Daniel Cosío Villegas, March 28, 1967, and with Arturo Arnaiz y Freg, April 4, 1967. The Hiperión group of the 1940's and 1950's included Leopoldo Zea, Emilio Uranga, Luis Villoro, Ricardo Onema, Jorge Portilla, Joaquín McGregor, Alejandro Rossi, Eduardo García Maynez, Francisco Larroyo, Oswaldo Robles, Gustavo R. Velasco, Santiago Ramírez, Francisco González Pineda, Lucio Mendieta y Núñez, González Casanova, and Víctor Urquidi; Spaniards involved were José Moreno Villa, Luis Recasens Siches, José Medina Echavarría, and Ramón Xirau. See Frank Brandenberg, *The Making of Modern Mexico*, p. 349. For a discussion of the philosophic and historical background of Gaos's contribution, see Romanell, *Making of the Mexican Mind*, p. 11, and John Leddy Phelan, "México y lo mexicano," pp. 309–318.

[8] Interviews, with Pere Bosch Gimpera, January 24, 1967; with Juan Comas, February 7, 1967.

history and in the history and culture of the Hispanic world. While these fields have not been among the most popular for postrevolutionary Mexican historians, for such Spanish refugees as José Miranda and Agustín Millares Carlo they were seen as a fascinating and altogether new aspect of their own national past. Well-known historians and men of letters, including Salvador de Madariaga, Victor Alba, Américo Castro, Ramón Iglesias, Carlos Bosch Gimpera, and José María Gallegos Rocafull were working and publishing important books and articles on issues related to Mexican history only a few years after they arrived.[9]

In the humanities, law, and sociology, in biology, physics, mathematics, and chemistry, Spaniards augmented all the faculties of the National University and have been well represented in the special technical universities and in the major provincial universities. In 1967, poet Luis Rius counted twenty-six full professors of Spanish origin in the National University Faculty of Letters alone, a number he considered to be but a modest indication of the extent of the Spanish contribution to Mexican intellectual growth.[10] While it is impossible to measure precisely the amount of influence of Spanish professors on their students, the sheer number of Spaniards teaching in the universities, in addition to their books and articles, obviously has produced an impact on Mexican academic life. Since the 1940's, it has been virtually impossible to attend the university, particularly the Faculty of Humanities, without encountering either a Spanish professor or a Mexican trained by a Spanish professor.

ARTS AND LITERATURE

The influence of Spanish participation in Mexican arts and literature is difficult to assess, since few of the Spanish writers or artists have directly "taught" their Mexican counterparts. Probably the Mexican environment has had a greater impact upon the exile writers and artists than they on it. Cut off from their homeland and its familiar surroundings, Spanish artists and writers often turned at once to the immense variety of Mexico for new inspiration.[11]

[9] See Carlos Martínez, *Crónica*, pp. 344–373.
[10] Luis Rius, "Maestros españoles en la UNAM," *El Heraldo*, March 7, 1967. Rius studied and taught in that faculty himself.
[11] As did Ceferino de Palencia. (See his *México inspirador*, p. 7.)

Their views of Mexico, however, have always been those of aliens rather than those of members of the community. Because they have been profoundly influenced by Mexico while retaining their Spanish outlook and orientation, their work has not fully reflected either Mexico or Spain. Rather it has tended to reflect the preoccupations of men in exile, their search for personal identity and for universal human values and characteristics.

The Republican exiles included a number of prominent artists,[12] whose creativity had been as much inspired by their sense of national identity as by international artistic trends. Exile for them was more than a break in the continuity of their lives, and, in nearly all cases, their work showed the impact of their separation from Spain, from their familiar surroundings, and from the original sources of their inspiration. Enrique Climent, for example, completely abandoned the forceful realism which characterized his Spanish paintings and turned instead to abstract art.[13] José Renau, who had established a reputation as a master of powerful political sketches during the Republic and the Civil War, found himself "disintoxicated" with the use of plastic arts for publicity. His interests turned to the aesthetic and political potential of large murals, such as those he found in Cuernavaca.[14]

Whatever the nature of the change that occurred in their art during exile, the Spanish painters could neither work closely with Mexican painters nor participate in the dominant trend in Mexican art, which at that time was still revolutionary.[15] The well-known Mexican artists were generally men of the Left who had sympathized with the Spanish Republican struggle. Alfaro Siqueiros went to Spain during the Civil War, and other Mexican artists, among them Diego Rivera, Juan O'Gorman, and Chávez Morado, had befriended the Spanish artists in exile.[16] Nonetheless, Mexico

---

[12] Such artists as Arturo Souto, Antonio Rodríguez Luna, Enrique Climent, Ramón Gaya, Miguel Prieto, Roberto Fernández Balbuena, Ceferino de Palencia, Cristóbal Ruiz, José Renau, and Antonio Clavé (Martínez, *Crónica*, p. 133).

[13] Ibid., p. 135.

[14] José Renau, "El pintor y la obra," *Las Españas* 2 (November, 1946): 12, 16.

[15] See Gilbert Chase, "The Artist," in *Continuity and Change in Latin America*, edited by John J. Johnson, pp. 106–111, 117.

[16] These artists were singled out specifically by Antonio Rodríguez Luna as some of the most friendly, though he had some reservations concerning the goodwill of Diego Rivera because, he said, Rivera was so intensely anti-Spanish that he found it difficult to sympathize fully with the refugees.

in the early 1940's still expected artists to reflect popular will and revolutionary ideals in their work. The Spaniards, *particularly* the Spaniards against whose country so much revolutionary ardor was directed, had no role to play in this school of art.[17]

In creative writing, as in painting, there was a severe break in style and content between what was written in Spain and what was produced in exile. Writers before the war frequently drew literary inspiration from political, cultural, and social innovations in Spain, but they rarely attempted to follow this practice in Mexico. Although, as already noted, collaboration between Spanish and Mexican writers was frequent, in all the periodicals which were not specifically Spanish the exile writers usually limited themselves to themes of universal or general professional interest. Articles which did not treat Spanish subjects dealt with persons of international reputation or used Spanish subject matter merely to illustrate abstract principles. With some notable exceptions, including Max Aub, Manuel Andújar, Ramón Sender, and the poet León Felipe, writers rarely made issues relevant to contemporary Spain or to contemporary Mexico or to their own personal experiences the subjects of their work.[18]

The Spanish exiles settled in Mexico at a time when themes of national concern dominated Mexican literature. Until the 1950's, most Mexican writers ignored European trends and criticized the *extranjerismo* of those of their compatriots whose writing seemed too cosmopolitan or abstract.[19] So long as local writers continued to seek a specifically Mexican style and content in their works, the newly arrived Spaniards had very little impact on their literature. Collaboration of Spaniards and Mexicans in all fields was certainly facilitated by their common Spanish language. Yet, for the Spanish writers there was also a language barrier. The exile writers

[17] Musicians and composers found it easier to make the transition to Mexico. Adolfo Salazar and Rudolfo Halffter, among others, were warmly welcomed and were quickly and deeply involved in musical developments and teaching in Mexico.

[18] For example, in *El Hijo Pródigo*, a general literary periodical published between April 15, 1943, and September, 1946, there appeared only six articles written by Spaniards on Spain, the Republic, the war, or their Mexican experience (excluding articles *en memoriam* to specific artists or heroes, which were more numerous).

[19] Joseph Sommers, *After the Storm: Landmarks of the Modern Mexican Novel*, p. 33.

drew their words from Spain and wrote as Spaniards to other Spaniards. Their meanings and inferences were neither familiar nor entirely clear to Mexicans.

Francisco Ayala, a prominent sociologist and writer in exile, considered this problem with regard to the exiles in all the Spanish-speaking Americas. He concluded that, during the first years of exile, Spanish writers were virtually without an audience outside their own group.[20] Luis Aranguren, a liberal intellectual leader in Spain, also noted enormous differences between the kind of work produced by the writers in Spain and the published work of the same men in exile. He concluded, however, that, in the long run, exile in other Spanish-speaking countries had revealed to the refugees more clearly than ever the intensity of their cultural and emotional ties to Spain.[21] Vicente Llorens Castillo, like Ayala an exile and a professor of Spanish literature, found that the Spanish language often proved a false friend: communication seemed so easy to the newly arrived exiles that at times both Spaniards and Mexicans failed to realize the extent to which they misunderstood or were being misunderstood.[22] For at least the first ten years of exile, Spanish audiences were not accessible to the refugee writers. Mexicans and other Latin Americans with their own national concerns neither understood nor were interested in the experiences which preoccupied the Spanish exiles, and few other Europeans outside Spain knew Spanish. The writers in exile, therefore, often wrote professional articles for scholarly journals or popular works for the general public, but they reserved their more intimate, more creative efforts for the very limited audience of their intellectual compatriots in exile.

OTHER FIELDS

No matter how many intellectual and cultural facilities were created in Mexico, there were many intellectuals, self-styled intellectuals, and would-be intellectuals in the emigration who eventu-

[20] Francisco Ayala, *El escritor en la sociedad de masas*, p. 18. Since leaving Spain, Ayala has lived in Argentina and in the United States.

[21] José Luis Aranguren, *Crítica y meditación*, pp. 172–177.

[22] Vicente Llorens Castillo, a lecture given at El Colegio de México, April 16, 1967. Llorens is currently preparing a book dealing with the contributions and experiences of Spanish writers in exile. He is a professor at Princeton University.

ally turned to other occupations. In a number of cases, Spaniards trained in a specific area were able to use their skills in a different but related field. As often as not, the alternatives they chose offered them substantial opportunity for individual success and remuneration.

For example, out of the long tradition of Spanish involvement in the literary arts, there emerged a small but influential group of writers and directors who contributed to the growing Mexican film industry. Their contributions were at times intellectual and artistic, but more often popular; for example, there were Spaniards involved in script-writing, acting, and directing for the Mexican theater. Some of them had had previous experience in Spain, others had not. They generally found in this industry a more than adequate means of earning their livelihood, and at times they also found an interesting medium for social or artistic expression. The Spanish films were often more "indigenous" than those of their Mexican colleagues. Such writers as Paulino Masip wrote or adapted the stories for Mexico's most popular "cowboy" movies in the late 1940's.[23] On an entirely different level, the social realities of Mexico never have been so vividly brought to the screen as they were in Luis Buñuel's powerful films, *Nazarín* (1958) and *Los olvidados* (1950).[24]

MEDICINE

According to Spanish sources, approximately five hundred Spanish doctors of medicine came to Mexico, doubling the total number of doctors in the country.[25] Among the Spaniards in exile was a substantial proportion of the members of the faculties of medicine

[23] Interviews with writer Max Aub, August 14, 1966; and with Sra. Fernanda de Masip, August 17, 1966.
[24] While the cinema attracted much Spanish participation in the 1940's, less attention was paid to the Mexican theater. A few Spanish actors and actresses played in Mexican productions, but the major Spanish contribution did not occur until the early 1950's, with Alvaro Custodio's Teatro Español de México (Interview with Alvaro Custodio, January 26, 1967; Martínez, *Crónica*, p. 72).
[25] Germán Somolinos, *25 años de medicina española en México*, pp. 19–20. Somolinos believes the high number of Spanish physicians in exile is due to a staunchly republican tradition among doctors in prewar Spain; the majority of these doctors had received part of their training at the Institución Libre de Enseñanza. Prime Minister Negrín had been a member of the medical faculty at the University of Madrid, and influenced many of his fellow doctors.

from all the Spanish universities,[26] as well as many internationally known medical specialists who had enjoyed lucrative private practices in Spain. Such fields as cardiology, ophthalmology, psychology, and gynecology, relatively undeveloped in Mexico, were represented by important figures in the emigration.[27] Mexico's subsequent medical advances in these areas owed much to these men and to the followers they trained.

During the 1940's and 1950's Mexico initiated major national health campaigns in which newly arrived Spanish physicians participated fully. For the first time important advances were made toward the eradication, or at least the control, of smallpox, malaria, tuberculosis, typhus, and leprosy, and efforts were significantly expanded in the fields of tropical medicine, sanitation, and nutrition.[28]

The Spaniards arrived just as Mexico was reorganizing and renovating its school of medicine and totally restructuring its general hospital, creating new services and improved research facilities. Spanish medical personnel were involved in all phases of the innovations, especially in aspects of research and teaching. Soon after their arrival, a new Cardiology Institute and an infants' and childrens' hospital were founded. During the 1940's the Ministry of Health sponsored new hospitals and clinics all over the country, and a Department of Rural Medicine was created within the School of Biology at the Polytechnical Institute.[29]

The better-known Spanish doctors were welcomed in Mexican universities as well as in several Mexican hospitals and clinics. Still, the large number of Spanish doctors who arrived in Mexico during 1939 and 1940 and their potentially competitive impact

[26] Mauricio Fresco, in a partial list, names sixty-nine professors of medicine from Spanish universities and twelve professors of pharmacology (*La emigración republicana*, pp. 73–76).

[27] Prominent doctors attained important positions in the universities of Mexico, Monterrey, and Tampico, and in the Nacional Politécnico. Spanish exile doctors also served in all of Mexico's major hospitals, as well as serving in or even founding a number of such smaller clinics and special institutes as the leprosarium. For the specific names of Mexican physicians and their university or hospital affiliations, see Somolinos, *25 años*, pp. 19–20.

[28] Xavier de la Riva Rodríguez, "Salubridad y asistencia médico-social," in *México, 50 años de revolución*, Vol. II: *La vida social*, 1962, pp. 380–442.

[29] Somolinos, *25 años*, pp. 16–17. See also Ignacio Chávez, *México en la cultura médica*.

initially caused both the general public and Mexican physicians some worry. As a result of Mexican concern serious attempts were made to limit those exiles who settled in the capital city to physician-academicians. Physicians who had not held university posts in Spain were not judged to be "intellectuals," and, therefore, they were supposed to scatter throughout the provinces. It was also considered desirable for the newcomers to enter the public sector of medicine before taking on private patients.[30]

Despite official efforts and the dismay of some Mexican physicians, Spanish doctors did in fact settle in large numbers in the Mexican capital and in other major cities. By November of 1939, Mexicans estimated that there were some two hundred Spanish physicians in the Federal District alone.[31] The Spaniards argued that Mexico City could easily absorb all the medical refugees, particularly those whose practice was in the specialized fields in which Mexican medicine was generally weak, and still be inadequately served medically.[32] Mexican doctors, nevertheless, continued to complain about the Spanish competition, accusing the Spaniards of charging too much for their consultations, of overemphasizing the commercial aspects of medicine, and of capitalizing on the prestige Spanish medicine enjoyed by pretending to be more capable than Mexicans.[33]

Complaints notwithstanding, there was little reason for serious discontent in the ranks of Mexican physicians. Although the Spaniards settled in urban areas and entered private practice, they rarely competed directly with Mexican medical personnel during the

[30] *Excelsior*, April 30, 1939, pp. 1, 6.
[31] *Excelsior*, November 17, 1939, p. 12.
[32] *Excelsior*, November 2, 1939.
[33] The Spaniards, at first, did generally charge more for their professional services, but, eventually, Mexican physicians came to charge roughly the same as the Spaniards for similar services (Interviews with Spanish physicians Germán Somolinos, November 11, 1966; José Puche, November 15, 1966; Blas Cabrera, December 22, 1966; Luis Fumagallo, December 22, 1966). According to the Spanish physicians interviewed, their practice of charging higher fees for their professional services was a service to Mexican and Spanish physicians alike, since all subsequently began to charge more, and thereby attained a more satisfactory living wage from their medical practice. According to Mexicans, medical charges were increased in keeping with the general rise in the cost of living during the war years.

early years of exile. Most of the time and attention of the emigré doctors was occupied in attending to the medical needs of the Spanish refugees. There were serious health problems within the Republican community, stemming from the physical privations experienced by some in leaving Spain and the difficulties of many in adjusting to the altitude and climate of Mexico.[34] Serving fellow refugees left Spanish doctors little time to seek new patients among the Mexican population. It also brought Spanish doctors little in the way of monetary remuneration. Until the penury common to most of the refugees was relieved, they received virtually free medical care.[35]

A large proportion of patients of the original Spanish refugee physicians is still composed of fellow Republicans and their children, some of whom receive medical care through the Beneficencia Hispánica, a medical clinic especially created for the Republican refugees.[36] The second generation of Spanish doctors, those who have received all or part of their medical training in Mexico (studying under Spanish as well as Mexican teachers), works in public or private medical practice in about the same proportion as Mexican-born physicians. They do not seem to be limited to predominantly Spanish patients.[37]

In the fields of physical and biological research and in pharmacology, Spanish scientists have, from the first, worked in close collaboration with Mexican scientists. Scientific facilities in the universities have been expanded and improved, and the number of

[34] Martínez, Crónica, p. 421.

[35] Interviews with Somolinos, Puche, and Blas Cabrera. See footnote 33, above.

[36] The Beneficencia Hispánica is a clinic, created so that the refugees would not become a burden upon Mexican health facilities. A large number of important Spanish physicians donated their time to the clinic; membership fees, initially quite low, have remained modest for any refugee or his family. The clinic, however, has been only moderately successful, since it duplicates—slightly more expensively—the services offered by the Sanatório Español; the sanatório was founded by and for the benefit of the old Spanish colony, but it is open to all Spanish-born residents of Mexico, or to those who have at least one Spanish parent. Many refugees have swallowed their political pride in order to take advantage of the facilities offered by the sanatório (Interview, Dr. José Harcourt, head of Beneficencia Hispánica, July 19, 1966).

[37] Interview, Dr. Jan Somolinos, who was working for the Social Security Administration, November 9, 1966.

private laboratories has increased significantly since the 1940's. It appears that in the fields of scientific research there has been no tension or competition between Spaniards and Mexicans.[38]

CULTURE AND THE WRITTEN WORD

Whatever their source of livelihood in Mexico, the exiles wished to preserve their identity and publicize the plight of their country. Intellectuals and writers were valued and respected throughout the community because they maintained, through their work, the vitality of Spanish culture and reminded the outside world of the Spanish exile. The widespread belief in the power and importance of the written word, moreover, attracted refugee Spaniards to work in institutions and enterprises which dealt directly or indirectly with the publication and distribution of literature and scholarship.

The Spaniards thus added their numbers to a wide range of academic and cultural institutions and associations existing in Mexico at the time of their arrival. But there was neither a sufficient number of these institutions to absorb all the Spaniards, nor an adequate number of outlets for their work. A significant aspect of the Spanish contribution to Mexico has been its role in expanding general cultural productivity and participation and in bringing the cultural contributions of both Mexicans and Spaniards to a wider public. The Spaniards have been involved in the expansion of the Mexican publishing industry from its modest and limited capacity in the 1930's to its present position, which includes some of the largest and most important publishing houses in Latin America. The number of periodicals of academic and cultural relevance in Mexico has more than doubled since the arrival of the refugees, and there is scarcely a single periodical in any field in which Spanish Republicans have not been involved.

PUBLISHING

The earliest published works of Spanish intellectuals in Mexico were those put out under the auspices of the Casa de España. The Casa de España–Colegio de México has continued to publish the

[38] The periodical *Ciencia*, founded in 1940, has been a testament to this cooperation. Although thus far continually directed by a Spanish scientist, *Ciencia* has welcomed Mexican contributions.

works of its members through its own publishing house and through that of Tezontle, which was created in May, 1940, for literary works considered to be outside the scope of the publishing facilities of the Colegio or of the important and growing publishing house, the Fondo de Cultura Económica.[39]

The Fondo de Cultura Económica was founded in September, 1934, by a small group of Mexicans. Their initial objective was to translate and distribute works in the field of economics and political economy hitherto unavailable in Mexico.[40] The members of the original governing body were, as they recall, more enthusiastic in their aims than experienced in the publishing industry.[41] Nonetheless, the company grew and expanded. It was soon publishing works in fields other than economics and even initiating the publication of original manuscripts by Mexican academicians.

The Fondo de Cultura filled a growing need for scholarly books in Mexico. Increasing facilities for higher education and a growing middle class had expanded the reading public. Furthermore, after the outbreak of the Spanish Civil War, in 1936, the Spanish publishing industry was virtually destroyed. Since a large portion of the books read in Latin America before the war had been printed in Spain, publishing houses in the Americas in the late 1930's and 1940's inherited a broad Hispano-American market.

The nascent Mexican publishing industry, and the Fondo de Cultura in particular, hoped to capture this market. But the industry was limited in its capacity to expand, primarily because of an insufficient number of Mexicans with the requisite skills in publishing. Among the Spanish refugees who reached Mexico from 1939 on, many had skills and experience gained in the publishing field in Spain, and they were anxious to continue their profession in Mexico. The refugees who sought employment in the Fondo de Cultura helped it become, within a relatively short time, the largest publishing house in Mexico and among the most important in all Latin America. By the early 1950's the Fondo was sponsoring ex-

---

[39] By 1950 the Fondo had incorporated the publishing houses of the Colegio and Tezontle (Fondo de Cultura Económica, Catálogo general, pp. 387–391, 401–402).

[40] Ibid., pp. xv–xvii.

[41] The original governing body consisted of Emigdio Martínez Adame, Eduardo Villaseñor, González Robles, Daniel Cosío Villegas, Jesús Silva Herzog, Eduardo Suárez, and Ramón Beteta (Ibid., pp. xvii–xviii).

tensive publication, both of original work and of translations, in seven academic fields, and the initial publishing house of economic material had grown to include a large number of fields and six special collections.[42]

Spaniards and Mexicans alike have noted the Spanish contribution to publishing houses in Mexico as crucial to the development of this industry. Spaniards, in addition to being deeply involved in the Fondo de Cultura, created a large number of publishing houses of their own, including Joaquín Mortiz, Seneca, Costa-Amic, EDIAPSA, Arcos, Proa, Vasca Elkin, Rex, Grijalbo, Catalonia, Ediciones Libro-Mex, Era, Centauro, Xochitl, Bajel, Leyenda, Esfinge, Oasis, Quetzal, Prometeo, Biblioteca Catalána, and many others. Some of these are highly specialized; others are large and general. Some were founded early in exile and have since grown; others have been founded recently; some survived only a few years.[43]

A number of Spaniards believe that their editorial skills and experience, coupled with the decline of the publishing industry in Spain, deserve the major credit for the flowering of Mexican publishing enterprises. Mexicans, on the other hand, argue that the important factor was the timing. The arrival of the Spaniards coincided fortuitously with the Mexican readiness to create and expand their own efforts in the field of publishing. The Spanish intellectuals thus profited from the existing conditions in Mexico,

---

[42] The fields established then were economics, history, sociology, politics and law, philosophy, anthropology, and science. The special collections included Biblioteca Americana, Colección Tierra Firme, Brevarios, Lengua y Estudios Literarias, Letras Mexicanas, also the former publishers El Colegio de México, and Tezontle. Among the many Spaniards who participated most actively in the Fondo were Eugenio Imaz, Sindulfo de la Fuente, José Gaos, Manuel Pedroso, Wenceslao Roces, José Alaminos, Florentino M. Torner, Joaquín Diez-Canedo, Jávier Márquez, Francisco Giner de los Ríos, Ramón Iglesia, José Medina Echavarría, José Roura-Parella, Juan Comas, and Vicente Herrero. See ibid.; see also Martínez, *Crónica*, p. 99. The Fondo split at the end of 1965 and many of its employees joined the newer Siglo XXI. The Spanish believe that they deserve as much credit as the Mexicans, or possibly more, for the growth and success of the Fondo.

[43] Martínez, *Crónica*, pp. 97–99; interview with Manuel Andújar, a writer and the owner of a large book-distribution center, Avandaro, February 27, 1967; Fresco, *La emigración republicana*, pp. 92–94.

and the Mexicans were able to derive maximum benefit from Spanish skills and cooperation.[44]

Spanish refugee writers were among the major contributors to their own and other publishing houses. Since the intellectuals in the Casa de España–Colegio de México were devoting full time to their scholarly activities, they wrote and published prodigiously. For many of the Spanish intellectuals and scientists, the years of chaos, war, and exile had meant years of severely limited productivity. Once settled in Mexico, they returned to their former professional and scholarly occupations with unprecedented energy. Furthermore, in Mexico, they were cut off from the Spanish students and admirers who knew and respected them, but they were familiar to relatively few Mexicans. In the absence of large personal followings, they concluded that their memory might be preserved in Spain and their fame earned in Mexico only by means of published writings.[45]

PERIODICALS

When serious difficulties beset the publication of the first Spanish literary periodical, *España Peregrina*,[46] its editor, Juan Larrea, and one of its chief contributors, León Felipe, began to make plans to replace it. The two Spanish poets approached the economist Jesús Silva Herzog, then secretary of the treasury and known to be sympathetically disposed toward the refugees. They asked him for financial support for the proposed journal, but Silva Herzog, instead of granting Mexican support to the Spanish venture, sug-

[44] Daniel Cosío Villegas, "España contra América en la industria editorial," *Extremos de América*, p. 310.

[45] Partial lists of early publications can be found in the *Boletín Informativo* of the Unión de Profesores, vol. 2 (January–November, 1944). Another partial bibliography of the books published by Spaniards in exile is in Julián Amo and Charmion Shelby, *La obra impresa de los intelectuales españoles en América, 1936–1945*, prepared by the Hispanic Foundation of the Library of Congress. This bibliography was printed, according to the editors, "because of the extraordinary number of publications by the Spanish in the New World" (p. vii). Another extensive bibliography of published works by Spaniards in Mexico appears in the Fería Mexicana del Libro, "España en América: La aportación de la emigración republicana española a la cultura continental," November 20 to December 15, 1960.

[46] See chap. 3, above.

gested a Mexican alternative. He proposed bringing together a group of prominent Spanish and Mexican writers who would be willing to collaborate in a journal which would be larger and broader in scope than *España Peregrina*. Larrea and León Felipe welcomed the idea and had no difficulty interesting other prominent scholars and writers in the project. In this manner, *Cuadernos Americanos* was born, its first issue appearing in January, 1942.[47] The initial board of directors included four Spaniards and six Mexicans, all of whom had held previous academic positions of importance in a variety of fields.[48]

The literary periodicals in which the Spaniards have been involved since their arrival in Mexico fall into three categories. The smallest number have been those almost exclusively Spanish in theme and participation, such as *España Peregrina*, *Litoral*, and *Las Españas*.[49] In another group are those periodicals founded either in part or almost entirely by Spaniards, in which both Spaniards and Mexicans have participated, such as *Cuadernos Americanos*, *Romance* (primarily a Spanish periodical), *Hijo Pródigo*, *Tierra Nueva*, and *Taller* (primarily Mexican periodicals), and the literary supplements to *Novedades* and *Excelsior*. In the third category are the periodicals which were entirely Mexican in origin and management, but which have welcomed Spanish collaborators and contributions. In this category are nearly all the remaining

[47] Interview with Jesús Silva Herzog, March 4, 1967; "Jesús Silva Herzog, León Felipe y los *Cuadernos Americanos*," in [Camino Galicia] León Felipe, *Antología y homenaje*, p. 8.

[48] The men who served on the first board of directors were, as director general, Jesús Silva Herzog, then secretary of the treasury and subsequently director of the School of Economics at the National University; as secretaries, Juan Larrea, ex-secretary of the Archivo Histórico Nacional de Madrid, and Pere Bosch Gimpera, ex-rector of the University of Barcelona; also on the board were Daniel Cosío Villegas, director general of the Fondo de Cultura; Mario de la Cueva, rector of the National University; Manuel Márquez, ex-dean of the University of Madrid; Manuel Martínez Báez, president of the Academy of Medicine, Mexico; Agustín Millares Carlo, professor at the University of Madrid; Bernardo Ortiz de Montellano, ex-director of the periodical *Contemporáneos*, and Alfonso Reyes, president of El Colegio de México.

[49] *Litoral* was a small literary periodical begun before exile by a group of prominent Andalusian intellectuals, directed by Francisco Giner de los Ríos. Only a few issues were published in exile. *Las Españas* is discussed in chap. 5, below.

literary and cultural periodicals published in Mexico and the daily press.[50]

A periodical of a different type, *Ciencia*, was initiated in 1940 and achieved immediate importance. Serving nearly all fields of science and medicine, *Ciencia* was founded and edited by the internationally prominent Spanish scientist, Dr. Ignacio Bolívar, and his son Cándido. It later was edited by Dr. Blas Cabrera. Since its founding it has served as an important source of information and exchange of ideas for the many Mexican and Spanish scientists who regularly contribute to its pages.

OUTSIDE MEXICO

Not all the Spanish refugees who came to Mexico chose to remain. Some accepted attractive offers in other countries of Latin America or in the United States. An even greater number left Mexico to work in various international organizations, employed either directly by the organizational secretariats, as in the United Nations or UNESCO, or filling the Mexican quota in various branches and committees of the United Nations, the Organization of American States, the World Health Organization, and elsewhere.[51]

A number of circumstances might account for the Spaniards' interest in the international organizations and Mexican interest in helping them find this type of employment. For the Spaniards, the most obvious attraction of such positions has been the relatively high salaries and the security offered. For those employed as Span-

[50] Interview with Francisco Giner de los Ríos, October 28, 1967; Antonio Alatorre, *Literatura de la emigración republicana española en México*, p. 4. I have omitted from this list of literary periodicals the countless periodicals of Spanish political groups and social associations. Nearly all the important Mexico City dailies—*Excelsior*, *Novedades*, *El Nacional*, and *El Popular*, and the *revistas*, such as *Tiempo*, *Sucesos*, and *Siempre*—have employed Spanish journalists, a number of whom have written regular columns for years.

[51] To give but a few examples: Pere Bosch Gimpera worked in UNESCO with Jaime Torres Bodet during the 1950's. Others who worked in the United Nations were Professors Miguel Marín (international law), Vicente Hurero (political science), Luis Recasens Siches (philosophy), and Manuel López Rey (criminology) (See Fresco, *La emigración republicana*, p. 161). José Echavarría, professor of philosophy of law, worked in UN-ECLA, and, later, Francisco Giner de los Ríos also joined the ECLA staff. Javier Malagón holds an important position in the OAS. Virgilio Botella Pastor has represented Mexico in UNESCO.

ish nationals by these organizations, the positions have proved the best means for the exiles to live outside of Spain without adopting the citizenship of any other country. Those individuals who first came to Mexico and then left, either to represent Mexico abroad or to work in the international bureaucracies, were not leaving a country to which they had a deep emotional attachment, outside of attachments to friends or family. In some cases they left precisely because they preferred life in Paris, Geneva, New York, or Washington to that in Mexico. In other cases, they left because they disliked Mexico or because they saw no opportunity to realize their ambitions there.[52]

It is reasonable to conclude that refugees who have chosen to live in Europe, the United States, or South America even though they are Mexican citizens, either have made little attempt to adjust to Mexican life or have failed in their efforts to do so. It is also probable that their sense of Spanish identity has continued strong throughout the years. As will be seen, moreover, these men and women are not alone among the exiles in wishing to remain overtly Spanish. In Mexico itself, there is an elaborate institutional structure which serves to insulate some refugees from direct confrontation with Mexican life and values and to remind even the best integrated and most successful of their original national and cultural identity.

[52] Mexican and Spanish informants frequently spoke about the work of the refugees in international organizations. The "international" alternative is most welcome to those Spanish exiles who, although grateful for their Mexican citizenship, are dissatisfied with life in Mexico. One Spanish interviewee, who now holds a position of prestige in Mexico, claimed that he was able to acquire the necessary status for success in Mexico only by having spent considerable time working outside Mexico as a technical expert in international organizations. On the Mexican side, informants concluded that the Mexicans do not object to being represented in international organizations by Spanish-born citizens, first, because the Spaniards do have the requisite skills, and, second, because Mexicans do not like to leave their country for long periods of time, thereby risking the loss of political contacts which traditionally have been important factors in professional advancement.

5. REPUBLICAN ASSOCIATIONS

From the beginning, the refugees assembled in Mexico City and the large provincial centers sought each other's company and familiar forms of activity. Although they adjusted to life in Mexico, most did not become absorbed by it for several years. The Spanish Republicans remained conscious of their separate identity as political refugees, and, in Mexico City at least, they were numerous enough to constitute their own community, where their social relations, cultural exchange, and politics were centered. These activities were interrelated in that no cultural association was without strong political goals, and social relations derived from common political and cultural objectives. The Republic's partisan political structure had been brought relatively intact from Spain. There was, however, far less organizational consistency between Spain and Mexico in the refugee's social and cultural associations.

Through a large number of formal and informal nonpolitical associations, the refugees were reminded of their common origin and their continuing responsibilities to Spain. They sought to maintain old ties and former activities, although the associations which developed in exile usually differed in orientation and function from any which had existed in Spain. Interest and participation in them has depended upon their continued relevance to the Spaniards' new condition as exiles. To a surprising extent, the refugees in Mexico have been able to renew their former patterns of social interaction and to formalize their shared concern for Spanish culture and for the preservation of their Spanish Republican identity. They have done so by holding intact old friendships and family groups, by educating their children in Spanish Republican values, and by associating with compatriots in exile with whom they share professional, regional, cultural, or social interests.

For the first refugees, those who arrived in Mexico in 1939, there were no formal associations except the Casa de España, which brought together only a few intellectuals. Most exiles registered with the SERE, but they came to this organization only out of financial need, or, occasionally, to locate a missing relative or friend. The first Spanish exiles in Mexico kept track of events primarily by regular meetings in public cafés, as had been their custom in Spain.

THE CAFES

No sooner did the refugees arrive in Mexico City than they sought out friends and acquaintances from Spain. The first important meeting places for refugees were the cafés of the downtown area,[1] public cafés, whose clientele at times, however, was exclusively Spanish. The cafés in Madrid had always served as more than informal places of meeting. They had been the recognized focal points for important discussions—*tertulias*—on cultural, political, and social issues of the day. During the Republic and before, they were the places in which the great professors of the Spanish universities met with their student followers in encounters which ordinarily were far more educational than social.

In Mexico when the Spaniards came there were already a few

[1] Simón Otaola, *La librería de Arana*, pp. 25–26. This book is largely devoted to a chronicle of one of the major cafés in Spanish exile life.

such cafés where intellectuals met: men involved in literature at the Café Paris; doctors and scientists at the Hotel Imperial. Where these café *tertulias* existed, the Spaniards joined the Mexicans and, within a short time, outnumbered them.[2] Since there were so few café *tertulias*, the refugees established their own, and carved out familiar patterns of social interaction: the Tupinamba, the Papagayo, the Latino, the Café do Brasil, the Campoamor, and others. Often before they had found permanent lodging or greatly needed work, writers, scientists, doctors, politicians, and others had established regular meeting places in the downtown cafés.[3] In these cafés a variety of *tertulias* were usually held: animated debates on literature, politics, and philosophy, past and future.

At first many Mexican intellectuals joined the gatherings of their Spanish colleagues, but gradually Mexican attendance declined. While they undoubtedly enjoyed the literary and philosophic discussions, the Mexicans were unprepared for the vociferous, unrestrained nature of Spanish debates. The high voices and the emphatic, argumentative manner in which the *tertulias* were conducted discomfited and annoyed the more quiet, courteous, and tactful Mexicans. In this setting, fruitful group conversations between the two nationalities proved difficult.[4] In his fictional account of a Spanish exile café, *La verdadera historia de Francisco Franco*,[5]

[2] José Moreno Villa, *Cornucopia de México*, p. 59; Carlos Martínez, *Crónica de una emigración: La de los Republicanos españoles en 1939*, p. 24.

[3] Martínez, *Crónica*, pp. 23–37. Without cafés, the Spaniards felt cut off from each other and from society, Martínez claimed. Cafés, therefore, were a social necessity and made life in exile tolerable. See also "Tertulias mexicanas," in *Boletín al Servicio*, September 21, 1939, p. 1. In *Librería de Arana* (p. 28–29), Otaola lists the cafés and those Spaniards who regularly attended each. The list includes almost all the well-known intellectuals and politicians who came to Mexico.

[4] Mexicans named as having attended the *tertulias* with the Spaniards were Manuel Martínez Báez, Martín Luis Guzmán, Alfonso Reyes, Daniel Cosío Villegas, and Ignacio Chávez, all of whom had had some experience in Spain. The younger men who joined Spanish *tertulias* included Ali Chumacero, José Luis Martínez, J. González Durán, and Octavio Paz. I discussed the early cafés with Max Aub, August 14, 1966; with Manuel Sánchez Sarto, March 15, 1967; with Juan Rejano, October 11, 1966; with Bernardo Giner de los Ríos, September 12, 1966; with Manuel Martínez Báez, April 27, 1967, and with Daniel Cosío Villegas, March 22, 1967; all of them had participated in the *tertulias*. Both Mexicans and Spaniards agree that the Mexican retreat was due in large part to Spanish boisterousness.

[5] Max Aub is himself an exile writer.

Max Aub describes how the unending and unendurable noise of the Spaniards and their perpetual plans for the time of Franco's death drive a harassed Mexican waiter to go to Spain and kill Franco himself in order to rid the restaurant of the Spaniards. The story, although playful in tone, is an effective caricature of Spanish café life and Mexican reaction to it.

In those cafés whose clientele was, or became, totally Spanish, the dominant theme of most *tertulias* came to be that of Spain: the Civil War, the unhappy stories of friends who had suffered Franco's revenge, the political feuds of Spain carried over into exile. At times such discussions proved only depressing and demoralizing, causing many who were intent upon making a reasonable adjustment to life in Mexico to react with aversion and cease attending. In some instances, however, conversations in the cafés led to the launching of new intellectual endeavors. The important publication *Las Españas* was born as a result of conversations at the Café Papagayo; so, too, were many of the ideas later incorporated into the Ateneo Español de México.[6]

The café *tertulias* eventually and inevitably declined as the exiles became more involved in their professional pursuits and moved from the center of the city to the suburbs, where they were no longer in close physical proximity to one another. During the mid-1960's, regular meetings were still held, but the attendance was very small. During the years spent in exile, the continual discussion of Spanish themes had gradually ceased to be relevant to most Republicans. While they continued to feel concern and interest in Spanish affairs, they no longer saw the value of discussing these feelings regularly in cafés.

THE COLEGIOS

One of the first steps taken by the SERE's Comité Técnico de Ayuda was to found a special school for the children of Spanish exiles in Mexico City. The Instituto Luis Vives was opened in

---

[6] Otaola (*La librería de Arana*, pp. 68–73, 120–124, 137–139) describes the café itself, as well as the people who came to the Papagayo and the many conversations and exchanges of ideas in which they engaged. Otaola provides anecdotes about the people who regularly participated in the café-*tertulias* and discusses the reasons they were there.

August, 1939, offering primary and secondary schooling to refugee children at a modest cost. A few months later, early in 1940, the Academia Hispano-Mexicana opened its doors, thanks to contributions from private subscriptions and a small amount of money from the Comité Técnico.[7] In 1941 the JARE financed and founded a third *colegio*, the Madrid, which for the first years of its existence offered only primary-school training. The three *colegios* have been among the most enduring institutions of the exile, and the most effective in preserving Spanish identity among children growing up in Mexico.

All three schools,[8] especially the Luis Vives and the Madrid, took as many pupils as their physical capacity would allow and accepted whatever payment parents were able to make.[9] Teachers' salaries and the purchase and maintenance of facilities at Vives and Madrid were covered in part by contributions from the SERE and the JARE until both organizations exhausted their funds. By that time a sufficient number of refugees could pay full tuition.

Spanish children, at the time of their arrival in Mexico, could have enrolled in Mexican public schools. In Mexico City few, if any, did, and comparatively few ever have attended public schools there. At first, the parents assumed that the *colegios* would be temporary, providing the children with a Spanish education in Mexico until they could return to the schools they had left behind. By 1941, it was clear that the schools were not temporary, and that

---

[7] *Cultural Creations of the Comité Técnico*, pp. 12–42; Martínez, *Crónica*, p. 418. In addition to the schools in the capital, the SERE established secondary schools, called Fundación Cervantes, in Tampico, Torreón, Córdoba, Veracruz, and Texcoco. These, however, functioned for only a few years.

[8] Information on the *colegios* was derived from interviews with the following: Dr. José Puche, head of the board of trustees of the Instituto Luis Vives, March 23, 1968; Francisco Giral, president of the board of trustees of the Colegio Madrid, April 4, 1967; Juan Bonet, principal of the Luis Vives, April 9, 1967; Jesús Revaque, principal of the Madrid, April 5, 1967; Bernardo Giner de los Ríos, president of the Institución Libre en el exilio, former professor at the Academia Hispano-Mexicana; various reports from about half a dozen students of the Hispano-Mexicana who attended the school at different times. Actually the earliest *colegio* established in exile was the Ruiz de Alarcón, which survived only briefly.

[9] The Colegio Madrid, besides requiring little or no tuition, at first kept the children in school for most of the day and provided them with meals so that both parents could work.

many years would pass before it would be possible to return to Spain. Still, the exiles were as intent as ever upon providing their children with a Spanish education.

The Spanish *colegios* filled and expanded over the years because the refugees welcomed the opportunity to offer their children education of the same kind and quality they would have had in Republican Spain. The *colegios* were all modeled on the educational philosophy of the Spanish Institución Libre de Enseñanza,[10] which had influenced Spain's twentieth-century intellectual renaissance. Had the Republicans won the Civil War, the Institución would have inspired the educational system of the nation. In spite of Franco's victory, the Republicans still wished their children to profit from the kind of progressive, liberal, secular Spanish education which had done so much to inspire the original Republic in 1931.

Republicans valued the *colegios* not only because the level of instruction was high, but because the orientation was Spanish. Children who had been brought to Mexico too young to remember Spain well, could learn in school what their parents discussed at home. Some of the refugee parents were content that their children should be raised in a Mexican environment and feel more a part of the country in which they lived than of the country of their birth. More, however, probably wished their children to share some of their own concern for their homeland. By exposing their children to school friends who were the sons and daughters of other refugees, many parents hoped to increase the likelihood that their children would marry within the Republican community by developing their feeling of identity as Spaniards.

Although the refugees all over Mexico were concerned about the kind and quality of schooling their children would receive, Spanish *colegios* were established successfully only in Mexico City. There was a larger concentration of refugee children in the capital than

[10] The Institución Libre is discussed in chap. 1. The educational philosophy was considered at that time to be liberal, progressive, and broadly based intellectually. It was, of course, secular. (See Jan Somolinos, "La Academia Hispano-Mexicana y su remoto inspirador," in *Boletín*, printed by the Corporación de Antiguos Alumnos de la "Institución Libre de Eseñanza," del "Instituto-Escuela," y de la "Residencia de Estudiantes" de Madrid, pp. 1–2.) Somolinos is a former student of the Academia.

in any other city, and, more important, there was a substantial number of unemployed teachers and university professors from Spain. To the Spanish teachers, the *colegios* were as necessary as they were to the children, if not more so. Whereas the latter could have attended the public schools (as they did outside of Mexico City) or other private schools (as many did in Mexico City), there were not an adequate number of positions in Mexican universities for the former, and Spanish teachers would have had to compete in public primary and secondary schools with Mexican teachers.[11]

In order to be accredited in Mexico, Spanish schools had to accept the requirement that courses in Mexican history and civics be taught by teachers *born* in Mexico, that a certain percentage of the teachers be of Mexican nationality, and that all schools follow standard Mexican textbooks. The first and third rules were honored, although attempts were made to secure Mexican teachers with moderately favorable views toward Spain.[12] The second stipulation was at first totally ignored both by the Spaniards and by Mexican officials, since virtually all of the original teachers in the Luis Vives, the Hispano-Mexicana, and the Madrid were Spanish. By late 1940, however, most of these refugee teachers had adopted Mexican citizenship, thereby satisfying the second requirement.[13]

Spaniards have been proud of the consistently high quality of education which has characterized the three *colegios*. Officials of both the Colegio Madrid and the Instituto Luis Vives have estimated that at least 90 percent of their students have gone on to successful university careers.[14] The same is almost certainly true of the Academia Hispano-Mexicana. Another source of satisfaction to the refugees is that, from the beginning, a number of prominent Mexican intellectuals have sent their children to the Spanish *colegios*.[15] Although the percentage of Mexican students in the Spanish

[11] They could have taught in rural areas but did not choose to do so for various reasons. See chap. 3.

[12] Interview with Jesús Revaque.

[13] Mauricio Fresco, *La emigración republicana española*, p. 145.

[14] Interviews with Francisco Giral and Dr. José Puche, on the boards of trustees of the Madrid and the Luis Vives, respectively.

[15] Interviews with Francisco Giral and Bernardo Giner de los Ríos. For example, Martínez Báez and Jesús Silva Herzog sent their children to the Colegio Madrid, Daniel Cosío Villegas sent his children to the Academia Hispano-Mexicana, and Antonio Martínez Báez sent his to the Luis Vives.

schools has been increasing steadily, it has never been very high.[16]
Some Mexicans were impressed by the fact that many of the teachers in the *colegios* had held chairs in Spanish universities. They
were attracted also by the fact that the three Spanish schools were,
in the 1940's, the only liberal, private, and secular primary and
secondary schools teaching in the Spanish language in Mexico.[17]
The number of Mexican-born teachers has been increasing, as well,
but it still comprises no more than about a third of the faculty in
any of the schools. Most of the original teachers have died or retired and frequently they have been replaced by younger Spaniards
who graduated from one of the *colegios*.

The children of the refugees thus grew up in two distinct envi-
ronments, the Spanish and the Mexican. For those who reached
maturity in the 1940's, the dominant influence was Spanish; for
those reaching school age in the 1950's, it was Mexican. Those who
attended one of the *colegios* before 1950 were usually left with a
strong commitment to Spain and a sense of community which, in
many cases, endured throughout the university years and after.
Even those who attended the *colegios* in the mid and late 1950's
acquired a sense of Spanish identity, which, since that time, has
been increasingly difficult to instill in the younger students. Although the *colegios* have continued to provide Spanish youngsters
with a modified Spanish education, the environment has been increasingly Mexican.[18]

ASSOCIATIONS

Commenting on their own exaggerated individuality, the exiles
sometimes claim that any three Spaniards will inevitably form at

[16] Some of the officials of the Madrid, the Luis Vives, and the Hispano-Mexicana have claimed that as high as 50 percent of the students are Mexican. There
is no way to determine the percentage, because in the official records there are
no distinctions made between students born in Mexico of Mexican parents and
those born in Mexico of Spanish parents. From the first years of the establishment of the *colegios*, nearly all the children have been of Mexican nationality.
Anecdotal information from former students and from parents of present students suggests that there are still relatively few Mexicans (of Mexican parents)
among the students, and that, until about 1960, less than 20 percent were Mexican.

[17] Mexicans also frequently send their children to French, American, British,
German, or other foreign schools, but for all of these the children must become
fluent in another language.

[18] Later chapters in this book describe the attitudes of the refugees toward

least two associations. Indeed, within a short time after leaving Spain, the refugees began organizing themselves for a variety of purposes. Many associations were short-lived, but new groups arose to supplement and replace the old. The total number of formal and quasi-formal groups founded in exile is unknown, but at least twenty associations—cultural, regional, professional, or educational—have been important either to the Republican community as a whole or to significant sectors within it. Some associations which existed in Republican Spain were re-created in exile; others were organized to facilitate contact among the scattered refugees or between Spain in exile and Spain. Most of the associations founded in Mexico have been social, recreational, and educational centers, where refugees can meet for specific or for general purposes.

Only a few of the associations of the Republican exile can be discussed in this chapter,[19] and those will include associations of varying size and objectives. Some of them are organizations which have been in existence for the entire span of the Republican exile, others were created early and have since been dissolved, and still others were founded a decade or more after the Republicans began their exile.

Junta de Cultural Espanola

The first intellectual association to be created in exile was the Junta de Cultura Española, established in Paris in 1939.[20] The initial objective of the Junta was to salvage what it could of Spanish cultural life by enabling Spain's artists and intellectuals to establish themselves productively in other countries. The Junta enjoyed considerable success in this endeavor and saw most of its members welcomed in the Spanish-speaking Americas. Before 1940, the Junta itself had left war-threatened France, where it could no longer function easily, and had established its central offices in Mexico,

---

Spain and Mexico, and discuss more completely the socialization of the younger generations into the Spanish Republican and Mexican communities.

[19] Such politically oriented but nonpartisan associations as the Movimiento Español de Liberación, Movimiento '59, Movimiento Europeista de México, and the Unión de Intelectuales have served political as well as nonpolitical functions. Some of these associations will be discussed in chap. 6.

[20] The Junta de Cultura was discussed in chap. 3.

the new center of refugee intellectual life. Negrín had previously given President Cárdenas approximately 50,000 pesos, earmarked for representatives of the Junta. This money was to establish a library, an intellectual center, and a literary periodical, *España Peregrina*.[21]

The aim of the Junta de Cultura, in Mexico as it had been in Paris, was to preserve the unity and collective spirit of Spanish intellectual life and to win friends for Spanish culture in those countries in which the Spaniards were guests. The members of the Junta contended that it was the responsibility of the representatives of the Spanish cultural community, while in exile, to continue in their work, so that the world would know that the exiles, and not those who surrendered to Franco, represented true Spanish culture.[22]

Neither the Junta de Cultura nor its journal, *España Peregrina*, lasted more than a year. Personal quarrels within the association between the two major editors of the journal, José Bergamín and Juan Larrea, made operation of the Junta nearly impossible,[23] and funds were quickly exhausted. Those who had worked with the journal were sought by the many Mexican literary periodicals that had emerged in response to the new literary talent available. The failure of the Junta de Cultura, caused by its founders' inability to work together meaningfully, marked the first of several failures for the Spanish cultural elite. The Unión de Intelectuales and the Ateneo Español as well would subsequently disappoint those who hoped to create in Mexico a flourishing and unified Spanish cultural center.

Union de Profesores Espanoles en el Extranjero

More than half of Spain's university professors went into exile. The majority, by far, settled in the various countries of the Americas, particularly Mexico. It was in Mexico, therefore, that the cen-

---

21 Interview with Juan Rejano, one of the members of the junta and editor of *España Peregrina*, October 11, 1966. See also *Cultural Creations of the Comité Técnico*, pp. 43–48.

22 The statutes of the Junta de Cultura were printed in *España Peregrina* 1 (February, 1940): 42.

23 Interviews with Juan Rejano; Francisco Giner de los Ríos, October 28, 1966; José Bergamín was also in charge of the first Spanish refugee publishing house, Seneca, founded in 1939 by the SERE.

tral body of the Unión de Profesores Españoles en el Extranjero (Union of Spanish Professors in Foreign Countries) was established, after having been organized in Paris in 1939.[24]

The Unión de Profesores served as an agency of mutual assistance, and more important, as a means of professional contact among the dispersed academic community. The original hope of the professors was to continue to collaborate in their intellectual activities, which would be useful to Spain upon their return. Later, as the prospects for an immediate return to Spain diminished, the Unión directed its efforts toward increased communication with Spain. Professors in exile tried to inform their liberal colleagues who had remained in Spain subject to Franco's censorship of the work being done by Spanish scholars fortunate enough to have escaped to countries where they could speak more freely. Any exile who had been a professor in Spain was considered a member of the Unión, regardless of individual political affiliations.[25]

In September, 1943, a large number of the most prominent of the professors who had taken refuge in the Americas met in Havana. Their objective was to make a public appeal, based on the principles of the Atlantic Charter, for the restoration of the Spanish Republic. The professors, still not doubting the imminence of their return to Spain, discussed all of the problems that return would cause. Despite a membership that ranged from conservative Catholic to Communist, the professors meeting at Havana were able to draft a statement of political purpose, defining the steps to be taken toward resolving some of the fundamental problems of Spain. They maintained that, as the intellectual leaders of Spain, and because they represented a broad political and regional spectrum, they had an obligation to speak on Spain's future.[26]

[24] Fresco, *La emigración republicana española*, pp. 57, 65–66. The first bulletin of the unión gave special thanks to Mexico for having made available such facilities as the Casa de España, the National University, the Polytechnical Institute, and the Universities of Morelia and Monterrey, all of which had welcomed many Spanish professors (*Boletín Informativo* 1 [August, 1943]: 1–2; ibid. 1 [February, 1944]: 1). In ibid. (1 [September–December, 1943]: 2) the secretary general of the unión, Dr. Mendizábel, states that 90 full professors and 150 associate professors went into exile, most of them to Mexico.

[25] Most of the associations of exiles did include some political limitations, especially against Communists (Interviews with Francisco Giral, present head of the Unión de Profesores and originally its youngest member, April 4, 1967).

[26] "La reunión de la Habana," *Boletín Informativo* 1 (September–December,

The major theme of the Havana conference, and the basis of unity among the exiled professors, was the conviction that the Franco rebellion had been destructive, immoral, and illegal, and that the intelligentsia, therefore, had a responsibility to work toward the liberation of Spain and the restoration of a democratic, republican form of government.[27] Above all, those attending the meeting stressed that the Spanish professors had a primary commitment to the future of Spain equal to or above any commitment to their personal academic future in the Americas.

From August, 1943, just prior to the Havana conference, through 1944, the Unión de Profesores published the monthly *Boletín Informativo*, which reported the activities of its members and printed lists of their works published in exile. Most of these works either were banned in Spain or had been "pirated" by Spanish publishing houses to be printed under the names of individuals loyal to Franco. The *Boletín* ceased publication in 1944 because of lack of funds. The Unión itself continued after 1944, but more symbolically than substantively.

By the mid-1960's, only a handful of older men who had been professors in Spain before the Civil War remained in the Unión; the Unión itself had long since ceased to be active. In 1967, members of the Unión who were living in Mexico, in collaboration with some liberal professors from the University of Madrid, began to discuss action which would reinvigorate the Unión de Profesores and allow it to resume an active role in Spanish affairs. The proposal involved recruiting new members, so that the association would not die with the last of the pre–Civil War professors. Two additional groups were to be invited to join an enlarged and restructured Asociación Internacional de Profesores Universitarios Hispánicos: the younger exiles who had become professors and taught in American or European universities, and the post–Civil War generation of professors in Spain, a large percentage of whom opposed the Franco regime.[28]

1943): especially pp. 9–11. (See also the inaugural address of Dr. José Giral in *Libro de la primera reunión de Profesores Universitarios Españoles Emigrados*, pp. 60–61.)

[27] Giral, *Libro de la primera reunión.*

[28] Interviews with Francisco Giral and Dr. José Puche. In a letter to the membership of the unión, the new proposals were explained: "Han surgido,

This action expressed both a realization and a hope. It is clear, on the one hand, that the exiled Republican intellectuals recognized that they no longer held a monopoly on resistance to Franco; the voices of young scholars inside Spain were as loud as and more effective than those of the refugees. On the other hand, it is not so clear what the nearly thirty years' separation had meant for the younger Spanish professors in exile. By their action, the older men were expressing their hope that their colleagues, who were born in Spain but had spent their adult lives outside of it, were still concerned enough about their homeland to wish to contribute to its future.

REGIONAL ASSOCIATIONS

The associations created by the exiles uniformly served in some way to reaffirm their political identity as refugees of the Spanish Republic. Among the most successful and enduring of these associations, however, were the regional clubs, most of which neither originated with the exiles nor were concerned with the defeated Republic. One of the most surprising developments of the refugees' early years in Mexico was their gradual, regionally based rapprochement with the *antigua colonia*. As previously discussed, the majority of the conservative and wealthy members of the Spanish colony were hostile to the arrival of Republican refugees. Yet, only a few months after the latter had arrived, some members of the colony began to welcome the "red" Republicans socially as fellow Spaniards and co-regionalists in some of the Spanish regional centers.

Regional centers had existed in Mexico as long as there had been sufficiently large and wealthy groups of Spaniards to maintain them. When the refugees arrived, in 1939, there already existed the Orféo Catalá (Catalonian), the Centro Vasco (Basque), the Centro León (Old Castilian), the Centro Asturiano (Asturian), and the Centro Gallego (Galician). The first two included more moder-

---

fuera de España, numeros jóvenes profesores y investigadores. Todos ellos, independientemente del país en donde ejercen y de su nacionalidad actual, mantienen interés sostenido por los problemas de España . . . Por otra parte, dentro de España, los intereses de las nuevas generaciones de profesores e investigadores se hallan en conflicto con patrones anticuados y medidas restrictivas que impiden, mientras subsistan, tantos su progreso como el libre diálogo."

ates and pro-Republicans than the others and also represented the strongest regionalism. They welcomed all fellow Catalans and Basques who were among the refugees, with the exception of the Communists, who formed separate regional groups. The Asturians also welcomed the refugees, but they added the stipulation that the center was to serve no political function. The Gallegans, on the whole somewhat more conservative, grudgingly invited the refugees from Galicia, but, in the end, a separate Republican Gallegan group was formed. The Leoneses rejected the refugees altogether, as did the general social clubs of the *antigua colonia*, the Casino Español and the Club España.[29] Where they were uncomfortable within the existing organizations, or where no such organizations existed, the refugees created a Casa Regional Valenciana, a Cultura Gallega, a (short-lived) Casa de Andalucía, and a Centro Montañés (also short-lived); the large numbers of refugees who considered themselves without regional ties, the *madrileño* group, formed a club called Los Cuatro Gatos.[30]

In the Centro Vasco and the Orféo Catalá the Republicans soon outnumbered the *antiguos residentes*. These two centers became by far the most important of the regional cultural and social centers for Spaniards in Mexico. The Orféo Catalá in particular has played a significant role in the preservation and encouragement of Catalan culture at a time when it has been strongly discouraged in Spain. Approximately twenty publications of literary, political, or Catalan nationalist orientation have been sponsored through the Orféo Catalá—some published for no more than a year or two, others having endured almost the entire span of Republican exile.[31] Besides its

[29] Information from Sergio Pich Romero, librarian of the Ateneo Español and active member of the Orféo Catalá. Members of the Orféo declared themselves ready to offer "moral and economic" help to the refugees almost immediately after the arrival of the first large groups (*Excelsior*, July 5, 1939, pp. 1, 11).

[30] Information also from Sergio Pich Romero. There were few pre–Civil War Spaniards from these regions or from Madrid living in Mexico; hence there were no existing regional clubs when the refugees arrived. The name "Los Cuatro Gatos" was intended to imply, humorously, that there were only a "few cats" (common *madrileño* expression) from Madrid to form such a club.

[31] Michael Kenny, "The Integration of Spanish Expatriates in Ibero-America," p. 102. Nearly all of the regional centers have published at least one regular periodical of regional news, nostalgia, and community activities. The periodical of the Centro Vasco is *Euzko Deya*, that of the Casa Regional Valenciana is *Senyera*, the Gallegan publication is called *Vieros*, and the major Catalan publications of general interest are *Pont Blau* and *Orféo Catalá* (Interview with the

extensive library, the Orféo Catalá also offers a variety of recreational, social, and cultural activities, intended to attract all persons of Catalan origin living in Mexico, regardless of political attitude or age.

The explanation for the durability and high level of participation in these clubs lies in the importance of regional ties for all Spaniards. The extent to which the people of Spain identify with their regional origins can hardly be overstressed. While strong separatist movements exist only among the Basques and Catalans, the Asturians, Gallegans, Valencians, and Andalusians have maintained separate cultural heritages as well. In Mexico, many Spanish refugees have considered it as important to sustain their regional culture as to support the cause of the Spanish Republic.

LATER ASSOCIATIONS OF THE REPUBLICAN REFUGEES

Refugees continued to emigrate to Mexico throughout the Second World War and the postwar period, swelling the ranks of some of the existing associations and leading to the creation of new ones. By the late 1940's, such agencies as the SERE, the JARE, and the Junta de Cultura no longer functioned, while some of the older groups declined rapidly as old members died or lost interest. Two new associations, Los Amigos de *Las Españas* and the Ateneo Español de México, were founded in the late 1940's, both dedicated to preserving the greatest possible unity in the gradually disintegrating Republican community. The new associations were also devoted to the task of redefining the role of the Spanish exiles at a time when their hopes for a return to Spain had dimmed. Both Los Amigos and the more significant Ateneo Español attempted to override the divisiveness of the Republican community in Mexico and to renew the spirit of involvement in Spanish problems.

LOS AMIGOS DE *Las Españas*

In October of 1946 a group of men and women, mostly writers and other intellectuals, founded Los Amigos de *Las Españas*, an association devoted to the publication of a new periodical which was

---

librarian of the Orféo, Juan Potao, April 19, 1968; visits to all of the other existing regional centers. See chap. 8, below, for further discussion of the *Orféo Catalá*). The important Catalan periodical, *La Nova Revista*, was also published in Mexico, under the auspices of the Institución de Cultura Catalana.

to provide both a cultural and a political forum. *Las Españas*, unlike most of the periodicals toward which the Republicans dedicated their efforts, was not intended for a general Hispano-American audience, but primarily for circulation in Spain. Its stated purpose was to contribute to Spanish culture from exile and to aid in the projects for the liberation of the country. For this reason the periodical, smuggled into Spain, always had a larger circulation there than in Mexico.[32]

As its name suggests, the basic theme of *Las Españas* has been the concept of not one, but many Spains, each of which deserves to be treated and understood separately; that not until Spaniards have understood their differences will they attain a meaningful unity.[33] Articles devoted to the folklore and culture of the various regions have appeared in nearly every issue. The editors believe that research into the cultural, political, and popular realities of the Spanish regions will yield the understanding necessary to recognize past mistakes and to find workable future alternatives to the present regime. *Las Españas*, according to its founders, was created in order to determine why the emigration failed to unseat Franco, why the war which should have been won was lost, and why the war occurred in the first place.[34]

Initially, *Las Españas* accepted the contributions of intellectuals from all political sectors of the emigration,[35] but the founders of the

[32] Anselmo Carretero, *Notas sobre "Las Españas,"* unpublished paper (pamphlet), by the editorial secretary of *Las Españas* (March, 1967); interview with Anselmo Carretero, July 21, 1966; editorial in *Las Españas*, November 29, 1946, p. 2.

[33] Carretero, *Notas sobre "Las Españas,"* p. 1. Not only is the federalist theme repeated editorially throughout the issues of the periodical, but it is also supplemented with books, published by the editorial staff, dealing with regionalism and the distinct aspects of the various "Spains." For example, Pere Bosch Gimpera, *Cataluña, Castilla, España,* and Anselmo Carretero y Jiménez, *La personalidad de Castilla en el conjunto de los pueblos hispánicos,* published together by *Las Españas*.

[34] *Las Españas*, "Por un movimiento de reconstrucción nacional," p. 1.

[35] Commenting on the founding of the periodical, Otaola notes: "Through its pages have passed writers, poets, philosophers, of all political shades—among them: José Bergamín, Juan Rejano, José M. Gallegos Rocafull, León Felipe, José Antonio Balbontín, Benjamín Jarnés, José Moreno Villa, María Zambrano, Manuel Altoaguirre, Herrera Petere, Sánchez Trincado, Vázquez Humasqué, Juan José Domenchina, Sánchez Vázquez, José Renau, Honorato de Castro, Juan D. García Bacca, Enrique Rioja, Adolfo Salazar, Margarita Nelkin, Luis Nicolau

periodical, with the exception of editor José Ramón Arana, were all members of the Frente Universitario Español (FUE). FUE, the former liberal student association of the Republic and the Civil War,[36] had been reconstituted not only in Mexico, but in all the countries of exile. It continued to exist clandestinely in Spain as well. The FUE's links with Spain were of considerable importance in its political orientation, and consequently in the policies of *Las Españas*. The founders of *Las Españas*, through the FUE, were in communication with liberals in Spain, who opposed Franco, but who were not necessarily Republican. Because *Las Españas* was written with a Spanish rather than an exile audience in mind, and because of its continued communication with Spain, its editors were among the first in exile to take a position against the future objective of a simple reconstruction of the Spanish Republic. They also were among the first to plead for moderation and compromise in place of total hostility toward the Franco regime.[37]

From the first, the *Las Españas* group rejected the idea of the violent reestablishment of the Republic in favor of a reassessment of Spanish problems and even a reevaluation of the Republic itself. The editors stressed the need to increase the understanding of the diverse and federalist character of Spain, among both Spaniards in exile and those in Spain, before creating a new political order.[38] Articles in the periodical, throughout its history, urged readers to cease basing their hopes for the future on a past which had been destroyed: "Those who carry the weight of the Republic, who do

D'Olwer, Fernando de los Ríos, Francisco Rivero Gil, Luis Carretero Nieva, Augustín Bartra, Rodolfo Halfter." (From Otaola, *La librería de Arana*, p. 70.)

[36] Interview with Antonio María Sbert, April 3, 1967. At that time Sbert was president of the FUE and had been involved in *Las Españas* since its beginning.

[37] Frente Universitario Español, *Coincidencia de propósitos*, pamphlet on the program of the FUE, printed by the Ateneo Español de México, 1956. Antonio Sbert, in an interview, defined the policy of the FUE and Las Españas as stressing "all that unites instead of that which divides."

[38] The cataclysm of the Civil War was so great, Ramón Arana claimed in an early editorial, that "there is no possibility there of restoring anything, because of that which has fallen, nothing remains but dust and bitterness. It is necessary to begin at the beginning . . . and construct again with that which is ours" (*Las Españas*, November 29, 1946, p. 2). Two years later, he again urged that in view of the natural tendency of the exiles to take up a new life and let old memories fade, it was essential to learn to understand the war and the course of history which brought about the war (Ibid. 3 [April, 1948]:15).

penance for it, walk a dolorous path for what is no more than a skeleton of a Republic . . . How long will we keep our morbid commitment?"[39] It would be better, argued the editors, to cease talking of the Republican form of government and to concentrate on the realities of Spain, to forget the political structure which had lost the war, to let the old political parties and institutions die, and to refrain from talk of heroics and violence.[40]

In 1949, *Las Españas* moved toward the position that it was not the major function of the exiles to bring down Franco, but rather to work for national reconstruction and reconciliation between the exiles and leaders in Spain.[41] This point of view lost many supporters for the periodical. In that period in the late 1940's, politically active exiles still believed that Franco could be defeated and that the exiles' responsibility was to do whatever possible in that cause. A number of leftist contributors[42] to the periodical criticized the idea of seeking increased understanding with forces in Spain, on the grounds that such a concept was defeatist and would be favorable to Franco. To radicals and Communists the proposal that the refugees abandon their posture of total hostility to Franco and seek areas of compromise was near heresy. The Communists thereafter not only ceased to contribute to *Las Españas*, but also actively attacked its position.[43]

The entire editorial board, as well as those who had sponsored *Las Españas*, found themselves divided over the appropriate policy for the periodical to follow, and, during the years 1953 to 1956, no issues were published. In July, 1956, the second series of *Las Españas* was begun. The orientation of the periodical remained fundamentally the same, but the editors and contributors were polit-

[39] Daniel Tapia, "La otra mujer de Lot," *Las Españas* 3 (July, 1948):11.

[40] Ibid. A number of articles in *Las Españas* deal with this theme; see also the editorial in the same issue of *Las Españas*, p. 2; and a more strongly stated article by Daniel Tapia several years later, "La generación del '29 y los heterodoxos en el exilio," *Las Españas*, 2d ser. (July, 1956):42.

[41] *Las Españas*, "Por un movimiento de reconstrucción nacional"; Anselmo Carretero. *Notas sobre*, p. 6.

[42] "Leftists," as used here, refers not only to members of the political parties of the Left, but to radicals without any party affiliations.

[43] See the discussion of the Communist party and its position with regard to *Las Españas* and intellectuals in general in chap. 6, below.

ically more conservative, less tolerant of leftists in general and of Communists in particular.[44]

From the start of the second series, the position of *Las Españas* has been that any future Spanish government will have to attend to the special needs of the Spanish people and should take into greater account the democratic and federalist traditions of Spain. That the government be specifically Republican in form is not a requisite, and reform within the context of even the Franco government is judged conceivable. The second series was named *Diálogos de Las Españas*, the implication being that a dialogue including Franco's supporters is possible.[45]

ATENEO ESPANOL DE MEXICO

The Ateneo Español de México became, with little doubt, the most important association of Spanish Republican exiles in Mexico. It was founded in 1949, at a time when the political and cultural associations which had existed or were founded at the beginning of the exile were already beginning to decline in importance. It was created, moreover, to serve as an alternative or a supplement to these existing associations. The Ateneo was intended as a cultural center, modeled upon and named for the famous intellectual center in Madrid.[46] Just as Spanish intellectuals during the Monarchy and the Republic had gathered in the Ateneo de Madrid to discuss intellectual currents and to encourage cultural and political changes, so, too, did the founders of the Ateneo Español de México intend that the exiles would gather there to keep alive the Spanish culture which they represented, and to do whatever possible to bring about a change of regime in Spain. The Ateneo was a political center in that its members were political refugees who wished to alter the existing government of their homeland, but its main emphasis was culture, and it avoided partisan ties. The governing body of the Ateneo staunchly insisted that Republicans of all points of view were welcome.[47]

[44] Carretero, *Notas sobre*, pp. 3, 51; editorial, *Las Españas*, 2d ser. (July, 1956):2, 31.

[45] Interviews with Antonio María Sbert and Anselmo Carretero. The *Diálogos* were still being published sporadically in 1968.

[46] "El Español de México," *Las Españas* 4 (January, 1949):6.

[47] Interviews, with Dr. José Puche, president of the Ateneo Español, and Dr.

100 EXILES AND CITIZENS

Although its primary function was to serve as a cultural center, the Ateneo over the years sponsored a wide variety of activities designed to attract maximum participation among the refugees, including social receptions, ceremonies of homage, and assemblies of protest or debate concerning Spain and the Republic. In the cultural realm it was initially divided into seven sections: art, the biological and medical sciences, physical sciences, philosophy and social sciences, literature, theatre and cinema, music and radio, and it sponsored, in addition, special lectures and general cultural activities.[48] The Ateneo also boasts a fairly extensive library of books, manuscripts, and periodical literature. Most of these have been donated by publishing houses and academic institutions; some have been purchased with funds contributed by its members.[49]

Whereas the Spanish Ateneo served as a center of reunion and discussion, its counterpart in Mexico has been occupied almost exclusively with prearranged meetings, lectures, and special entertainment. At its peak of activity, in the early 1950's, it was not uncommon for lectures or other events to fill every night's program completely, sometimes playing to virtually nonexistent audiences; at other times, especially on the occasion of a relevant political discussion, Spanish Republicans would fill every available space.[50] There are still frequent and varied events which take place in the Ateneo, although the audiences usually tend to be smaller and older than they were a decade or more ago. Nonetheless, the Ateneo is the only creation of the emigration which Republicans of all ages and nearly all political tendencies have continued to frequent. It is the only center which still attempts to cater to the interests of all.

The initial impetus for the creation of the Ateneo came from the group originally involved in the publication of Las Españas. Many of them were active, as well, in the Unión de Intelectuales, created in 1947.[51] Most of the men who were active in the founding of the

Joaquín D'Harcourt, the past president, November 15, 1966, and July 17, 1966, respectively.

[48] Ateneo Español de México, Memoria, 1950, pp. 1–7.

[49] Ibid., p. 7.

[50] Martínez, Crónica, pp. 39–41; Otaola, La librería de Arana, pp. 152–158.

[51] This "Association of Intellectuals in Exile" was founded in 1947 and began to decline by 1950, a fact which Marxist theoretician Wenceslao Roces and Spanish writer in exile Max Aub, both members of the unión, trace in part to

Ateneo over twenty years ago continued on the board of directors.[52]
A few younger men assumed positions of responsibility as librarians
or as heads of the various cultural sections, but a number of persons
in their late thirties and forties, who reported frequent attendance
in the past, claimed that by the late 1960's they found little of
interest in the Ateneo. Many resented the advanced age and con-
servatism of the administration and believed the center to be
doomed to the gradual decline and dissolution to which other Spanish organizations had succumbed when the old leadership refused
to give way to new ideas and younger men.[53] In 1967 there were
about 750 dues-paying members,[54] but most functions had been
opened to the general public. Considerable effort had been exerted
to attract young people in their late teens and early twenties to the
Ateneo, and such experiments as a dramatic club were fairly successful.

Among the associations, the Ateneo has made the strongest appeal
for unity over and above partisan conflicts in the Spanish Republican community. There is no political faction of the emigration
whose members have specifically avoided the Ateneo, but some
Socialists and Anarchists have objected to the supposed Communist
sympathies of a few of the founders and leaders. None of the administrators have had known affiliation with the Communist party,
but many of the sponsors were previously identified with the leftist,
radical, pro-Negrín factions of the exile.[55] Communist members of

---

the fact that the ateneo, once founded, served the purpose for which the unión
was intended. Other, more important reasons for the dissolution of the unión are
discussed below and in chap. 6. The initial inspiration for the creation of the
ateneo owed much to artist and critic Ceferino de Palencia, who was a major
contributor to *Las Españas* (Otaola, *La librería*, pp. 137–138; Martínez, *Crónica*,
p. 39).

52 Dr. Joaquín D'Harcourt was president until 1966 when another of the
original members, Dr. José Puche, took over the position. José Luis de la Loma
has been the secretary of the ateneo since its founding; Arturo Saínz de la
Calzada, Antonio María Sbert, Daniel Tapia, and others have always served in
important posts in the association. Many of the original founders have died, but
those who remain continue to exert a strong voice in the operation of the ateneo.

53 All of those interviewed who were between the ages of approximately
thirty and forty-five years in 1966 and 1967, and who claimed to have attended
frequent meetings at the ateneo in the past, said they now attended much less
frequently, if at all.

54 Interview with Dr. José Puche, March 28, 1968.

55 Among the earliest and most enthusiastic supporters of the ateneo were

the emigration, as all others, have been welcome. Positions of leadership, however, have generally been held by men with no strong party affiliation. It has been the policy of the association that any group, whether inside or outside the emigration, may use its facilities for almost any purpose. Nearly all of the nonpolitical and some of the political associations of the emigration have held meetings there at one time or another.[56] In 1960, members organized a commemoration of the 150th anniversary of Mexican independence and the fiftieth anniversary of the Mexican revolution, in honor of which the Republicans donated money for the construction of a Mexican school.[57] Political refugees from other countries, especially those from Latin America, were also welcome at the Ateneo, and groups from Colombia, Nicaragua, and prerevolutionary Cuba took advantage of Spanish Republican hospitality to hold meetings there. During the 1960's a group of leftist Mexican students began to meet there fairly regularly, and a group of Mexican geologists came there each week.[58]

Thus the Ateneo has remained a useful and functioning entity. It is not, however, a dynamic association, and as a cultural center it has been limited by the fact that it has served as a place for formal meetings rather than for informal conversation. Nor has it succeeded, despite strong efforts, in its objective of providing a nonpartisan forum and center of activity which would facilitate the eventual political unity of the exiles. True, most general political debates, formal acts of protest, and manifestations of solidarity with Spanish opposition forces have been held in the Ateneo. It has

---

the men who had joined the leftist Unión de Intelectuales. Disappointed by the Communist direction which the unión followed, they left it and joined the ateneo, hoping the latter would serve to unite intellectuals and cultural leaders on a broader base and less politically than the former. These men, in many cases, were also contributors to *Las Españas* until it became more conservative in its second series.

[56] For example, the alumni groups of one or another of the Spanish *colegios*, the Spanish Medical Association, the Union of Journalists, the various youth movements, and many other associations.

[57] Ateneo Español de México, *Memoria, 1960*, pp. 6–7.

[58] Information from José de la Loma, secretary of the ateneo, and its librarian, Sergio Pich Romero. Not only did the Cubans occasionally use the facilities of the ateneo, but Fidel Castro and his followers were trained in Mexico for guerrilla warfare by Alberto Bayo, a former commander in the Spanish Republican army.

also served as the base for such attempts at political union as the Movimiento de Liberación Española[59] and the Movimiento '59.[60] But none of the political factions of the Republic-in-exile have been willing to surrender their autonomy in order to act through the Ateneo.

In 1952, soon after its founding, the Ateneo itself sponsored a meeting of all political parties and organizations to discuss the political problems of Spain and possible solutions to them. Invited were the two Republican parties, the two Socialist groups, the Catalan and the Basque parties, the Communists, and the Anarcho-syndicalist group. The results of this effort are indicative of the obstacles inhibiting the Ateneo, or any other body, from playing a meaningful political role in the Republican exile. The major Socialist party replied that it could not act on the invitation without consulting the party as a whole at its annual congress in Toulouse, France. The Communists refused because the Socialists had been invited. The other parties failed to respond at all, and finally the proposed meeting was cancelled.[61]

Such associations as those described above divide the Republican exile community as much as they unite it. Yet the fact that most older exiles participate at least nominally in one or more of the Spanish associations reminds them of their ties to Spain and increases their sense of responsibility toward their homeland. The associations which have emphasized intellectual, social, and cultural activities have endured because they have given a focus and meaning to the refugees' life in Mexico. Although the refugees could not restore the Republic to Spain, they have taken comfort in the fact that they have been able to preserve Spanish culture in exile and to increase the appreciation of that culture throughout the countries in which they have taken refuge. Since the Civil War, there has

[59] The Movimiento de Liberación Española was founded by the famed general José Miaja, as a union of Spaniards above political affiliations, in 1955. A number of prominent people in and out of the various political groups were affiliated with it; there were branches in Argentina, Brazil, and France, and a bulletin was published for a few years. The objective of this group was to win support from important people in Spain, especially in the military, for the establishment of an opposition government (Interview with Colonel Vicente Guarner, president of the Movimiento [now practically inactive] since the death of Miaja in 1958).

[60] See chap. 6 for a full discussion of the Movimiento '59.

[61] Ateneo Español de México, *Memoria, 1952,* p. 1.

grown up in Spain a new generation, which, despite the repression of the Franco government, has succeeded in reviving the quality and intensity of Spanish intellectual and cultural life. The associations created in Mexico and elsewhere for that purpose, therefore, have come to serve primarily a social function for the exile community and are of relatively little importance to Spain.

To the children of the refugees, who rarely participate in their parents' activities, the clubs, centers, and societies of the exile seem largely exercises in nostalgia, inappropriate to conditions of life in Mexico. The younger people are, for the most part, prepared to let the responsibility for the preservation of Spanish culture rest with those in Spain. They prefer to devote their energies to their personal and professional pursuits rather than to work for the benefit of the Spanish Republican community in exile; and they have no wish to insulate themselves from Mexico with a network of Spanish associations.

6. A POLITICAL EXILE

The Spanish emigration, although an economic and intellectual success, has been less successful politically. None of the political groups has been able to unite or to coordinate its efforts for positive action over prolonged periods of time. Personalism, local issues, and the changing international political scene have contributed to the creation (and the destruction) of coalitions and to the constant ideological reevaluations characteristic of all the exile parties. The political failure, however, has probably been due more to the events of the Cold War and to the relations between Spain and the rest of the world than to specific personal or organizational shortcomings among the refugees. Decisions made by Spanish Republican political leaders in Mexico have been profoundly shaped by the actions of politicians in Spain, Western Europe, and the United States, actions over which the Republicans have had neither influence nor control. The various directions taken by the exile parties in Mexico are thus best understood if prefaced by a review of the overall context in which political activity took place.

Personalism and Opposing Views

Nearly all the exiles who left Spain held strongly to their political beliefs, which covered a wide ideological spectrum. Political divisiveness had deepened and become more bitter as the war progressed. By the time they reached Mexico, however, most of the exiles had lost their taste for the partisan rivalry which characterized the war and was to be even more bitter in its aftermath. Political activity thus declined drastically during the first years of exile, especially for those refugees living in the Mexican countryside and in provincial towns. The demands of adjusting to life in exile, the problems of finding work, and the rebuilding of family ties left little energy for Spanish partisan activity.

Yet, it was extremely difficult to avoid political involvement altogether, even for those who wished to do so. The sustenance and care of the refugees during the early months of exile were derived largely from the resources and administration of the SERE and the JARE.[1] Both organizations were involved in the selection of refugees and their transport from France to Mexico. Both offered emergency aid and subsidies to needy refugees. They also invested funds in agricultural, financial, and industrial enterprises which provided employment for many of the refugees during their first months or years in Mexico.[2] These vital refugee organizations, furthermore, represented the two major personal and political divisions of the Republic: the SERE was administered and supported by the last Republican prime minister, Juan Negrín, and the JARE by his rival, the Socialist leader Indalecio Prieto.

Negrín and Prieto, each controlling a portion of the funds re-

---

[1] The SERE and the JARE are discussed in chap. 2.

[2] In 1940 the Comité Técnico reported that it was employing approximately seventeen hundred persons, most of whom were in the Federal District ("Informe del Dr. Puche," *Boletín al Servicio de la Emigración Española*, July 6, 1940, pp. 6–7). Mauricio Fresco (*La emigración republicana española*, pp. 168–179) gives a complete list of the enterprises founded by the Spanish refugees, but he does not distinguish between those founded by investments from the SERE and the JARE, or by private sources. Few of the SERE or the JARE enterprises survived more than a year or two.

maining to the Spanish Republic, vied with each other to win the gratitude and trust of those who accepted the aid and services they offered. Competition between the two organizations for refugee support resulted in inefficient management of funds, duplication of efforts, and increasing personal hostility between the two leaders.[3] The antagonism between the leaders and between their respective supporters continued long after the SERE had exhausted its funds and the Mexican government had taken over the management of the finances of the JARE.[4]

Negrín enjoyed a substantial following among leftist intellectuals

---

[3] Cipriano de Rivas-Cherif, *Retrato de un desconocido: Vida de Manuel Azaña*, pp. 42–43. In the matter of transporting refugees from France to Mexico, the two associations did not compete seriously, since the JARE did not begin to finance the refugee evacuation until about the time the SERE announced that its funds had been exhausted. In July of 1940 the officials of the SERE and the JARE argued over who should finance the ship *Cuba* while it remained stranded in Santo Domingo. The SERE officials claimed that they had exhausted all of their funds and that the JARE should begin to take responsibility for the transportation of refugees. The correspondence between the two groups is reprinted in the *Boletín al Servicio*, July 20, 1940, pp. 1–2; ibid., August 8, 1940, p. 1; ibid., August 13, 1940, p. 1.

[4] In January, 1941, the Mexican government for the first time assumed a role in the management of the funds of the Spanish emigration. In Mexico at that time—perhaps due in some part to the hostilities in the Spanish political community—rumors were circulated describing corruption in the administration of the JARE finances, and Mexican officials heeded the rumors to the extent of demanding that the JARE establish a limited-liability company, administered jointly by Spaniards and Mexicans, to handle the funds. When this was not done to Mexican satisfaction, the Mexican government assumed financial control of the JARE. To the men who worked with the JARE, and even to some refugees who opposed it, the action of the Mexican government in exercising control over the funds was considered a manifestation of Mexican distrust of the refugees, and as such, a humiliation to the exile as a whole ("No hay política de emigración," *Solidaridad Obrera* [Anarchist], December 15, 1942, p. 1). Even the hostile Negrinist, *El Socialista*, regretted the incident, although the writers "were not surprised by it" ("Fin de una experiencia," 2 [January, 1943], p. 6). The most severe criticism came from the Socialist organ *Adelante* ("Las cosas en su punto," May 15, 1943). To many refugees who had long objected to refugee economic aid based on political support, however, the incident called attention to the bickering and ill will which characterized relations within the Republican community. It is fair to say that the majority of the refugees, whatever their misgivings with regard to the implications in their Mexican action of 1943, welcomed the fact that the funds would thereafter be controlled by a neutral body and would no longer be used as a political tool by any Republican group. An account of this issue can be found in Lois Smith, *Mexico and the Spanish Republicans*, pp. 217, 271–272; also in Félix Palavicini, *México: Historia de su evolución constructiva*, IV, 274–275.

both within and outside the Socialist party, particularly among the youth who had been members of the JSU during the war.[5] His followers agreed with him that, as the last prime minister of the Republic, he remained its sole leader in exile. Negrín had been appointed to the post of prime minister by President Manuel Azaña in May, 1937. The appointment had been approved by the Cortes, and the Cortes had left the government in Negrín's hands in its last meeting, in February, 1939, at Figueras, near the French border.[6] In the same month, Azaña and the president of the Cortes, Diego Martínez Barrio, both resigned their offices. Since President Azaña died in 1940, and the full Cortes was disbanded in exile, Negrín claimed that his Popular Front government was the only authority to have survived the defeat and was, therefore, still in effect.[7]

The exiled *Negrinistas* favored the broadest possible Republican unity and continued militant activity directed toward bringing down the Franco government. They sought to re-create the coalition of political groups which had existed under the wartime Popular Front, and they thus united in exile to carry forward the interrupted war against Franco. At the very least, the Negrinists insisted, Spanish Republicans in exile should maintain their contacts with groups in Spain which still opposed Franco and do whatever possible to aid them in continuing the struggle there. The Popular Front, of course, had included, and was intended to include, the Communist party. The Communists, early in exile, lent strong verbal support to Negrín's militant policies.

Prieto's belated opposition to the role of the Communists in the wartime Popular Front government had been the factor most responsible for gaining him broad support within the Republican parties, as well as the loyalty of most of the Socialist party hier-

[5] The JSU dissolved within a short time after the war, its members thereafter joining the Negrín or Prieto Socialist parties, or the Communist party, or else abandoning their political commitments altogether. It was Negrín's misfortune that many of those most strongly sympathetic to his position were not committed to any party organization and after exile preferred to leave politics to the politicians.

[6] Prieto disagreed totally that the meeting at Figueras proved Negrín's position (Prieto and Negrín, "Epistolario"). The matter is described in several of their letters.

[7] Juan Negrín López, *Un discurso*, p. 61. This was one of the major points of argument in the correspondence between Negrín and Prieto. See Prieto and Negrín, "Epistolario."

archy. In exile Prieto spoke for the bulk of the Socialist party, the two Republican parties (the Izquierda Republicana and the Unión Republicana), and the two Republican-type Catalonian parties (the Esquerra Republicana de Cataluña and the Acción Catalana Republicana).[8] These political groups had worked together since the time of the Casado coup, which brought down Negrín's government at the end of the war. Once in exile, the immediate major political objectives of these parties were identical. They were determined to eliminate the Communist stigma from the image of the Republic and to convince France, the United States, and Great Britain that they should rectify past negligence by coming to the aid of the defeated Republic. The ultimate objective, as expressed by Prieto's supporters, was the restoration of the Republic of moderates and liberals, characterized by the government of 1931.[9]

The Socialists and Republicans, like the Negrinists, believed that the people of Spain longed for liberation from Franco's rule and wished for the return of a Republican government. Nevertheless, they objected to Negrín's desire to work from exile to foment internal conflict in Spain, just as they had rejected Negrín's maintenance of continued resistance at the end of 1938. With the country in ruins, physically and economically, the people exhausted by the war, and Republican leadership in Spain virtually destroyed, there seemed to them little merit in provoking further violence. Moreover, Socialist and Republican moderates had learned during the Civil War that in times of crisis the people tended toward extremist alternatives. The moderates had lost control of the Republic soon after the Civil War began; they were not

[8] These parties in Mexico were led by Indalecio Prieto, Alvaro de Albornoz, Diego Martínez Barrio, Antonio María Sbert, and Pere Bosch Gimpera, respectively. The Partido Nacionalista Vasco was another moderate liberal party which might have cooperated with the groups mentioned here, except that its political emphasis was more on Basque nationalism than on Spanish political problems. Neither was the Catalan Socialist group, the Movimiento Socialista de Catalunya, involved in the Junta. (Spanish Junta of Liberation, *Press Conference*, p. 10; *La Junta Española de Liberación ante la Conferencia de San Francisco de California*, p. 21; Interviews with Antonio María Sbert, September 26, 1966; Pere Bosch Gimpera, January 24, 1967.)

[9] Antonio María Sbert, "Los catalanes en el Pacto," in *El pacto para restaurar la República española*, pp. 61–64 by Juan Bautista Climent; Indalecio Prieto, "La reconstrucción de España," in Climent, *El Pacto*, p. 40; Alvaro de Albornoz, *Izquierda Republicana en la Junta Española de Liberación, informe pronunciado en la asamblea*, pp. 15–16.

anxious to resort to arms again.[10] Finally, unlike the Negrinist Socialists, the Communists, and the Anarchists, all of whom insisted that Franco could only be overthrown militarily, the Prieto Socialist and Republican groups professed the belief that Franco would fall because of his own unpopularity and inability to rule. The Spanish people, they trusted, would not long tolerate fascism.

Toward a Government in Exile

The Socialists, Republicans, and other moderates hoped to restore the original institutions of the Republic which they considered to have been corrupted by Communist influence during the war and lost in the Republican defeat. They were bitter because contemporary international opinion, even after the Civil War, so frequently interpreted the liberals' battle to save the Republic from Fascist rule as a Communist effort to destroy Spain. The Communists' role in the Popular Front government, it seemed, had turned much international public sympathy away from it, and many years were to pass before outside groups "remembered" that the prewar Republic had been liberal, not leftist.[11]

The nations of Europe and America which had refused to go to war on behalf of Spain in 1936 took up arms against Franco's allies shortly thereafter in the Second World War. In August, 1941, Great Britain and the United States signed the Atlantic pact, in which they promised, should they win the war, to protect the right of any people to choose its own form of government.[12] From the point of view of the exiles, an Allied victory in the Second World War could mean a Spanish Republican victory as well, but only if

[10] Indalecio Prieto, "La reconstrucción," pp. 38–39; Diego Martínez Barrio, *Informe político en la asamblea celebrada por Unión Republicana en el exilio*, pp. 13–17.

[11] One of the earlier articles in defense of the basically moderate political composition of the Spanish Republic was Philip B. Taylor's "Myth and Reality: How Red Were the Spanish 'Reds'?"

[12] In the Socialist newspaper *Adelante* (pro-Prieto) a cartoon appeared indicating the extent to which the Spanish Republicans had put their faith in the Atlantic Charter. The cartoon, entitled "Una esperanza," depicts a lovely young princess behind locked prison doors. A gruff and evil-looking guard is walking by and asking her, "Pero ¿crees que alguién se acuerde de ti?" She answers, "Sí, espero una carta del Atlántico" (*Adelante* 2 [August, 1943]:4). In 1943 it still seemed likely that the provisions of the Atlantic Charter might revive the Republic.

the Republicans could reestablish their claim to represent Spain's sole legitimate and popularly elected government.

In November, 1943, an Allied success seemed likely, and representatives of the Socialist and Republican parties united to form a political union called the Junta Española de Liberación. The members of the Junta feared that if the major Western powers continued to believe that the Republican government was dominated by Communists, these powers would favor the restoration of the Spanish Monarchy instead of the Republic which replaced the Monarchy in 1931.[13] Therefore they repudiated the Communist-tainted Negrín government and based their own authority on the fact that they represented the major political parties of the Republic of 1931. The Junta directed its activities toward two major objectives: to be named the official representative of the Spanish Republic at the meeting of the United Nations which was to be held after the war,[14] and to form an appropriate government-in-exile, acceptable to United Nations members.[15]

Although the Junta Española de Liberación was hailed as the first meaningful alliance of Spanish political parties, it did not include the Negrinist Socialists, the Communists, the Basque Nationalist party, or the Anarchist CNT. Its detractors, pointing to these exceptions, denied that the Junta could legitimately claim to represent the Republic in exile.[16] Junta leaders officially stated that all

[13] Because the Republic had existed for less than a decade, the Monarchy still might have been a logical alternative to replace the Franco government. There was, and still is, a pretender to the throne, and then, as now, he was mentioned frequently as a possible compromise solution for the Spanish political future. See Climent, *El pacto*, p. 7; Spanish Junta of Liberation, *Press Conference*, p. 18.

[14] At the Moscow conference of October, 1943, the United States, the United Kingdom, and the Soviet Union had pledged to create a general international organization upon the Allied victory (*Everyman's United Nations: A Basic History of the Organization, 1945–1964*, p. 5).

[15] Climent, *El pacto*, p. 11; Martínez Barrio, in ibid., p. 26; Spanish Junta of Liberation, *Press Conference*, pp. 10, 20–21; *La Junta Española de Liberación ante la Conferencia de San Francisco*, p. 2.

[16] In the political press of all the parties not involved in the junta, the Socialists and Republicans were blamed for arbitrary exclusiveness and for having falsely claimed to be the political voice of the exile. See, for example, the criticism by Isabel de Palencia in *Smouldering Freedom: The Story of the Spanish Republicans in Exile*, p. 162. Isabel de Palencia did not belong to any party in exile, but she had been ambassador to Sweden under the Negrín government and was closely tied to the Negrín group.

groups save the Communists were welcome to join the Junta and that it was hoped the other groups would enter. Even the Negrinista group would be welcome "if it would free itself of the Communist influence to which it owes its force."[17] No outside party, however, had been invited to share in the original formation of the junta or to serve on its governing board.[18] In fact, the members of the Junta neither expected nor wanted the opposing groups to join. The Republican and Socialist parties shared a basic political orientation which the others did not, and the entry of dissident groups, it was deemed, would serve only to disrupt the existing unity.[19]

The Spanish Junta de Liberación was optimistic that its representatives would influence the prospective members in favor of the Republic at the founding conference of the United Nations in San Francisco, April 25–June 26, 1945.[20] Thanks to an invitation by President Franklin D. Roosevelt, a delegation of the Junta was able to attend the conference as official observers without vote. The Spanish Republicans presented their case, reminding the World War II Allies that the war against fascism had begun in their country. They won their point. The San Francisco conference adopted a Mexican resolution which denied membership in the United Nations to states whose "regimes have been installed with the help of armed force of countries which have fought against the

[17] "Movimiento para formación de un gobierno español en el destierro," *Adelante*, January 1, 1944, p. 4.

[18] The governing board consisted of Indalecio Prieto, Manuel Alber, Carlos Esplá, Pedro Vargas, Diego Martínez Barrio, Félix Gordón Ordas, José Andreu Abello, and Pere Bosch Gimpera, representing the Socialist, Republican, and Catalan parties respectively. See Spanish Junta of Liberation, *Press Conference*, p. 10.

[19] Alvaro de Albornoz, president of the Izquierda Republicana and the last to adhere to the junta, gave as the major reason for his support the fact that the four groups mentioned above were not participating in the junta. Conflicting political philosophies, he felt, would hinder any progress the Junta might make (Albornoz, *Izquierda Republicana en la Junta Española de Liberación*, pp. 6–8). In his speech of adherence, Martínez Barrio also warned against the inclusion of elements who wished only to destroy Franco but shared none of the goals of the Junta for the future of Spain (Martínez Barrio, *Informe político*, pp. 3–16).

[20] *Adelante* reported that despite "Negrín's damaging attitude and actions," world opinion was modifying in favor of the Republic. According to this article, representatives of the junta had won significant support in the United States and throughout Latin America (*Adelante*, January 1, 1945, p. 1).

United Nations so long as these regimes are in power."[21] This resolution, although expressed in general terms, was aimed specifically at Franco.

Having succeeded in gaining the passage of this resolution, the Junta claimed credit for a full victory. The action by the United Nations was viewed by members of the Junta as the first step in the inevitable defeat of Franco. In a press conference soon after the San Francisco meeting, Prieto himself confidently predicted that the repudiation of Franco by the members of the United Nations would be followed by their withdrawal of diplomatic relations with Spain. The next step, then, would be the reconstitution of the Republican government in Spain under United Nations auspices.[22] In order that this might be accomplished, therefore, the Junta de Liberación and the Permanent Committee of the Spanish Cortes devoted themselves to the task of appointing an appropriate government in exile, which, it was hoped, would soon be recognized by the major world powers.

In 1945, over the protest of Negrín, the Cortes was called to meet in Mexico City. Martínez Barrio, acting as next in line to the deceased former president of the Republic, Azaña, named José Giral prime minister. Giral formerly had been a close friend and collaborator of President Azaña and was the latter's choice for prime minister in 1936. He seemed the epitome of the political spirit of the original Republic. As an internationally respected scientist who had not been involved in the political feuds between Prieto and Negrín, he enjoyed a position of wide prestige and trust both within and outside the emigration.[23] With the establishment of the Giral government in 1945, the Junta de Liberación rested on its laurels and, considering its functions accomplished, voluntarily dissolved itself.

The events leading to the establishment of the Giral government

[21] *El problema de España ante el mundo internacional, resolución aprobada por la Asamblea General de las Naciones Unidas, texto y discusion de la misma*, p. 14; *Everyman's United Nations*, p. 156. The United Nations' ban on admission of the Franco government and its subsequent change in position is discussed in *Spain and the Defense of the West* by Arthur Whitaker, pp. 344–350. It is also discussed more fully later in this chapter.

[22] "Una jornada histórica, el acuerdo de San Francisco" (*Adelante*, July 1, 1945, p. 1). Indalecio Prieto, press conference, reprinted in ibid., p. 3.

[23] See "Homenaje a Don José Giral," Mexico, 1963. José Giral was an eminent chemist and one-time close collaborator of Azaña; he was former minister of the navy and had been prime minister of the Republic briefly in 1936.

constituted a major crisis for the supporters of Negrín. They vigorously protested the summoning of the Permanent Committee of the Cortes to name a government, claiming that such a government already existed, under the authority of Negrín. Realizing that the actions of the Junta and the Cortes were intended specifically to undermine his claim to leadership of the Spanish Republican government, Negrín publicly raised three major objections to the proposed summoning of the Cortes. First, he maintained that his was the only legitimate government in exile. Second, he characterized the Permanent Committee of the Cortes as merely a group of former deputies who were committed to Prieto and not representative of the former Republican Cortes as a whole. He insisted, therefore, on the need to consult with other former deputies who were not on the committee. Third, he questioned the legality of Martínez Barrio's action on the grounds that the latter had resigned as president of the Cortes in 1939 and had only later disclaimed the resignation.

In order to bring his disapproval to public attention, Negrín offered his own resignation, expecting that the deputies of the Cortes, when put to the test, would not allow him, the duly appointed prime minister, to resign. He misjudged their temper. Martínez Barrio, after succeeding in having himself promoted from president of the Cortes to president of the Republic, accepted Negrín's resignation and then appointed Giral to succeed Negrín as prime minister.

The Giral government was located in Paris, but it was structurally ready with ministries and committees to assume authority in Spain whenever Franco fell. The government began with the support and participation of all the parties of the former Junta de Liberación, as well as of the Basque Nationalist party, and it had the tacit acceptance of the Anarchists. Despite its auspicious beginnings, however, the government lasted only about a year. Giral not only had to face the failure of the members of the United Nations to take any additional steps toward the overthrow of Franco and the restoration of the Republic, but he also had to contend with the increasing confusion and vindictiveness of Spanish politics in exile.[24] Once the Junta dissolved, whatever semblance of political

[24] Interview with Francisco Giral, son of José Giral, and currently the president of the United Republican group, the ARDE, April 4, 1967.

unity had existed disappeared. From that time on, all parties worked individually and often at cross-purposes.

When, by 1946, it became apparent that the enthusiasm for replacing Franco's regime with the Republic was waning among United Nations members, Giral decided to broaden his political base by admitting an Anarchist representative and a Republican recently escaped from Spain. In order to attract more determined support from the Soviet Union, he also allowed limited participation of the Spanish Communist party in his government. His major objective, consistently, was to gain increased international support, if not from the Western powers, then from the Soviet Union. The Socialists, as well as the Anarchist representative, however, preferred to leave the government, rather than see it dependent upon an ideological group with which they were incompatible. Once the Socialists withdrew, the Giral ministry collapsed.[25] Giral was succeeded as prime minister at the beginning of 1947 by Socialist Rodolfo Llopis, thereby bringing the Socialists back into the government. The new government soon thereafter lost the support of the Republicans.

In the meantime, during 1946 and 1947, Prieto had had conversations with the Monarchist group, the major opposition organization in Spain. These talks culminated, in 1948, with an alliance between Socialists and Monarchists, the Pact of San Juan de Luz.[26] The various Spanish and regional Republican parties and the independent political groups supporting the government in exile did not follow the Socialists' lead and refused to join them in adhering to the San Juan pact.[27] For the Republicans in particular it was easier to conceive of a reconciliation with the Communist

[25] Various articles written in the early 1940's reflect these concerns. For example, "Movimiento para formación de un gobierno español en el destierro" (*Adelante*, January 1, 1944, p. 4); Ovidio Salcedo, "Posiciones y orientaciones de las Juventudes Socialistas" (lecture, February 9, 1944, at a meeting organized by the Juventud Socialista, pp. 10–20); José Fernández, "Nuevas juventudes" (*Adelante*, September 15, 1943, p. 3). Interviews with Socialist party officers Víctor Salazar and Enrique López Sevilla.

[26] Within the Republican party there was a faction favoring continued cooperation with the Communists. Perhaps for this reason the Republicans have been somewhat more open in their attitude toward the Communist party than the other two groups.

[27] Fidel Miró, *¿Y España cuando? El fracaso político de una emigración*, p. 58; Stanley Payne, *Franco's Spain*, p. 118; Whitaker, *Spain*, p. 168.

party than with the Monarchists, since the very idea of restoring the Spanish Monarchy, in any form, contradicted their single objective of reestablishing the Republic.[28] The Llopis government fell shortly after the signing of the pact and was followed by the government of Alvaro de Albornoz, which was supported solely by the Republican parties. The Albornoz government, like those which have followed it (Félix Gordón Ordas, Claudio Sánchez Albornoz, Luis Jiménez de Asua), has been a symbol of the Republican existence, but without real influence or importance, either internationally or among the exiles.[29] Political parties have continued to function, but without regard to the existence of a government in exile.

The Spanish Story in International Relations

The early actions and reactions of Spanish politicians followed as though consciously orchestrated by the major powers in the United Nations. Later it became evident that Franco had indeed managed to outlive his erstwhile allies in Italy and Germany and

---

[28] "El Izquierda Republicana no pertenece a la Alianza de Fuerzas Democráticas," originally printed in *Izquierda Republicana*, the organ of that party, on January 8, 1949, and quoted here as reprinted in *El Socialista* 7 (January, 1949): 2. The article refers to the Alliance of Democratic Forces, founded in 1944 in Spain, which included the remnants of the Spanish leftist parties and which briefly discussed the formation, with the Monarchists, of a common front against Franco. The Republicans stated that their party neither planned to participate in the leftist Alliance of Democratic Forces nor to join the Socialists in signing a pact with the Monarchists. They condemned the San Juan pact as useless and damaging. The Monarchists, for their part, had brought together in 1945 the political moderates and traditionalists in a Confederación de Fuerzas Monárquicas, which proposed the pretender, Don Juan, as an alternative to Franco. The exiles, who participated in neither group, were displeased when the two groups began to discuss forming a common union. Some Anarchists proposed throwing exile support toward the alliance, but other exile parties declined to do so (Miró, *¿Y España cuando?* pp. 54ff.). Finally, the talks between the alliance and the Monarchist confederation broke down, and the latter turned instead to sign the San Juan pact with the exiled Socialists. The San Juan pact was short-lived, however; many conservatives among the Monarchists objected to a pact with the exiled Socialists, and when Don Juan began holding friendly talks with Franco, shortly after signing the pact, Prieto withdrew from his commitment (Payne, *Franco's Spain*, pp. 115–116, 118; Whitaker, *Spain*, p. 168).

[29] By the early 1950's most of the officials and ministers of the Republican government in exile had left the official seat of the government in France and settled in other countries of exile (Interview with Alfonso Ayensa, February 21, 1967. Ayensa served in the Republican government in France until 1952; he then went to Mexico).

was wiping the tarnish of fascism from his international image by cooperating with the anti-Communist efforts of the governments of the United States and western Europe. As Franco successfully consolidated his regime in Spain, the Republican presence receded on the world stage and the politics of exile ceased to have meaning to anybody outside of the exile itself.

The United Nations resolution of 1946 not to accept the constitutionality of the Franco regime had given the Republicans in exile hope for further action on the part of the major powers to bring about the end of the Franco government and the restoration of the Republic. Between February and December of 1946, the "Spanish question" was frequently discussed in both the General Assembly and the Security Council. In February, forty-six out of forty-eight countries represented in the General Assembly voted in favor of a mild Panamanian resolution suggesting that the members of the United Nations "should take into account the letter and spirit of the [previous United Nations'] statements [at San Francisco] in the conduct of their future relations with Spain."[30] In June, a fact-finding committee appointed by the Security Council labeled the Franco regime a "potential menace" to international security,[31] and, in December, the General Assembly voted a formal censure of Spain, recommending that its members withdraw recognition from the Franco government and that Spain not be permitted entry into any of the international organizations associated with the United Nations until a democratic regime had been restored. The General Assembly resolution also recommended that an economic blockade be established against Spain and that other measures be undertaken to hasten the downfall of the Franco government.[32] Spain was isolated economically from Europe when France closed the Pyrenees border; aid to Spain was not included in the Marshall Plan, the country was denied admittance to the United Nations and

[30] *El problema de España ante el mundo internacional*, p. 14. The conference at San Francisco was discussed earlier in this chapter. The resolutions against Franco's admission to the United Nations were reiterated at Potsdam, July-August, 1945.

[31] *Everyman's United Nations*, p. 156.

[32] In 1947 the Spanish Republicans in exile were invited to send a delegation to the meetings of UNESCO. This was considered a great honor, and a form of assurance that the United Nations would not abandon Republican Spain (*Las Españas* 2 [November, 1947]:2).

later to the North Atlantic Treaty Organization. Spaniards suffered from dismal economic conditions throughout the 1940's. Yet the regime did not topple, and Franco used the economic crisis to his own political advantage by identifying himself with feelings of injured national pride.[33]

The General Assembly's recommendations that members withdraw recognition of Franco and seek means to bring down his government were, in large part, ignored. By 1948 the Cold War had begun and the Western powers were less anxious to punish the anti-Communist government in Spain. Spain, whose government until 1950 was considered unworthy by democratic Europe, gradually began to earn a welcome into the Western community of nations. In November, 1950, the United Nations overruled its previous recommendations, resolving that diplomatic recognition did not constitute a judgment of the domestic policy of a government, and concluding that the nonpolitical, technical agencies of the United Nations were intended for the benefit of all peoples, regardless of the government under which they lived. Each member nation, therefore, was to decide independently whether or not it would recognize Spain, and each technical agency of the United Nations would be able to rule separately regarding Spain's participation in its programs. Spain was admitted formally into the United Nations in December, 1955,[34] and within a few years all United Nations members except Mexico and Yugoslavia recognized the Franco regime.

Mexico

The Spanish Republic continues to have a special meaning in Mexico because the Mexican government has persistently refused to recognize Franco as the legal ruler of Spain. When the Spanish government in exile was founded in 1945, the Mexicans allowed the Republicans to reopen the old Spanish embassy, which had been

[33] Payne, *Franco's Spain*, p. 35; Alvaro de Albornoz, *El gobierno de la República española en el destierro a los gobiernos y a la opinión pública de todos los paises democráticos*, p. 7. Albornoz, the head of the Izquierda Republicana, argues that the economic blockade did not strengthen Franco's position. Economic sanctions failed, he claimed, because they were not accompanied with any other action which would have weakened Franco's hold.

[34] *Everyman's United Nations*, pp. 156–157.

closed since the end of the Civil War.[35] The Spanish Republican ambassador and the members of the diplomatic staff have been invited to attend all official functions in Mexico since 1945, and formal diplomatic relations have been maintained between the Mexican government and the Republic.

The symbols of recognition have been reserved for the Republic. On the other hand, all important commercial and political business between Mexico and Spain is carried on between the Mexican government and the official "representatives" of Franco in Mexico. The Republicans do not object to cordial economic and commercial relations between the governments in Spain and Mexico. Because such relations do exist, it has been possible for the Republicans, most of whom have now become naturalized Mexican citizens, to send money to relatives in Spain, to travel to Spain, and even to invest in Spanish enterprises. Spaniards, those supporting the regime as well as those who have had political difficulties with it, have also been able to emigrate easily to Mexico.

The Republican embassy, meanwhile, is open for business, and a secretary handles various administrative matters on behalf of those exiles who have not taken Mexican citizenship, or who have had personal or financial matters pending in Spain since the Republic. The embassy's administrative tasks have been diminishing over the years, and there is presently little serious work facing the Republican consul, who nonetheless appears at the embassy for a few hours nearly every working day. At this time there is no indication that the present situation is about to change.

Most observers, both Republican and Mexican, think that when Franco dies and another government replaces him, the Mexican government may reconsider its recognition of the Spanish Republic. If the government which follows Franco is a liberal and more progressive one, it is extremely likely that diplomatic relations between Mexico and Spain will be regularized. The effect this will have upon the political life of the Spanish exiles is difficult to predict, but, since participation in Spanish Republican politics has declined dramatically, Mexican recognition of Franco's success may affect the community as a whole only in symbolic ways.

[35] The building was closed because, as far as Mexico was concerned, there was no legal Spanish government after the defeat of the Republic, until the appointment of Giral.

POLITICAL PARTIES AND GROUPS AND THE SEARCH FOR UNITY

The same political entities which were active in the Civil War and which struggled for power during the early years of exile have continued to dominate political activities of the Spanish Republic in exile. All of the parties have split at times into dissident factions, and on a few occasions these splits have been formalized. All of the parties have united for political action with one or several of the other political groups. All have witnessed a severe decline in active membership, and none has attracted the younger people of the emigration in substantial numbers. The hierarchy of leadership has been slow to change, and, in most of the parties, remains relatively unchanged, despite the fact that most of the major political leaders of the Republic have died.[36] All the political groups have attached their policies to projects and preparations for the defeat of Franco and the restoration of the Republic. Yet relations among the political groups, defeated together by the forces under Francisco Franco, have been more discordant than cooperative. Until shortly after the Second World War, the emigration as a whole looked upon the programs and policies of the various parties as relevant and important to the Spanish future. By the mid-1950's, political activity and interest generally declined, and, by the late 1960's, the political participation of Republican refugees in Mexico had become minuscule. Issues of political debate since have tended to be more abstract and ideological than concrete. There is little expectation, even among those still politically active, that they or the parties of exile will play significant roles in Spain's political future.

Círculo Cultural Jaime Vera

In exile, those who accepted Negrín's authority and supported his claim to leadership of the Republic in exile found themselves thoroughly alienated from most of the party hierarchy which supported Prieto's policies. In January, 1942, the Negrinista faction attempted to enhance its political influence in the party by forming a group called the Círculo Cultural Jaime Vera. In November, 1942, as the hostility between Negrín and Prieto grew more intense, the Jaime Vera was expelled altogether from the formal party

[36] By the mid-1960's, Negrín, Prieto, Alvaro de Albornoz, Martínez Barrio, and José Giral had all died.

structure. The group existed thereafter as an entirely separate
entity under the presidency of Ramón Lamoneda, a former deputy
of the Cortes. The Jaime Vera element considered itself the only
legitimate Socialist party, supporting the only legitimate Republican government, that of Negrín.[37] Nearly the entire Socialist party
bureaucracy and most of the membership, however, rejected the
Negrinist position.[38] The party considered the Jaime Vera to be but
"a small dissident group" and renounced Negrín both as a Socialist
and as a Republican leader.[39]

The Negrinist Socialists believed that only if the emigration were
united could Republicans cooperate effectively in exile, and they insisted that political groups in exile would have to work with the
existing opposition groups still inside Spain to overthrow the Franco
government by violence. As a basic policy the Jaime Vera proposed to expand its base by uniting with other political groups,
particularly with the Communists and with uncommitted leftists
in the emigration, in order to create a "popular front" kind of cooperation in exile.

The first of such unions was the Unión Democrática Española
(UDE), whose intent was to bring together all the exiles and direct
their efforts toward political action.[40] The UDE was formed during
the early months of exile as a coalition of members of the Jaime
Vera, of Communists, and of a number of individuals, either uncommitted or only nominally committed to other parties. It lasted
only a few years. By March, 1943, *El Socialista*, political organ of
the Jaime Vera, began to report the gradual dissolution of the UDE,
because of opposition from the Prietists, who were in the process of
forming the Junta Española, and of lack of cooperation from the

[37] "Creación del Círculo Cultural Jaime Vera," *El Socialista* 1 (January,
1942):1–4. The legitimacy of both the Jaime Vera and the Negrín government
were the primary themes of *El Socialista*, especially during the first series of its
publication, 1942 to 1943. They were also the themes of *República Española*,
published from May, 1944, to May, 1945, by those who were sympathetic to
Negrín but not necessarily Socialists. See, for example, the editorial in the first
issue (May 15, 1944, p. 1).
[38] I use "Socialist party" to refer to those who accepted Prieto's leadership
and retained the structure of the old Spanish Socialist party. The dissident
Socialists are referred to specifically as the "Negrín Socialists" or the "Grupo
Jaime Vera."
[39] Editorial in *Adelante*, August 1, 1945, p. 1. *Adelante* was the organ of the
major Socialist party.
[40] "Catorce de abril, manifiesto de la U.D.E.," *El Socialista* 1 (April, 1942):1.

Communists. The Communists, still officially supporting Negrín, declined to follow his leadership in efforts directed at political action in Spain. By mid-1943, the UDE collapsed totally, leaving the Jaime Vera considerably weakened.[41]

The collapse of the UDE was followed by a period of bitter debate (1944–1946) over the merits of continued cooperation with the Communists. Many of those who had participated in the Jaime Vera or been sympathetic to its position now withdrew their support and joined the majority of refugees who denounced the Communists. The Communist party, although verbally advocating a policy similar to that of the Negrinistas, actually insisted on working independently of the Socialists and other radicals in building its own ties with opposition groups in Spain. To the Socialists of the Jaime Vera, Communist independence constituted a betrayal both of Negrín[42] and of Republican unity. Still the Jaime Vera continued to favor cooperation of the two political groups, even though this cooperation was not reciprocal, and despite increasing misgivings about its outcome.

In 1945 the Jaime Vera was confronted with the formation of the Giral government, whose primary objective was to win recognition of the Spanish government in exile from the major world powers; Negrín and his Socialist followers considered this objective unrealistic and wrong. After some hesitation, the Jaime Vera decided not to oppose the new government for fear it would then lose face internationally, but the members of the group determined not to participate in Giral's ministries.[43] Negrín himself announced that

[41] For example, the editorial in *El Socialista* 2 (March, 1943):1, was subtitled, "¿Es posible la unidad?"; see also "El partido Socialista y el valor de la conducta" (*República Española*, August 31, 1944, p. 4). *El Socialista* stopped publication between December, 1943, and March, 1944, due to opposition from the anti-Communist factions in the emigration and the uncooperative attitude of the Communists themselves. See section on Communist party.

[42] In Fernando Vázquez, "Juntas que no juntan" (*El Socialista* 3[March, 1944]:1). Vázquez blamed the Communists as well as the Prietist Republican faction for creating disunity and hindering common action with their separate entities. See also the article mentioned above, "¿Es posible la unidad?" (p. 4); and Enrique Angulo, "La vuelta de la linea" (*El Socialista* 5[April, 1946]:2), which accused the Communists of seeking understanding with the reactionary anti-Communist forces rather than working with progressive and worker elements.

[43] *El Socialista* 4(September, 1945):6, announced the policy of the Jaime Vera and listed the other parties which remained outside the government: the Com-

although he disagreed totally with the new government's policy of attempting to regain control of Spain by currying international goodwill, he had no choice but to wish the Giral government success, because its failure, he feared, would mean a failure for all the refugees.[44]

It was reasonably clear by 1947 that the newly formed United Nations organization was not going to take the initiative in ending the Franco regime. The Negrinistas, satisfied in having judged correctly the lack of potential foreign support, were nonetheless dismayed at the consequences of the exiles' inability to attain their ends. When the United Nations failed to act positively in behalf of the Republicans, many refugees who up to this time had maintained some faith in the efficacy of political action in exile gave up hope and abandoned political participation altogether.

It was at this point that the Jaime Vera made one last attempt to unite the Republican emigration behind the banner of Negrín and the Popular Front. The organization founded a new movement called "España Combatiente" in December of 1947.[45] España Combatiente was intended to reinspire the disillusioned exiles with the desire to unite and to act, not, this time, by leaving the Spanish solution to the European powers, but by acting in collaboration with opposition groups inside Spain to bring about the fall of Franco. The Communists verbally supported the Jaime Vera in this objective, but again, due to the independent activities of the Communist party in Spain, relations between the two groups ultimately grew hostile.[46] No significant portion of the emigration ral-

munists; a small faction of the Republican party; and the UGT (the syndicalist arm of the Socialist party). The writers believed that the policy of the government was altogether contrary to their own and that, if Negrín were to support it, his name would be "sterilized."

[44] Juan Negrín López, "Discurso," *El Socialista* 4 (September, 1945):1–4.

[45] "Declaración de 'España Combatiente,'" *El Socialista* 6 (January, 1948):5; "Ante el primer congreso de España Combatiente," ibid. (March, 1948):3. The president of España Combatiente was Julio Alvarez del Vayo, then residing in New York.

[46] This information was derived from several conversations with Enrique Angulo, former director of *El Socialista* and son-in-law of Ramón Lamoneda, president of the Grupo Jaime Vera. Speaking for the Communist policy, poet and party official Juan Rejano noted that the party usually preferred to follow an independent course and to convince others of the efficacy of joining in its efforts (Interview, October 11, 1966).

lied to España Combatiente, and, within a year of its founding, it had ceased to exist.

Partido Socialista Obrero Español

After the dissolution of the Junta de Liberación, the Socialist party policies became more rigid—neither open to broad cooperation with other groups nor sympathetic toward dissidents within the party. Not only did party leaders expel many individuals, they also kept a tight rein on such semiautonomous groups as the UGT and the Socialist Youth. The Socialist Youth were (and continue to be) censured frequently by older political leaders for their willingness to cooperate with groups outside the party, as well as for their tendency to look to the anti-Franco leaders in Spain, rather than to the party bureaucracy in exile, for direction.[47]

The Socialists also opposed any attempts on the part of non-partisan groups to investigate alternative solutions for the future of Spain. For example, when the Unión de Profesores Españoles en el Extranjero met in Havana to discuss the future of Spain and the Republic, the official Socialist paper, *Adelante*, strongly criticized the professors for undermining the political structure of the Republic in exile.[48] Although the Socialists continued to share with

[47] There was no Socialist Youth group in exile from the time the original Spanish youth groups of the Civil War were old enough to join the main party, in the mid-1940's, until the mid-1950's, when a few of the young people who had grown up in exile, responding to the renewed activity of the youth in Spain, decided to form their own group. They considered themselves to the left of the party bureaucracy in exile, or, as one of them noted, their ideology resembled the old Caballero-type socialism more closely than it resembled the Prieto philosophy (see chap. 1). The younger people resented the older leaders for having ignored the youth and for maintaining an overly sectarian and conservative position with regard to Spain. The older leaders, on the other hand, dismissed the "youth" as romantic and unrealistic, given their complete ignorance of Spain and the Socialist experience in Spain. This problem, of course, has not been unique to the Socialist party, although that party has dealt more harshly with its youthful dissenters than have most of the other groups (Interviews with Rafael Fernández, head of Young Socialists, March 8, 1967; Francisco Lurueña, April 22, 1967; party intellectual Enrique López Sevilla, February 23, 1967; Víctor Salazar, secretary of the UGT in exile, March 4, 1967).

[48] According to the Socialist press, however, the professors were implying by their action that political parties had outlived their usefulness; they were setting themselves up as a "cultural autocracy" superior to the political structure ("Un manifiesto de los intelectuales," *Adelante*, January 15, 1944, p. 4). The issue of the intellectuals and their attitude was further debated in later issues of *Adelante*. See also "Ratificación de un criterio," ibid., January 15, 1945, p. 1.

the Republicans and the Anarchists a basic fear and distrust of Communist influence in exile groups, all attempts at joint action extending beyond a shared anti-Communist posture failed. Republican and Anarchist leaders have frequently blamed the rigidity of the Socialist party for these failures.[49] So great was the hostility of many Socialists to Negrín that they considered their first task of exile to be his removal from power.[50]

Once the Negrinist Jaime Vera had been expelled, Prieto's primary objective as chief of the Socialist party-in-exile was to restore the party to its pre–Civil War condition, before Communist pressure had robbed it of much of its independence and had wooed Socialist youth into the Communist-dominated JSU. To accomplish this objective, the party hierarchy considered it desirable to maintain an orthodox ideological posture and to limit the cooperation of its members with other groups, hence the party's exclusivist policies after the dissolution of the Junta de Liberación. Leaders devoted their attention to defining the party's position vis-à-vis Spain and their efforts toward building and coordinating the organization of Spanish Socialist party groups in all countries of exile.

Although Prieto spent his exile years in Mexico, and many prominent Socialist leaders have lived there, the official center of party activity has always been France.[51] This is because most of the UGT workers remained in France in their exile, and, moreover, it

[49] For example, Anarchist Miró, ¿Y España cuando? (pp. 15–17, 47–50, 74–79); Máximo Muñoz, "Grandeza y tragedia de la emigración republicana española" (lecture, presented February 22, 1958—Muñoz had been an important member of the Socialist party but was expelled; he gave this speech in his own defense); interview with Francisco Giral, head of the combined Republican parties, the ARDE, April 4, 1967.

[50] The significance of the Negrín-Prieto opposition was discussed by the Republican party leader and admirer of Prieto, Alvaro de Albornoz, "El llamado pleito Prieto-Negrín," in the Socialist press (Adelante, August 15, 1945). Albornoz praised what he considered to be Prieto's liberal and democratic views as contrasted with the extremist, unrealistic, and dictatorial tendencies of Negrín, and he emphasized that the dispute between the two leaders affected not only the Socialist party, but the entire future of the Republican emigration. This article by a Republican party leader was used to buttress the many editorials and articles in Adelante condemning Negrín.

[51] Interview with Víctor Salazar, secretary of the Socialist UGT of Mexico, March 4, 1967. The Spanish workers did not feel the same pressure to leave France as did the professionals and intellectuals, because in most cases their labor was needed in France, and the language barrier was not so great a problem for them as it was for those who worked with words and ideas.

was much easier to maintain communications with Spain from France than from Mexico. Representatives of the party, from all countries of exile as well as from Spain, have met annually at congresses held in Toulouse, to discuss and vote on party policies. The resolutions voted at the Toulouse congresses are binding on the entire membership.[52] The consequent limitation of the autonomy of local leaders constitutes another reason for the Mexican-based party's lack of flexibility.

At the annual congress in Toulouse in 1946 (and at each subsequent congress), the Socialist representatives agreed that neither the party nor its members should cooperate with Communists or with the Jaime Vera in any kind of endeavor.[53] Shortly thereafter, the Socialists withdrew from the Giral government and began conversations concerning possible cooperation with the Monarchist groups in Spain. These conversations suggested that the same party which had organized the Junta de Liberación, in 1943, so that Monarchists would not inherit the Spanish government after the fall of Franco, was willing three years later to consider sharing the government with its erstwhile enemies. The Socialist shift in position reflected the deterioration in the exiles' political hopes between 1943 and 1946. Despite all the efforts and the high expectations of 1945, at the end of 1946 Franco still had the recognition of the major world powers, and was effectively consolidating his rule in Spain.

The Socialist party in exile faced its most serious crisis in the 1960's, which, ironically, derived from the very success of socialism in Spain. As long as Franco's repression of political opposition remained complete, the Socialists in exile had nearly full control of the direction of the party, both inside and outside Spain. The party continued to exist clandestinely in Spain despite the repression, but it remained small and almost completely dependent upon

[52] According to Salazar, representatives come to Toulouse from every major city in Mexico, and there are delegates from most of the other American countries, as well as from France and Spain. The largest number of delegates, of course, comes from the major centers of emigration: Mexico City, Paris, and Toulouse. The annual congresses are held in secret so that the Spanish delegates can leave Spain and return unnoticed by the authorities. (See the discussion of the Spanish Socialist party in Whitaker, *Spain*, pp. 180–182.)

[53] Article in *El Socialista* 4 (August, 1946):4. Interviews with Enrique López Sevilla and Víctor Salazar.

aid and direction from outside. In the late 1950's the internal situation began to change. Franco, reasonably certain of his own leadership position, relaxed some of the restrictions on political and intellectual activities: opposition groups were allowed to organize and to speak more freely, and, to a degree, censorship was relaxed.[54] As a result of the limited liberalization, important movements of a liberal and socialist type developed in Spain. They were led by such young intellectuals as Enrique Tierno Galván and Luis Aranguren and appealed particularly to young people in Spain and in exile. These Spanish movements, however, had nothing to do with the old Civil War and exile Socialist party structures.

The exile leaders in Mexico have agreed that Tierno Galván and Aranguren and others like them in Spain are the most relevant figures for Spanish socialism, but the older men have been unwilling to accept the leadership of the younger Spanish intellectuals. The exiles have objected particularly to the fact that socialists in Spain have based their movement upon a willingness to cooperate with a wide variety of leftist opposition groups, including the Communists. Furthermore, the exile party, which through the years has maintained an orthodox ideological position, has accused the socialist movement in Spain of lacking the proper ideological foundations. The Spanish socialist activists, as one exile leader insisted, represent an attitude more than they represent a political philosophy. Compromise is difficult: the older Socialists believe in the value of their long experience in forming and directing the party. However, they cannot deny that the movement in Spain is more vital, and far more involved in the actual struggle taking place against Franco, and, therefore, more appealing to Spaniards as well as to many young exiles.[55] The party in exile retains the

[54] See Arthur Whitaker, *Spain*, pp. 155–195, for a discussion of the various opposition groups. Most of the activity Whitaker describes did not come to public attention until the late 1950's. Dionisio Ridruejo, in *Escrito en España* and in a lecture at Harvard on May 7, 1968, confirms the opinions of many refugees who have been in touch with events in Spain, in pointing to a definite liberalization occurring in the late fifties, and attributing it to Franco's closer ties to other European countries, to increased tourism, and to Franco's sense of increased security. The liberalization, of course, is far from complete, and Spaniards who wish to speak freely usually find it necessary to do so outside Spain.

[55] Interviews with Socialists Víctor Salazar, Enrique López Sevilla, and the leader of the Socialist Youth, Rafael Fernández, March 8, 1967. Many of the impressions recorded above come from a debate at the Ateneo Español de México

loyalty of a few older workers in Spain who remained there after the Civil War and who still consider themselves members of the old UGT. Their loyalty, however, represents the survival of pre-Civil War socialism only in its trade-union form.

The Republican Parties

Prior to the establishment of the Spanish Republic, all those in Spain who favored supplanting the Monarchy with a republican form of government were called Republicans, whatever their political ideology. After 1931, the term "republican" came to refer to specific political entities. These groupings, while not ideologically based in any one class or doctrine, advocated a republican form of government which would move in a progressive and socializing, but not Socialist, direction. Most Spanish intellectuals supported the Republican parties, particularly the Izquierda Republicana, Manuel Azaña's party,[56] and their influence dominated Republican policies. After the defeat in the Civil War, the Republican parties had no defined ideology to maintain. Moreover, the Republican intellectuals in exile rarely participated in partisan politics. Of all the exiles, they were among the first to lose faith in the efficacy of partisan action for the liberation of Spain.[57] As they became in-

---

on February 16, 1967. On the panel were López Sevilla, speaking as a Socialist theoretician, Rafael Fernández, speaking for the young people, José Bullejos, defending the position of the old Civil War Socialist hierarchy, and Manuel Ortuño, a Socialist in his thirties, recently arrived from Spain, defending the newer Spanish Socialist movement. The issue of debate was a book by Bullejos on the bases of socialism, *Problemas fundamentales de España* (Mexico, 1966).

[56] For example, more than half the executive council of the FUE and a high proportion of the professors at the Havana conference were Republicans, or had been, in Spain. Dr. José Giral, who directed a section of the Havana conference, had been Azaña's choice for prime minister of the Republic and was later the first prime minister of the Republic in exile. The president of the FUE in exile, Antonio María Sbert, was also president of the Esquerra Catalana; Giral, Sbert, Bosch Gimpera, Mariano Ruíz Funes, Luis Nicolau d'Olwer, Francisco Giral, Felipe Sánchez Roman, and others, all identified to some extent with the Republican parties, were on the original board of directors of the Unión de Intelectuales; they later abandoned it, because they considered the Communists to be dominating its activities and rendering it useless. See the discussion below on the Communist party in exile and Frente Universitario Español (FUE), *Coincidencia de propósitos*; Unión de Profesores, *Boletín Informativo* 1 (September-December, 1943); Unión de Intelectuales Españoles en México, "Constitución," in *Las Españas* 2 (September, 1947):12.

[57] After the defeat of the Republican government in Spain, the term "republi-

volved in their separate professional or academic careers, they tended to cease political activity altogether, or else they preferred to work within their professions, for instance, in the Unión de Profesores or the later Unión de Intelectuales. Their parties, therefore, which had been small in Spain because they were parties of the educated classes rather than of the masses, were smaller still in exile because so many of their members preferred nonpartisan political activity.

Initially, there were two major Spanish Republican parties and two Catalonian parties of a Republican type in exile, each of which resembled each other ideologically.[58] They were the Izquierda Republicana, the Unión Republicana, the Esquerra Catalana, and the Acción Catalana Republicana. The Izquierda Republicana and the Acción Republicana merged into a single party in 1959,[59] after the deaths of their respective leaders, Alvaro de Albornoz and Diego Martínez Barrio. The new party, called the Acción Republicana Democrática Española (ARDE),[60] was, in 1968, under the leadership of Francisco Giral, son of former Prime Minister José Giral.

Because the Republicans have been dedicated to the restoration of the republican form of government in Spain, but have not been bound to follow any specific ideology, they have shown more flexibility than the Socialist party in seeking alliances. For example, the Republicans have not made anticommunism an article of faith, although, in practice, the Republican and Socialist parties have acted together against the Communists. On the few occasions, however, when the objectives of the Communist party appeared to coincide with those of the Republicans, the latter have cooperated to some extent with the former. Hence, the Republican Prime Minis-

can" seems to have returned to its original, nonpartisan definition, one which included all those who wished to bring about a liberal, democratic, and republican form of government. Hence, Juan Marichal has declared that more than 40 percent of the population in Spain is "republican" (*El nuevo pensamiento político español*, p. 96). The statement does not refer to the strength of the Republican party but to the existence of "republican" sentiments.

58 There was a somewhat separate Republican group called the Ateneo Pí y Margall, which maintained its independence with a handful of members. It was never a factor of political importance in the exile.

59 The action appears in Ateneo Español de México, *Memoria* (1958), p. 8.

60 Although the Catalan parties shared a similar political orientation, they preferred to remain solely identified with the Catalan state, and did not join the ARDE (Interview with Pere Bosch Gimpera, January 24, 1967).

ter José Giral did accept a certain amount of Communist participation in the first Republican government in exile, while the Socialists withdrew from his government for that very reason.

The Republicans have tried to unite the exiles on the basis of shared objectives for the future of Spain, rather than on strictly partisan lines. They have appealed to the politically inactive but concerned exiles who ignore politics on a day-to-day basis, but who will respond to a crisis situation concerning Spanish Republicans for Spain.[61] The Republicans have been more active than any other political group in the Ateneo Español, a nonpartisan association. Whereas members of the Socialist and Anarchist groups have been reluctant even to attend certain meetings at the ateneo, for fear of becoming involved in political debates with members of the Communist party, the Republicans not only have attended but have sponsored debates which include representatives of all political coloration.[62] The leaders of the ateneo also appear to have been far more willing than others to accept a secondary role to opposition groups inside Spain, and they have been actively seeking to increase and improve contacts between the Republican leaders in exile and the new, younger leaders of the moderate political groups in Spain.[63]

The Communist Party

Of all the parties in exile the Communists appear to have best preserved their structure and level of activity. Although the party

[61] "Los partidos no sirven . . . se han hecho viejos, sus hombres no inspiran confianza, sus métodos estan gastados; sus programas, sus ideologías, sus modos de gobierno, no coinciden ya con las realidades españoles. . . . Hay que hacer algo que no es un nuevo partido, sino otra cosa diferente. Algo tán claro como esto: agruparse para encauzar un movimiento de opinión latente ya, que será muy pronto para España un imperativo inexcusable. Los Republicanos tienen derecho a exigir a los españoles, sean o no hombres de partido, que seleccionen, con conciencia del momento histórico que vivimos, un grupo de hombres cuyas palabras pueden tener un eco de esperanza" (Mariano Granados, *Una solución española, informe aprobada por la Asamblea General de Unión Republicano*, pp. 33–34).

[62] Interviews with Enrique López Sevilla (Socialist), February 23, 1967; Ricardo Mestre (Anarchist), March 5, 1967.

[63] See the discussion on the role which Republican exiles should play in the Spanish opposition movements in Marichal, *Nuevo pensamiento político*, pp. 91–97. Dionisio Ridruejo praised the ARDE for its receptiveness to new alternatives in Spain (*Escrito en España*, p. 252); Francisco Giral, president of the ARDE, was instrumental in carrying out the negotiations which led to opening the Unión de Profesores to young Spanish professors (see chap. 5).

has modified its attitudes and policies in relation to shifts in the international Communist position, its activities have focused exclusively on Spanish issues, and at no time has it been involved in matters concerning Mexico or any other country.[64]

During the first years of exile, before it was possible for any of the exiles to return to Spain, the Communists supported the Negrinist group's efforts to restore Popular Front unity among the parties in exile. Later, the Communists abandoned their allies in exile to form, in 1944, the Junta Suprema de Unión Nacional, which sought to attract support from diverse opposition groups then organizing in Spain. In Mexico the Junta Suprema remained the exclusive domain of the Communist party.[65] The Junta Suprema itself had only a small following in Spain, but it set the precedent for future Communist policy. Subsequent opposition fronts organized by the party in Spain were more successful. As nearly all factions inside and outside Spain agree, the Communists have been the most effective of all exile political groups in retaining a foothold in Spain.[66]

In Spain, the Communists have cooperated with any party willing to work with them and the party has enjoyed considerable success in influencing both intellectual groups and landless peasants. Most often, it has worked within the official labor-union groups, judging these groups to be the most important source of potential opposition to the Franco regime.[67] Official policies in Spain have also aided the Communist efforts. Despite its frequent expressions of ardent anticommunism, the Franco government, at times, has been surprisingly tolerant of Communist activity. Although the Communist and the Socialist parties are illegal in Spain, the government seems less wary of the political influence of the former.[68]

---

[64] Interviews with Juan Rejano, October 11, 1966; Wenceslao Roces, January 6, 1967. *España Popular*, the political organ of the Communist party, publishes more articles of international concern than does any other Spanish political-party press, but the articles rarely are critical of Mexico.

[65] Interviews with Rejano and Roces; Fernando Vázquez, "Juntas que no juntan," *El Socialista* 3 (March, 1944):1.

[66] Ridruejo, *Escrito en España*, p. 264. The Communists organized and sponsored a great deal of guerrilla activity in Spain between 1944 and 1949 (Payne, *Franco's Spain*, pp. 116–117). In interviews with refugees, there was near unanimity in naming the Communist party in exile as the one working most effectively in Spain.

[67] Whitaker, *Spain*, pp. 185, 385; Ridruejo, *Escrito en España*, pp. 244, 264.

[68] Whitaker, *Spain*, p. 184.

Since the main thrust of the Communist party in exile has been to involve itself in Spanish opposition movements, party leaders have frequently directed Spanish Communists in Mexico to return to Spain, legally or illegally, and to help organize opposition groups. Expressing their pride in the fact that so many of them have been active in Spain, instead of sitting in comfortable exile, the Communists have accused members of other partisan groups in exile of excessive talk about bringing down the Franco government and a minimum of concrete action.[69]

In Mexico the party structure was supplemented by a large number of associations established under party auspices for women, youth, and intellectuals, or for some specific purpose or some regional group. These associations often attracted persons who were not members of the party, but who were in sympathy with it. Some of the associations were closely tied to the party and shared its headquarters.[70] The larger and more active of them attracted a broader membership within the emigration and were more autonomous.

The most important and most long-lived of such groups is the Comité de Ayuda a los Presos Españoles, an association of exiles who regularly send money to the families of persons held in Spanish jails for political crimes, as defined by the Franco regime. A few of those whose families receive aid have been in prison since the Civil War, although by the early 1960's most of the original prisoners had been released or had died. Since frequent political arrests have continued throughout Franco's rule, there continue to be large numbers of families who might benefit from stipends from the Mexico "Committee of Prisoner Aid." Although the aid is channeled through Communist organizations in Spain, exile spokesmen claim that it goes to persons with a variety of political views.[71]

[69] Interviews with Rejano and Roces. Critics of the Communists argue that although the Communists do return to Spain more frequently than members of other groups, they do not necessarily participate actively in opposition activity there.

[70] An official file of associations of the Spanish Republic in exile, provided by the Spanish Republican Embassy in Mexico City, lists several groups which meet at the party headquarters. These groups have long been nearly or totally inactive.

[71] Interview with Juan Rejano, October 11, 1966. Some critics of the party claim that, on the contrary, the funds are used mainly for Communist needs and causes.

While nearly all the political groups in Mexico have established similar programs for aiding political prisoners within their parties, none is so large or effective as the Communist Comité de Ayuda.

Another group largely within the Communist domain since the early 1950's is the Unión de Intelectuales Españoles en México. Founded in September of 1947 and enthusiastically welcomed in the pages of *Las Españas* by intellectuals of all political convictions, the Unión de Intelectuales attracted a large following. Intellectuals inside Spain, mostly Communists, initially encouraged its formation, with the goal of increasing communication and positive action between intellectuals inside and outside Spain. Non-Communists who joined the original association wished to increase their contact with colleagues still in Spain and hoped that they would be able to communicate as fellow intellectuals rather than as partisan representatives.[72]

The stated objectives of the Unión de Intelectuales were to offer material and cultural aid, as well as moral support, to Spanish intellectuals, to promote and defend Spanish culture against the persecution of the Franco government, and to work toward the liberation of Spain.[73] Not only did the intellectual union fail in its objectives, it failed as well to hold its members. The non-Communists, for the most part, left the association, usually with bitterness, within a few years of its founding. They accused the Communist party of using the group as a political tool, thereby destroying the possibility of fruitful, intellectual cooperation.[74]

The Communists, for their part, blamed the intellectuals in exile for refusing to involve themselves in meaningful political action. In the view of party members, the Unión de Intelectuales could have achieved its goals only through concerned and organized political activity. Communists criticized, and continue to criticize, the

[72] Interviews with Francisco Giral, April 4, 1967; Max Aub, August 14, 1966; Antonio María Sbert, September 24, 1966. The original board, including its president (Honorato de Castro), vice presidents, secretaries, treasurer, and other directors, was composed of twenty-three important intellectuals, representing a variety of fields and political factions. *Las Españas* (September, 1947), p. 12, carried a list of the members of the Unión de Intelectuales and published its constitution.
[73] Paraphrased from the constitution, Unión de Intelectuales (in *Las Españas*).
[74] Interviews with Giral, Aub, and Sbert. Poet León Felipe was one of the few who were not members of the Communist party who remained for several years in the union.

non-Communist intellectuals for stressing cultural ties between exiles and Spaniards but refusing to follow the Communist lead in acting politically to help bring down the Franco regime.[75] The division between Communist and non-Communist intellectuals was clear by 1950, and it was a source of chagrin and annoyance to both. The former asserted that the persistent unwillingness of the latter to see the relation between politics and culture contributed to the impotence of exile activity as a whole.[76] Hence, since the early 1950's, there has been practically no Communist support given to efforts by non-Communist intellectuals to establish closer ties with Spain.

Naturally, the Communists consistently criticized the large number of formerly radical Republican intellectuals who used the fact of exile as an excuse to abandon their former Communist sympathies and turned against the party. Many Spanish intellectuals, particularly the younger men, either were members of the party during the war, or were as favorably disposed toward it as they were toward Negrín's Popular Front policy. Once in exile, these same men withdrew from their partisan involvement and sought instead to increase cooperation and activity among intellectuals, as already noted, through such associations as the initial Unión de Intelectuales, as well as through such periodicals as *España Peregrina* and the later *Las Españas*. As the intellectuals grew increas-

[75] See the article by party leader and secretary general of the Unión de Intelectuales, Wenceslao Roces, "Los intelectuales españoles," in *La cultura de nuestro tiempo*, pp. 25–28. Roces criticizes the intellectuals of the past for not acting in solidarity with the Spanish people, and praises those in exile and in Spain who, he hopes, will continue to act together in the struggle against Franco. In his article following, "Grandes tareas comunes," in the same pamphlet (pp. 30–31), he asks that intellectuals work together, not only against Franco, but against the defeatists within the emigration represented in the Albornoz government (in exile).

[76] In an article critical of the intellectuals, Juan Rejano complained that the same lack of unity which had brought about the political dissolution of the emigration had also adversely affected the activities of the exiles with regard to Spain. He criticized those who tried to separate the political from the cultural. The duty of the intellectual, according to Rejano, lay equally in both lines of activity: unless Spain could recover her lost liberty, there would be no Spanish culture. The intellectuals' emphasis on *arte puro* only served to aid the reactionaries, he believed ("Deberes de los intelectuales españoles en la hora actual," *Nuestro Tiempo*, September 1, 1950, pp. 16–24. The article was reprinted from a lecture given under the auspices of the Unión de Intelectuales).

ingly anti-Communist,[77] the Communists in their turn treated the intellectual community with increasing contempt. Nonetheless, the Communists regretted the loss of support of those who had once been their best propagandists.[78]

Although the Communists in exile are substantially stronger than any of the other political groups, perhaps the most important general effect of the Communist party in exile has been that all the other exile parties have considered its existence and strength to be threatening and harmful to their basic goals. With the politically active exiles divided into ardent Communists and passionate anti-Communists, concerted political action has remained an impossibility.

The Anarchists

It is perhaps improper to speak of the Anarchists in terms of their role in Spanish Republican political life, since the Anarchists are not a political party and do not engage in partisan activity. It is also misleading to consider them within the context of Spanish Republican refugee groups, since the Anarchists never were favorably disposed toward the Republic during its existence. They participated in the Civil War and cooperated with Republican parties through their labor union, the CNT, because they recognized Franco and his allies as an enemy common to the Republic and to Anarchism. After the war, however, they made little effort to support outside groups which were trying to reestablish the Republic.[79] In exile there was a certain amount of cooperation between the Anarchist CNT and other political entities, but the cooperation was directed toward the overthrow of Franco, not toward the Republican alternative to his regime.

[77] In interviews with members of the Communist party, I was given names of several men prominent in the world of arts and letters who, I was told, had once been members of, or sympathizers with, the party, and who had since turned against it. In some cases I spoke with the men themselves and asked about their political past. None of them admitted to having had Communist ties. Since there is no proof in either direction, their names are not mentioned here. That a large number of intellectuals did defect from the party, however, is a fact corroborated by both Communists and non-Communists among the refugees.

[78] One response from the Communist party was a series of printed attacks against the periodical *Las Españas*. This will be discussed in chap. 8.

[79] "El factor determinante," editorial, in *Solidaridad Obrera*, August 5, 1942, p. 1.

The CNT was the strongest labor syndicate in Republican Spain, and, while not all of its members were confirmed Anarchists, most of the members shared the Anarchist orientation of the leadership. In exile, the hierarchy of the CNT continued to speak for the political and ideological position of the Spanish Anarchist community, although its policies frequently have been challenged by individual exile CNT members.[80] Whereas the Socialist UGT syndicate is dominated by the Socialist party, there is no Anarchist party and the CNT syndicate can speak only for those who choose to follow its directives. It is in the nature of Anarchist philosophy that all factions are allowed to determine their own political behavior.

The majority of the exiled members of the CNT, like those of the UGT, remained in France. Unlike the Socialist theorists, however, most of the important Anarchist theorists also remained in France. For them, Toulouse has always been a far more important center of activity than Mexico, although it should be stressed again that the policies decided by Anarchist or CNT leaders at Toulouse, unlike those of the Socialists, have not been binding on exiles elsewhere.[81]

The Anarchist exiles who sought refuge in Mexico were obliged to work in cooperation with the SERE and the JARE in order to emigrate to Mexico. They complained of discrimination from both organizations as well as from the Mexicans involved in the selection process.[82] They preferred the JARE, slightly, over the SERE, because of the former's unequivocal anti-Communist position. Although the Anarchists distrusted all of the parties of the Republic, they remained particularly bitter toward the Communists because of Communist Civil War policies.[83] Whenever the Anarchists decided that their goals could be reached only by uniting their efforts with other political groups in exile, the intensity of their anti-com-

[80] The two major publications of the CNT in Mexico, *Solidaridad Obrera* and *Tierra y Libertad*, were both concerned with philosophical and practical questions of anarchism as well as with items of syndicalist interest.

[81] Interviews with Juan Montserrat, one of the committee of syndicalist leaders of the CNT, and H. Plaja, Anarchist theoretician and writer, March 12, 1967.

[82] See Silvia Mistral, *Exodo: Diario de una refugiada española*, pp. 148–153; "La JARE y la CNT," in *Solidaridad Obrera*, May 5, 1942, p. 3. Interviews as noted above.

[83] See chap. 1, above.

munism led them into somewhat unwilling cooperation with moderates and conservatives who shared their hostility.

Just as the Civil War caused the Spanish Anarchists to break their long tradition of nonparticipation in any government and to join in the war efforts, so, too, the conditions of Franco's rule in Spain brought them to consider limited cooperation with other exiled Republican groups in order to defeat Franco. Immediately after the Civil War, Franco began with determination and considerable success to eliminate all Anarchist-syndicalist influence from Spain. Exiles, therefore, concluded that the survival of Spanish anarchism depended upon the overthrow of his regime and accepted the fact that alliances, on a temporary basis at least, were essential. Although Anarchists could not conceive of an alliance with the Communists or with Communist sympathizers, they expressed a willingness to work for limited objectives with non-Communist sectors of the emigration, with the understanding that they would form no lasting political ties with any outside group.[84] One sector of the CNT supported the Giral government—not as a government per se, but as a non-Communist body providing a focus for the opposition of Franco.[85]

Some Anarchists have consistently argued in favor of joining in formal alliances with other parties for specific objectives. But the majority have opposed the complete commitment of the CNT to political unions, arguing that in the long run even successful action by the united parties in exile would not ensure continued Anarchist-syndicalist influence inside Spain. In practice, there has never been any concrete or long-term cooperation between Anarchists and other groups. The distrust with which most Anarchists view the organized political structure of the Republic in exile has been more than returned by the people in control of that structure.

Although during the 1940's the CNT favored cooperation with other anti-Franco groups for limited objectives, those groups did not invite the Anarchist syndicate to participate in the formation of the Junta de Liberación. The Republicans and Socialists responsible for the creation of the Junta worked alone to formulate its structure and goals, and only afterward did they invite the CNT to join. The

[84] "El factor determinante," *Solidaridad Obrera*, May 5, 1942, p. 1.

[85] Miró, *¿Y España cuando?* pp. 40–50, 59–60. As previously noted, there was one Anarchist representative who served briefly in Giral's government.

CNT, resenting the secondary role to which it had been assigned, rejected the invitation—officially on the grounds that, as a syndicate, it had no reason to participate in a political union. The invitation refused, the Socialists declared that Anarchists had no place in the Junta in any case, because the latter had not accepted the Republic in 1931.[86] While the Anarchists continued to avoid any formal political unions, the CNT would have welcomed, at any time, the formation of an enlarged syndicalist union with the UGT. The UGT, however, remaining fully integrated into and controlled by the Socialist party, never indicated any enthusiasm for such an alliance.[87]

In the mid-1950's, the CNT participated in discussions held regularly in the Ateneo Español by representatives of the non-Communist parties of exile. Although the discussions produced no concrete results and were soon abandoned,[88] they served to involve the CNT for the first time in the political deliberations of the Republican parties. In 1961, the CNT established its headquarters in the Centro Republicano, which is also the headquarters in Mexico for the offices of the Republican and Socialist parties and the UGT. From this location, surrounded by the offices of the other political groups, the CNT became, physically at least, part of the established Republican structure in Mexico.

The CNT in exile, using as a base of operations the large Anarchist/CNT center in Toulouse, has devoted considerable energy to maintaining contact with the old revolutionary groups of libertarian syndicalists, in Spain, and to sending aid to its followers in prison or otherwise in need. There are few such followers left in Spain, however, due to the effectiveness of Franco's repression of the libertarian (Anarchist) syndicates.[89] Some feel that the CNT, once the largest workers' association in Spain, may have been reduced to the smallest.[90]

[86] "La CNT explica su posición ante la unidad antifranquista," *Solidaridad Obrera*, February 26, 1944, p. 1; "El pacto de unidad para la liberación de España," *Adelante*, December 19, 1943, p. 1.

[87] Miró (*¿Y España cuando?* pp. 47–48) describes discussions concerning such a syndicalist union, which took place around 1953. The union never materialized.

[88] Ibid., p. 84.

[89] By 1943 Franco had arrested the entire national committee of the CNT underground (Payne, *Franco's Spain*, p. 118).

[90] Ridruejo, *Escrito en España*, pp. 347–348.

Should there be a change of regime to one which would again tolerate independent labor organizations in Spain, many of the workers who, before the Civil War, would have been influenced by revolutionary anarchism, are likely at present to be moving toward socialism or Christian Democracy. This, in part, may be because of Franco's successful repressions, but perhaps it may also be related to the increasing industrialization of Spain. Since the early 1950's, the organized laborers in Spain have belonged only to the government-sponsored and controlled vertical unions,[91] although independent workers' groups have been organized successfully by Christian Democrats and to a smaller extent by Anarchists and Socialists.[92] For the first time in over a century, however, the libertarian movement has lacked an active core of loyal workers to carry its message.

The major CNT faction in exile has taken the position that the Spanish workers' abandonment of anarchism is a temporary phenomenon and that workers and peasants will recognize instinctively the relevance of Anarchist ideas, once these ideas are made available to them. Therefore, they argue, even if anarchism is weak in Spain, when Franco dies the workers will reject the syndicalist organization he imposed, and the CNT will resume its old vitality. In the meantime, the exile leadership believes it useless and probably destructive for the CNT to try to spread its ideas through any of the existing labor unions in Spain, except possibly in a limited way within the remnants of the old UGT. To work through government unions, they reason, would compromise the revolutionary and libertarian principles of anarchism to such an extent that the CNT would be destroyed. Therefore, CNT leaders have concluded that the only role remaining to them in exile is to maintain their militancy and to prepare psychologically and tactically for the revolution which will follow sooner or later upon Franco's death.

The Anarchists in exile are by no means unanimous in this assessment of the situation. A minority has always believed in the efficacy of some measure of political union, either with other exile groups or, more recently, with workingmen's associations existing

[91] See Fred Witney's history of the labor movement in Franco's Spain, *Labor Policy and Practices in Spain: A Study of Employer-Employee Relations under the Franco Regime.*
[92] Payne, *Franco's Spain*, pp. 90–91.

in Spain. Although the leadership of the CNT has remained consistently opposed to such alternatives, there is a growing concern
among Anarchists in exile to seek new tactics more appropriate to
the present situation. It is clear that the exiles have not been able
to save their Spanish-based unions from destruction, and, in view of
the extreme weakness of the Anarchist-syndicalist movement in
Spain, it is difficult for many Anarchists to continue to believe in
the workers' instinct for libertarian revolution. Division and dis-
sent have increased, and, in the early 1960's, the CNT acknowledged a decisive split within its ranks. Most of the dissenters simply
ceased to participate in or to support the activities of the central
body of the CNT, but a small group took more definite action. Considering themselves the modernizers of anarchism, they began,
around 1960, to hold separate meetings and, in 1962, they sponsored a new publication called *Comunidad Ibérica*.[93] By 1966 the
CNT had responded by expelling the major figures in the dissident
group. Fidel Miró, editor of *Comunidad Ibérica*, protested his expulsion from the CNT Assembly by accusing his opponents of antiliberal, Bolshevik-type sectarianism.[94]

The specific issues for which Miró and his followers were expelled, and the basic area of controversy within the Anarchist
group, concerned the Anarchist relation to the government-organ-
ized unions in Spain. The CNT leaders censured Miró for nego-
tiating with, and encouraging aid to, the Spanish government's
vertical syndicates. Miró and his supporters insisted that the CNT
had to spread its message through existing institutions in Spain or
resign itself to playing no role at all. In the opinion of the dissident group, those within the CNT who persisted in "purism" and
noncooperation with outside unions had divorced themselves from
the Spanish people. Moreover, in opposing all innovation and
modification in their strategy toward Spain, they would be doomed
to eventual disappearance, for they were awaiting a libertarian
revolution that never would come.[95]

[93] *Comunidad Ibérica* began publishing at the end of 1962; *Tierra y Libertad*
continued publication as the official organ of the CNT.
[94] Miró, "Las prácticas totalitarias y el dogmatismo significan la muerte,"
Comunidad Ibérica 4 (May–August, 1966):47–53.
[95] Ibid., pp. 49–50; interviews with Fidel Miró, August 9, 1966, and Ricardo
Mestre, who had been involved with both groups but not committed to either
point of view, March 5, 1967.

Those in sympathy with the dissenting group would have liked to modify the old Anarchist dedication to total revolution and total destruction in favor of a more gradual program of change toward a libertarian society. The long-awaited violent revolution no longer seemed either possible or desirable. They wished, instead, to work within existing conditions in Spain to bring about a more democratic regime, and then to encourage that regime to move in a libertarian direction.[96] They considered their more orthodox colleagues to be out-of-date "traditionalists." The "traditionalists," in turn, believed that the "modernizers" had altered Anarchist principles beyond recognition and substituted a petty bourgeois liberalism in place of a revolutionary ideal. The orthodox libertarians believed not only that anarchism would survive despite Franco, but that it could only survive if it did not alter its ideals.

Spanish Youth

There is no Spanish political party in Mexico which has been successful in recruiting young people to its ranks. Although youth groups exist for Socialists, Republicans, Communists, and Anarchists, who are approximately thirty or under, these groups have become little more than paper organizations.[97] There is no doubt, moreover, that the majority of members of the regular party structures are over fifty. In other words, most of the people who have shown consistent interest in Spanish Republican politics were politically active before emigration.

Having grown up in Mexico and witnessed the increasing dis-

[96] Miró, "Las prácticas," *Comunidad Ibérica*, pp. 51–53. Anarchists are not all divided into one or the other of these points of view, and most of them would fully agree with neither. The description here is intended, primarily, to indicate the nature of the dialogue which is taking place, and the possible directions for the Anarchist movement in the future.

[97] The party leaders of the Republicans, Socialists, Anarchists, and even Communists all stated that their youth groups were of no numerical importance. One of the active young Socialists claimed that there were about seventy nominal members of the Socialist Youth, of whom less than 10 percent were active. Interviews with Alfonso Ayensa, July 19, 1966; Jacinto Segovia, March 4, 1967; Enrique López Sevilla, February 23, 1967; Fidel Miró, August 6, 1966; Juan Montserrat, August 12, 1967; Wenceslao Roces, January 6, 1967; and Rafael Fernández, March 8, 1967. There is, in fact, near unanimity among refugees on the lack of political enthusiasm among the exile youth. (The information which follows in this chapter has been taken from the interviews noted above and from other more informal conversations.)

illusionment of their elders, younger refugees have only rarely been motivated to participate in exile politics. Those raised in Mexico have been more interested in the political, economic, and social problems of Mexico than in those of Spain. Even the few who have strong feelings of identity with Spain have not necessarily felt tied to the institutions and aspirations of the Second Spanish Republic. They may wish to see political change in Spain, but they do not see change necessarily in terms of the reestablishment of the political system created by their parents.

While most of the second generation in exile have been apathetic about their parents' political and emotional ties to Spain, there have been short-lived instances of significant numbers of the young people being mobilized to political activity. The inspiration invariably has come as a result of incidents of protest among students in Spanish universities. At the same time that the sons and daughters of those who remained in Spain began to protest the lack of political, intellectual, and religious freedom, so too did some of the sons and daughters of the Republicans in exile protest the ineffectuality of their elders in their efforts to liberate Spain from Franco. However, not only has the number of youth in Mexico concerned about Spain always been small and its political associations short-lived, but its goals have been only vaguely defined.

The single most significant political effort of Spanish youth in exile was the Movimiento '59, named for the protests of Spanish students against the 1959 visit of President Dwight Eisenhower to Madrid.[98] The movement attracted persons ranging in age from their late teens to their early thirties. Some of them were involved in the youth sections of the Republican, Socialist, Communist, or libertarian Anarchist political groups, but the majority had no political ties whatever. The youthful leadership of the Movimiento '59, for the most part, wished to avoid a partisan approach to activism.[99] The older leaders of the official political parties in exile, fearing Communist influence, were more opposed to the creation of a nonpartisan or multipartisan union of youth than they had been

[98] *Movimiento Español 1959: Hojas de información*, January, 1961, p. 3; Whitaker, *Spain*, pp. 80–82, 349.

[99] Interview with Ignacio Villarrías, February 24, 1967. Villarrías was one of the founders of the Movimiento.

to the young people's apathy.[100] The older politicians did nothing, therefore, to encourage the movement, and at times attempted to discourage its activities.

The objective of the members of the Movimiento '59 was to co-ordinate their efforts with those of the student opposition in Spain. Besides sending money for bail to arrested students and dissemi-nating information by radio and press concerning the student op-position in Spain, the group made strong appeals to the rest of the youth in exile to renew their ties with their country of origin.

At its peak of activity, in mid-1960, the Movimiento '59 claimed some three hundred active participants and one hundred dues-paying members.[101] The founders of the movement took pride in declaring that most of the participants, whatever their political views, had no formal party ties at all, and that, further, for the first time in exile, a union including all political tendencies had proved possible. By 1961, however, it had become apparent that even the youth in exile were not immune to political factionalism. Largely in response to pressure from older political leaders in these parties, those in the movement who were members of the Socialist, Republican, and Anarchist/CNT parties withdrew their member-ship and formed a separate group. Left within the movement were the Communist youth and the larger group of young people who had no political party commitments. The Communists, as an or-ganized minority in an association lacking a determined political orientation, had a strong voice in directing its activities. The older politicians who had insisted that any association which included Communists risked being dominated by Communists, now saw their fears realized—a self-fulfilling prophecy.[102]

By 1963 the Movimiento '59 had practically ceased to exist. Its dissolution was due, in part, to the political conflicts and hostility which surrounded it. In larger part, however, the movement dis-solved because of its own fundamental artificiality and ineffective-

[100] Interview with Rafael Fernández, March 8, 1967. Fernández was one of the younger participants in the Movimiento, and he is the present head of the Young Socialists. He left the 1959 movement due to pressures from older leaders of the Socialist party.

[101] Interview with Villarrías. See footnote 99, above.

[102] The Movimiento '59 was discussed in a large number of interviews, and in nearly all cases was described in critical terms or dismissed as a well-inten-tioned but futile effort.

ness. The students in Spain rarely consulted the Spanish youth in exile. Among the refugees, those who were not against the movement did not take it seriously, and nearly everyone agreed that youth associations in exile served little purpose.

The Socialist, Republican, and Anarchist groups which abandoned the Movimiento in 1961 formed another group, the Junta Coordinadora, in 1962, in response to widespread strikes and subsequent government repression in Spain. At the peak of the crisis, youth in Mexico collected between four and five thousand dollars in aid for Spanish strikers, published a bulletin, and, like the '59 group, sponsored a radio program of news and information concerning Spain. Within a little more than a year, however, the Junta Coordinadora disappeared. Once the critical moment in Spain had passed, there was no further contribution the group was prepared to offer, and, without long-range plans, its continued existence could not be justified.

A still more recent group for "young" refugees (some of whom were approaching their forties) was called the Grupo de Ayuda de Primero de Mayo, founded in 1967. Its directors have tried to maintain contact with student leaders in Spain in order to extend any aid the Spanish groups might request of them. Its aims, although similar to those of the Movimiento '59, were far more modest and the participants were very few.[103]

Political beliefs and ideologies remain alive among the exiles, both old and young, despite the fact that the political organizations are dying. Older refugees, even those who do not participate in any of the exile political groups, still tend to uphold their ideologies and to debate their positions on the present and future of Spain. Their Mexican-born offspring, obviously, are not oriented to events in Spain, but it would be wrong to assume that they, therefore, have been unaffected by Spanish Republican politics. Events may well prove that the sons and daughters of the Spanish exiles have been able to take the political ideals of their parents and grandparents and to use them creatively in expanding the horizons of political activity in Mexico.

[103] Interview with Ignacio Villarrías. He was also on the board of directors of the Grupo de Ayuda.

7. HISPANISM AND HISPANO-AMERICA

The arrival of the Spanish exiles in Mexico and the other countries of America marked the first mass emigration of Spaniards to Latin America since the end of the colonial period. Hence, the refugees were aware that their experience in Mexico would significantly affect the Mexicans' assessment of the Spanish Republic and their future attitudes toward Spaniards in general.

The Republic, more than any previous government in Spain, had tried to draw closer politically and culturally to the democracies of Spanish-speaking America, and relations between Spain and Mexico were better during the period of the Spanish Republic than at any time since Mexican independence.[1] Spanish Republican efforts to improve relations between the two countries were substantially rewarded by the Mexican government's unwavering support and friendship during the period of Republican need. Mexican aid was

---

[1] Marcelino Domingo, *El mundo ante España: México ejemplo*, pp. 252ff. Marcelino Domingo was the minister of public instruction in the Republican government. See also discussion and references in chap. 2.

viewed as more than a gesture of political friendship. To the embattled Republicans it symbolized a unity of peoples and ideals, the Mexican Revolution at one with the Spanish Republic:

> Hoy es el día de fiesta, camaradas,
> México, pueblo hermano
> Nos manda sus fusiles, victoriosos
> en la revolución de los centauros:
> en la revolución de Pancho Villa,
> en la explosión agraria de Emiliano
> Zapata! ¡Viva el Pueblo mexicano. . . . !
>
> .   .   .   .
>
> Tres hurras por el pueblo mexicano
> y tres vivas a Cárdenas soldado
> Cárdenas del petróleo y Cárdenas del agrio.[2]

When Cárdenas, noting that the course of the war was going badly for the Republicans, stated that, should the worst come to the worst, Mexico would be a fatherland for the Spaniards, his offer was considered to imply a commitment which was spiritual as well as political.

The Republican sympathizers who fled Spain to escape Franco's reprisals and to avoid living under his rule saw Cárdenas's generosity as their only hope. The refugees who were given the opportunity to emigrate to Mexico considered themselves the most fortunate of the exiles. It seemed that they had many things in common with the Mexicans, among them their cultural heritage and a struggle for social justice and progress. They hoped the similarities would help make Mexico a second homeland during the time they must spend there. Mexico offered them the opportunity to work and to become citizens, and, despite the initial hostility of some Mexicans to their arrival, the welcome they received in Mexico appears to have been far more generous than that which they received anywhere else.[3]

It was not easy, however, for this group to adopt a new homeland

---

[2] Celso Amieva, "Los fusiles de México," written in Spain, 1936, published in a collection of his works, *El paraíso incendiado, 1936–1939.*

[3] See chaps. 2 and 3. For example, those who went to Santo Domingo before coming to Mexico reported that the officials of that country offered to allow the Spaniards to settle, then required that they pay for each member of their families before permitting them to disembark. Other difficulties were encoun-

after having suffered and sacrificed so greatly for their own country. Most of the refugees quickly became disillusioned with their divided and ineffective political parties, but even those who avoided participation in groups of Republican exiles, political or nonpolitical, remained concerned about the political future of Spain. Although some exiles adjusted easily to Mexico and did not devote themselves to planning a Republican reconquest of Spain, none forgot that they were Spaniards with a loyalty to their Spanish compatriots in exile, and with a loyalty to Spain.

What then was to be the nature of their loyalty to Mexico? Mexico was a temporary home, or so most of the refugees believed when they arrived. The majority of them, however, gladly accepted Mexican nationality, and felt bound to repay with good works and exemplary citizenship the enormous debt of gratitude they owed. They also felt an obligation to demonstrate their loyalty to Mexico, "not to oppose themselves to the Mexicans, or be indifferent toward them," but to identify themselves with the Mexican zeal for justice, culture, and progress, and to be enthusiastic collaborators in seeking these goals.[4] The new arrivals were advised by their cultural and political leaders to unite with the Mexicans in every aspect of their lives outside of the political realm—even to call themselves Mexicans, because "to be Mexican is to be much more Spanish than the Spaniards of Franco."[5]

During their first years in Mexico, some of the most prominent men of the exile community, many of whom had been among the political and intellectual leaders of the Republic, wrote articles and books on the precise nature of their loyalties and debated it among themselves. Their statements, which will be summarized below, sometimes reflect their good intentions toward Mexico and, at other times, their resentment toward their critics. Most of what was written was intended for Mexican as well as for Spanish readers, for both groups wondered what kind of adjustment the refugees would make to life in Mexico and how long and how deeply they would remain Spaniards.

tered, especially in Cuba, but also in Venezuela, Chile, Argentina, France, Great Britain, and the United States.

4 Taken from an editorial "Sentido de la emigración española en México," *Boletín al Servicio*, August 15, 1939, p. 1.

5 Ibid.

In the first year of exile, Paulino Masip, one of Spain's leading writers and journalists, published a series of "letters" to his fellow refugees in Mexico.[6] The letters, published together in pamphlet form, were intended to provide a basis of orientation for the thousands of confused refugees who were trying to make a life for themselves and their families in Mexico. In the letters Masip emphasized that, whatever had happened, they were all still Spanish Republicans with obligations as both Spaniards and Republicans. But he also reminded his readers that they were far from their own country and that there was no immediate way to return. As refugees, therefore, they must regard Mexico as their home, not as a place of temporary asylum. In no case were they to waste their years in Mexico isolated "in a sealed tower of rigid españolismo."[7] Masip tried to resolve the dilemma of whether to become Mexicanized or to remain Spanish with the soon familiar suggestion that to act as Mexicans in Mexico was "the best and only decent way to be Spaniards" and "each good work one of us does is an argument in favor of the Republic."[8]

HISPANIC UNITY

The first refugees who came to Mexico sought a unity between their emotional ties to Spain and their physical presence in Mexico, between their commitment to a Republic which had failed and their gratitude to the people who had made a successful revolution. The fact of the Republic's military defeat was easier to accept if it could also be believed that Republican ideals still had meaning in the countries of Latin America. If Spain represented only one lost battle in an overall struggle which was continuing throughout the Spanish Americas, then the refugees could continue to serve their country although very far from it.

The Spain which the Republicans had tried to create, they claimed, had not died, because Republicans still lived: "España no se ha muerto. La vivimos nosotros."[9] "Among us still beats the

[6] Paulino Masip, *Cartas a un emigrado español.*
[7] Ibid., "Carta septimo," pp. 68, 71.
[8] Ibid., "Carta cuarta," p. 37.
[9] Fragment of "España viva," a poem by Francisco Giner de los Ríos, published in part in *España Peregrina* 1 (August, 1940):7–8.

popular spirit of Spain, generous, alive, giving itself once again to the New World."[10] The Spaniards began to speak in terms of a definable entity which was a Hispano-American world and to hope that their Mexican counterparts would share their ideal. If there could be a creative and productive unity of peoples, then, indeed, the individual success of any refugee in any field in Mexico would be a symbol of the continuing vitality of the Republic, and it would also help to repay the debt which the Republicans owed to Mexico. At the very least, the exiles felt, if their own cause could be identified with the goals of the Mexican revolution, then those Mexicans who thought of Spain only in terms of its imperialism and its colonial exploitation might reexamine their negative attitudes, thereby bringing the two peoples closer together.

A basic factor in the hispanism of the refugees was, and to some extent still is, the idea that there exist two Mexicos and two Spains: the Mexico of the revolution and the Mexico of the reaction, the Spain of the Republic and the Spain of orthodoxy and fascism. In Mexico the forces of the "revolution" were the government, the party in power, most of the middle class, and the workers who approved of the objectives of the revolution and had therefore approved of the Spanish Republic. The "reaction" was represented by those groups which had profited from the dictatorship of Porfirio Díaz and still wielded political and economic power usurped from the Mexican people and by the irreconcilable Catholics who would never accept the separation of church and state.

Like the Mexicans, the democratic Republicans had sought independence from a common imperialistic, orthodox, monarchic past.[11] The Civil War had been the battle of the poets against the clerics, with the poets of Spain and Mexico supporting the same side, the side of creative effort.[12] The Republican surrender signified the defeat of what might have been a fruitful *hispanismo* of unity and progress in the Hispanic world. Against this *hispanismo*, according to refugee literature, the victorious Fascists created a reactionary

[10] "Doce de octubre fiesta del Nuevo Mundo," editorial in *España Peregrina*, October 12, 1940, p. 52.

[11] José Gaos, *En torno a la filosofía mexicana*, II, 78.

[12] Juan Larrea, "Nuestra alba de oro," *Cuadernos Americanos* 1 (January–February, 1942):71.

movement they called *Hispanidad* to encourage their counterparts in the Americas in antirevolutionary, pro-Nazi doctrine.[13] The refugees maintained that, despite the sadness of exile, they had more in common with what they found there than with what remained in their own country.[14] The representatives of "wandering," exiled Spain, of "España peregrina" (pilgrim Spain), therefore opposed the Spain of conquest and colony, for they too had fought for an independent future against the orthodoxies of the past.

These were the ideals with which many exiles began their lives in Mexico. Since monarchic Spain had accomplished the conquest but had forgotten the Americas after the wars of independence, since Fascist Spain only wanted to renew the old imperialism, the Republicans in exile considered it to be their mission to unite the spirits of the old and new worlds on the basis of equality:

> Qué hilo tán fino, qué delgado junco
> de acero fiel—nos une y nos separe
> con España presente en el recuerdo
> con México presente en la esperanza
>
> .   .   .   .
>
> España que perdimos, no nos pierdas,
> guárdanos en tu frente derrumbada,
> conserva a tu costado el hueco vivo
> de nuestra ausencia amarga,
> que un día volveremos, más veloces,
> sobre la densa y poderosa espalda
> de este mar, con los brazos ondeantes
> y el latido del mar en la garganta.
>
> Y tú México, pueblo abierto
> el agil viento y a la luz del alba
> indios de clara estirpe, campesinos
> con tierras, con simientes y con máquinas
> proletarios gigantes, de anchas manos

---

[13] F. Carmona Nenclares, "Hispanismo e hispanidad," *Cuadernos Americanos* 3 (May–June, 1942):43–55. "Hispanidad" refers to the antiliberal movements throughout Latin America during the late 1930's and 1940's. They were encouraged by Franco and identified themselves with the traditional Catholic Spain he claimed to represent.

[14] José Gaos, "La adaptación de un español a la sociedad hispanoamericana," *Revista de Occidente* 4 (May, 1966):174. See also "Doce de octubre" (editorial), *España Peregrina*, p. 52.

> que forjan el destino de la Patria
> pueblo libre de México:
> Como en otro tiempo por la mar salada
> te va un río español de sangre roja,
> de generosa sangre desbordada . . .
> Pero eres tú este vez quien nos conquistas
> y para siempre, ¡oh vieja y nueva España![15]

Because it was not possible for Franco's Spain to become identified with the progressive spirit of the Americas, nor for Spanish liberals to live in their homeland, the only alternative for the Republican exiles was to accept America as their home and to adapt to life in Mexico.

The Mexicanization of the Refugees

Some of the most important Spanish writers preferred to deemphasize the differences between Spaniards and Mexicans. The philosopher José Gaos, for one, believed in the rapid Mexicanization of the Spanish immigrants and in the future of Mexico. In his view, Spain and Mexico were more a double country than two separate countries; they had shared common battles against a common past.[16] In this last battle, he would put his faith in the forward march of Mexico instead of mourning over the decline of Spain:

The theme of Spain for Spanish thinkers is the theme of a decadence which must be remedied; for many it is the theme of a greatness which must be restored, more than that of new progress to go on attaining. The theme of Mexico for Mexican thinkers is the theme of establishing their independence from that decadence which is not their own, of moving down the path of greatness without outside obstacles, a path which promises to be much newer and much more sure. For behind all of Mexico's negative self-criticism lies the essence of its development, the confidence of one who, never having caused his own downfall, can only raise himself the more; while behind the animated Spanish self-exaltation lies the essence of Spain's development, the insecurity of one who, having fallen on his own, knows that it is possible to fall.[17]

[15] Pedro Garfias, "Entre México y España," *España Peregrina* 1 (June, 1940): 230.

[16] Gaos, *En torno a la filosofía*, II, 76.

[17] Ibid., p. 65 (my translation).

That the Hispanic world shared basically the same cultural and
philosophical foundations meant, for José Gaos, that refugees from
Spain in Mexico could not consider themselves to be *desterrados*
("exiles") but rather *transterrados*, that is, transferred from one
part of their homeland to another. They were not *expatriado* from
Spain, but *empatriado* to Mexico.[18]

Sociologist José Medina Echavarría wrote in terms of Hispanic
man, and noted that the positive experience of the Spanish Republicans in the Americas, in the midst of a troubled world, had revealed
to him the extent to which all Spanish-speaking people were linked
to one another. He saw it as "laboratory proof" of the existence of
"Hispanic man."[19] Another writer, Juan Vicens, remarked that a
great good had come from the Spanish tragedy, since, for the first
time, distinguished Spanish intellectuals could acquire a clear view
of the Hispano-Americas. Though the intellectuals were lost to
Spain, they could continue their creative efforts, thanks to their
brotherhood with the American nations.[20]

A symbol of Hispano-American brotherhood was the literary periodical *Romance*, founded in 1940 by Latin American and Spanish
leftists, dedicated to the principle that there must be greater unity
among progressive writers of the Spanish-speaking countries. The
aim of *Romance*, as stated in one of its early editorials, was to realize the dream of a spiritual unity, much more profound than language and origins, to allow the active, creative work which rose
from each country to spread through the rest. "Despite the material
distances, many feel a sense of Hispanic culture, of rich and varied
shades, not yet fully realized but with an immense future before
it."[21]

None of the Spaniards pretended that in Mexico they could find
the Spain they had left behind. None of them denied that there

Ibid., p. 83; and in "La Adaptación," *Revista de Occidente*, p. 177.

[19] José Medina Echavarría, "Cuerpo de destino," *Cuadernos Americanos* 1
(January–February, 1942):38–42. See also Medina Echavarría's Introduction
(p. 9) to his *Responsabilidad de la inteligencia*.

[20] Juan Vicens, "La bibliografía hispánica," *España Peregrina* 1 (August,
1940):17–21.

[21] "Sobre la unidad espiritual de los pueblos de América," editorial in *Romance: Revista Popular Hispanoamericana*, March 15, 1940, p. 7.

were deep cultural and historical differences to which each would have to be especially sensitive.[22] Mexico, nonetheless, was a country in which they felt they could find a place for themselves and their families without vastly readjusting their habits or their values. They stated their intention of serving Mexico, but they saw no need to imitate the Mexicans in superficial things. Paulino Masip advised them on this matter "to go on pronouncing the S's and the zetas, to feel no obligation to eat enchiladas," but to make every effort to "draw into the living force of the country."[23] The manner in which each was to do so was left to his choice and abilities.

In this manner, in the years after 1939, the cream of Spain's intelligentsia, the men and women who represented Spain's continuing liberal hopes, discovered America. Their imagination was deeply stirred by the enormous potential they found there. They had left the past behind in Spain, their future was in America, but they would make it their inspired goal of exile to ensure that the future of America would also be the future of Spain.

THE REPUBLICANS, THE BEST OF SPAIN

When they first arrived, the Republicans wished to present themselves as representing the best that Spain had to offer to its former colonies. They did so, often by comparing themselves with the group they initially regarded as the antithesis of all their good intentions, the group which in Mexico was known as the Honorable Spanish Colony or the *antigua colonia*. This group was composed of those Spaniards who, over more than a century, had come to Mexico, to make a better economic life for themselves, or to avoid being drafted to fight in the very unpopular Spanish nineteenth-century wars. They had worked hard, in many cases they had made a great deal of money, but they generally were disliked by the Mexicans

---

[22] José Moreno Villa, in his *Cornucopia de México*, describes the differences in the Spanish language (pp. 5–6), the importance of Mexico's pre-Columbian past in its influence on the present (p. 67), and the great difference in historical sense between Mexico and Spain (p. 105). José Gaos discusses the influence of Spain and Mexico on each other, and the distinctiveness of each, in "La Adaptación," *Revista de Occidente*, pp. 176–177; the same theme appears in his *En torno a la filosofía*, p. 63.

[23] Masip, *Cartas*, "Carta septima," p. 92.

and were considered to have been of little if any value to Mexican development.[24]

The Spanish emigrants who came before the Republicans were rarely professionals or intellectuals. They worked in small stores and bakeries, often in *cantinas* (bars); many began as the hated foremen of the Mexican *haciendas* and later became the wealthy owners of the same *haciendas*. Many lost their land during the revolution, but, in general, the Spanish colony grew increasingly wealthy over the years.[25] These Spaniards, who came to Mexico from the time of the colony until 1939, often believed that they would return to Spain once their fortunes had been made, to become rich *indianos*. Most, however, stayed and saw their children and grandchildren born in Mexico. They neither returned to Spain nor mixed with the general population. In the opinion of the Mexicans, these Spaniards, or *gachupines*, had brought little in the way of cultural or even economic improvement to the Mexican nation (with few exceptions), yet their wealth was earned at Mexican expense. Moreover, they mixed so little and were so often on the side of political, economic, and religious reaction that the Mexicans, outside of the race-conscious, religious, upper class, resented them.[26]

Certain elements in the *antigua colonia*, as noted earlier, had joined the Mexican press, the orthodox Catholic Mexicans, and the generally conservative or reactionary Mexicans in attempting to keep the Republicans out of Mexico. The members of the *antigua colonia*, for the most part, were hostile to the exiles during the first few years, although in time certain individual or regionally based friendships were formed across the two groups.[27]

[24] These are the *gachupines* discussed in chap. 3. The Mexican view of the group is presented by Mauricio Fresco, in *La emigración republicana*, p. 26; and by Félix Palavicini, *México: Historia de su evolución constructiva*, IV, 256.

[25] Fresco, *La emigración republicana*, p. 26.

[26] Ibid. Fresco tries to give as fair an appraisal of the *antigua colonia* as possible. Many of the Republicans interviewed agreed that the "reactionary" element in the Spanish colony was at times exaggerated, and that basically these Spaniards, who were not intellectually oriented, were apolitical or simply conservative.

[27] The wealthy and well-known industrialist Carlos Prieto was often singled out by prominent Republicans interviewed as one whose attitude was unlike that of the Spanish colony generally. He offered material help and encouragement to many of his countrymen, although he was not politically a leftist nor even especially liberal. His motives were judged to have been elitist—humanitarian and cultural. The *antigua colonia* as a whole had celebrated Franco's victory

During the early period of exile, the Republicans liked to portray the *antigua colonia* as the "other Spain," whose allies were the anti-revolutionaries of the "other Mexico." The newly arrived Republicans could find no group more different in every way from themselves and their ideals. To remind either the refugees or the Mexicans of the contrast was useful propaganda to the former. The unfavorable comparison with the Spanish colony quickly became a favorite theme, sometimes exaggerated in its proportions, of the Republican and pro-Republican writers: "Neither do we wish to cease to stress the singular phenomenon which is implied by the presence in America of thousands of Spaniards who have not come to make a fortune, and do not wish to make one . . . because their vocations lead them to disciplines which do not include such preoccupation. For the first time Spaniards are coming to America without desiring to conquer anything. . . . They are coming to live simply and to work in peace and liberty."[28]

Paulino Masip assured the Republicans that they were different from those who had preceded them because, as political emigrants who left Spain against their will, they did not come to Mexico with ambitions or seeking adventure.[29] Many of the Republicans continue to believe that their presence has helped to change the unfavorable impression Mexicans had had of the Spaniards. By having behaved in what they consider to be a totally different fashion from their predecessors, they have sought to prove that the "new Spain" which they represent is superior to the old. As León Felipe wrote in a poem dedicated to Lázaro Cárdenas:

> ¡Está muerta! ¡Miradla!
> Miradla
> Los viejos gachupines de América,
> Los españoles del éxodo de ayer. . . .[30]

Another way in which the exiles could show themselves as the "best of Spain" was to champion the cause of the Mexican Indian.

(*Excelsior*, March 29, 1939, pp. 1, 2). They were not sympathetic to Mexico's policy toward the Republic. As already noted, antipathies between Republicans and the *antigua colonia* declined over the years.

[28] From an editorial in *Boletín al Servicio*, August 24, 1939, p. 1.

[29] Masip, *Cartas*, "Carta primera," p. 8.

[30] From a long poem by León Felipe Camino Galicia, *El español del éxodo y del llanto, doctrina, elegías y canciones*.

Editorials in both *Romance* and *España Peregrina* applauded the
progress of the Congreso Indigenista Interamericano, a meeting
sponsored by Cárdenas and held at Patzcuaro in early 1940 to consider positive legislative measures in favor of the Latin American
Indians.[31] The writers of *España Peregrina* expressed their regrets
that there were no Spanish delegates at the congress, and stressed
that this was not due to disinterest or disapproval, but only to the
fact that the Spanish Junta de Cultura lacked the material means
to send a representative. They viewed the Mexican intention of rescuing the Indian from the poverty and obscurity in which civilization had left him as a policy in the best humanitarian tradition of
popular Spain.[32] In expressing these feelings, the exiles wished to
identify themselves with, hence to prove the existence of, the continuing humanistic, progressive Hispanic tradition. The social
worth of the Indian had divided Spanish opinion from the sixteenth
through the eighteenth centuries, and Bishop Bartolomé de las
Casas, who had defended the Indians, belonged to the Spain which
the Republicans claimed to represent. Las Casas received his due
homage from Mexicans of the mid-twentieth century, but the liberal, humanistic Spain which he symbolized was little known.

THE REFUGEES AND MEXICAN POLITICS

The refugees established what they thought to be their appropriate position with regard to Mexico and Spain soon after their arrival: they were Spaniards, still fervently loyal to their cultural
traditions and to their recent political dreams for their own country. Ideologically, they were solidly in the camp of those Mexicans
who shared the same dreams of progress, and they wished to contribute to Mexico in any area they could, save one—the political
realm. This certainly was not because they lacked political concern.
As has been noted previously, nearly all of them had been, in some
way, politically active in defending the Republic; moreover, they
were perfectly willing to continue their battle, now a verbal battle,

---

[31] See the editorial, "Acercamiento al problema indigena," in *Romance*, April
15, 1940, p. 7; also "El primer congreso indigenista americano," *España Peregrina* 1 (April, 1940):40.
[32] The exile writers may have hoped, moreover, that such public praise of
government policy would be favorably viewed by Mexican officials.

against the "other Spain," those serving Franco in Spain and in Mexico's Spanish colony.

They were determined to have nothing to do with the "other [conservative] Mexico." Nor would they actively support their much-admired Mexican progressive, leftist counterparts in any way which might bring upon them the charge of political interference. Although there were no formal restrictions against political activity by refugees who had adopted Mexican citizenship, virtually all of them refrained from becoming politically involved. The policy of nonparticipation was determined at an early stage of exile and endured through the years, because it was deemed a necessary condition for living in harmony with the Mexicans.[33]

This decision is well illustrated by writings which were intended or, in any case, used for orientation of the new refugees. In these, there was unanimity of opinion against political activity:

Only one field is closed to you, Mexican politics, in all other areas . . . do as the Mexicans.[34]

We are all political exiles and will exercise political action. This is not to suggest that we will intervene in the politics of our host countries, which would be impertinent and foolish.[35]

We have not come to Mexico to take part in Mexican politics, for the very statement presupposes an insensitivity which cannot be attributable to us. On this matter, if there were any doubts, they were not those of the exiles . . . but those of persons who undertook to invent our intentions. Now there are no more doubts. . . . On the other hand, we can and we must take part in Spanish politics.[36]

Even the journals of the various political parties of the exiled Spanish Republic virtually ignored the day-to-day political events of Mexico, except to praise one or another political leader for his attitude toward Spain or toward the refugees.

Spanish Republican writers either avoided Mexican topics altogether, wrote in terms of general praise for Mexico, or carefully disclaimed any political intentions whatever. José Moreno Villa

---

[33] This point is further discussed in the chapters following.

[34] "Sentido de la emigración," in *Boletín al Servicio*, August 15, 1939, p. 1 (my translation).

[35] Masip, *Cartas*, "Carta cuarta," p. 31 (my translation).

[36] "El emigrado y la esperanza," in *Boletín al Servicio*, December 15, 1939, p. 1 (my translation).

claimed, as did many of his compatriots, that in Mexico politics of any kind ceased to be of interest to him.[37] José Gaos took the position that intellectuals had no significant role to play in politics and that political activity would be only a frustrating experience for them.[38] In neither of the two early books on Mexican life written by refugees, *Cornucopia de México* by José Moreno Villa and *La esfinge mestiza* by Juan Rejano, is there any discussion which goes beyond the views of a casual tourist; nor are there any negative comments on what they might have perceived, even as tourists. Juan Rejano specifically stated that controversial subjects were outside the realm of his book:

It is a minor book. In its pages are collected some impressions of cities, landscapes or customs. There are a few notes on various aspects of Mexican life. On the other hand, topics which touch on problems and on men who play a dramatic role in their resolution have been deliberately omitted. So too are politics, social questions, economic conflicts, and racial disputes. It does not even deal with art and literature, which to some appear dangerous. After having thought much, I understood that the Mexico of great and passionate struggle was still too fresh in my eyes for me to be able to reflect upon it without fear of serious errors. . . . Besides, my status as a Spaniard welcomed by this country compromises my present situation.[39]

The periodical *Romance*, intended as an organ of Hispano-American solidarity, politically progressive and leftist in tendency, did entertain some articles of political relevance. The director of *Romance* was the same Juan Rejano quoted above, but the editorial board and collaborators were a mixed group of Latin Americans and Spaniards, and most of the politically relevant editorial mate-

---

[37] Moreno Villa, *Cornucopia de México*, p. 106.

[38] Gaos, *En torno a la filosofía*, p. 72. See also his statement in a debate sponsored by and published in *Cuadernos Americanos* 15 (May–June, 1944):32–48. In the debate there were two Latin Americans, Mariano Picón Salas and Jesús Silva Herzog, and three Spaniards, Gaos, José Medina Echavarría, and Juan Larrea. The Latin Americans generally agreed that intellectuals had an obligation to participate in the solution of political and social problems of their nations, whereas the Spaniards took the position that intellectuals should not bear the responsibility for the political future of their nations. Their sense of personal failure with regard to the Spanish Republic could scarcely have been more evident.

[39] Juan Rejano, *La esfinge mestiza: Crónica menor de México*, p. 9 (my translation).

rial was unsigned. Moreover, the comments with regard to the Mexican political system were seldom, if ever, negative.

The refugees, as Spaniards and foreigners, realized that any participation in Mexican politics was likely to be misunderstood, not only by their enemies but even by some of those who had shown them much sympathy in the past. Mexican intellectual and political society was polarized, with the *indigenistas* on one side and the *hispanistas* on the other. "The reaction in general was *hispanista* and the Revolution, *indigenista*."[40] The *indigenista*, the group with which the exiles felt the greatest kinship, identified itself in terms of the Mexican Indian past as opposed to the Spanish heritage. The *hispanista*, the group which was considered pro-Spanish, was specifically pro-Franco and reactionary. The Republicans found full favor in neither camp. Feared by the conservative hispanists as Communists and revolutionaries, and distrusted by many of the progressives as Spaniards, the refugees sought to allay the negative predispositions of both groups.

DECLINE OF THE IDEAL

By the end of 1942, the theme of the Hispanic world and the future of Spain and America had either ceased to appear in Spanish writing or had changed character altogether. *Romance*, the voice of the ideal of Hispanic unity, ceased publication in May, 1941. Many of those who had collaborated on *Romance*, as well as many of the refugees who had worked on *España Peregrina* until its finances were exhausted, joined with Mexican intellectuals in what was to be a much more important effort, the periodical of general Latin American culture, *Cuadernos Americanos*. A number of writers also contributed to *El Hijo Pródigo*, *Tierra Nueva*, *Rueca*, and the literary supplements of *Novedades* and *Excelsior*, all of which were published during the 1940's, many for the first time. As fruitful collaboration between Spanish and Mexican intellectuals increased, however, the idea faded that there existed a spiritual unity between Spaniards and Hispano-Americans simply because it was possible to work together productively.

The brotherhood of peoples remained a basic ideal, but the form and emphasis of its expression changed, and the change was re-

[40] Gaos, "La adaptación de un español," pp. 169–170.

flected in the literary journals after 1942. *Romance* had stressed the importance of the linguistic unity of Spanish-speaking peoples, despite national and racial differences. Its stated task was to re-create a "loyal communion among the peoples of the various Span-ish-speaking countries," and to find a universality in Hispano-American thought.[41] *Cuadernos Americanos*, on the other hand, was much more concerned with the specific struggles of Latin America, and particularly those of Mexico, whose citizens included the dis-tinguished Spaniards on its staff.[42] *España Peregrina* had devoted a large number of articles to developing the idea of shared aspects of Spanish and Mexican culture. Such literary periodicals as *El Hijo Pródigo*, which appeared just a few years later, in 1943, contained many articles on cultural activities in Spain and in Latin America, but virtually none on the idea of unity between Spanish and Latin American peoples.

It was obvious that Hispanic unity was not going to reappear after more than a century of American independence merely be-cause representatives of Spain's cultural elite had come to Mexico and to other Spanish American countries. It was equally obvious that, even if the democracies of the Spanish-speaking world were to draw more closely together, they would not include Spain among them so long as Spain continued to be ruled by Franco. Implicit in all the refugees' early idealism of Hispanic unity had been the faith that they would soon return, victorious, to Spain, and, remembering their exile, would draw their homeland closer to the Americas. Be-fore the Republicans could promise a new Hispanic unity to the Americas, they would have to recapture Spain for themselves. Their attention turned increasingly in that direction.

Finally, it must be said that underlying the many statements by the Republicans concerning "their mission as exiles," their "debt to Mexico," and the nature of the broader understanding they hoped to create, there was often more than a hint of paternalism. Behind Spanish promises to work for Mexico was the assumption that Mexico really needed their work, their skills, and their intelligence. Whether or not this paternalism existed in all or nearly all cases, the Mexicans who felt it staunchly maintained that the Spaniards

[41] Initial editorial in *Romance*, February 1, 1940, p. 2.
[42] Jesús Silva Herzog, "Veinte años al servicio del mundo nuevo," *Cuadernos Americanos* 119 (November–December, 1961):7–18.

were unnecessary to Mexican progress and gave them little credit for their contributions to it. The Spaniards, for their part, resented the lack of appreciation and, at the same time, grew gradually more disillusioned with the ideals of the Mexican revolution as manifested in the political and social realities of the day. Although they continued to find much to admire in the Mexican system, few considered the Mexican revolution worth emulating in terms of the future Spanish Republic.[43]

Spaniards throughout the 1940's continued to remind each other and the Mexicans that the refugees had an obligation to contribute the best of their abilities to Mexico, but, as the international political scene changed, their eyes turned increasingly toward their homeland. Writers who, in 1939 and 1940, wondered how exiles would be able to begin a new life in Mexico, were more concerned after 1943 with enlarging the prospects for their return to Spain.[44] By 1944 the outcome of the Second World War looked promising for the Allies, and the refugees were increasingly hopeful that Franco would fall, with the other Fascists, thereby permitting them to return to Spain. Virtually all the reports printed in Mexico portrayed conditions in Spain as wretched and opposition to the regime as growing stronger.[45] The stories served to give exiles the sometimes unshakable impression that Franco would be ousted, if not by international effort, then by popular revolution, and that the exiles would then be needed and awaited in Spain. As the prospects of returning to Spain seemed more real, most of the exiles began to dwell increasingly on that return rather than on their future life in Mexico.[46]

> ... después de haber sembrado en medio de volcanes
> lo mejor de nosostros, el beso y la palabra.

[43] Changing Spanish and Mexican attitudes toward one another will be discussed in the chapters following.

[44] See chap. 6.

[45] See, for example, Isabel de Palencia, *Smouldering Freedom: The Story of the Spanish Republicans in Exile*, pp. 138–142; also the frequent articles in *Boletín al Servicio*, *República Española*, *España Peregrina*, *Adelante*, *España Popular*, *Solidaridad Obrera*, *Boletín Informativo*, and other publications—that is, nearly every early political or literary journal of the emigration.

[46] Certainly, of those interviewed, the overwhelming majority did come to Mexico with the idea that they would soon return to Spain. Until after the Second World War, more than half continued to believe they would return.

Nos llevaran las ondas sin querer ni queriendo.
El destino es más fuerte que nuestra voluntad
y a cada quien señala su tarea en el mundo.[47]

The Spaniards judged that, although they might give their best efforts to Mexico, their final destiny would lie in Spain.

Before the end of a decade of exile, however, these hopes of return had declined, and with them much of the sense of purpose underlying the Spanish Republican community. No longer believing that Spain and Mexico shared common goals or a common destiny, nor expecting that they would ever return to lead Spain, the refugees settled in Mexico as a Spanish-speaking but alien group. Through the 1950's and 1960's, although the exiles experienced a multitude of individual satisfactions and successes, there was also a growing sense of political frustration and disillusionment among them. Unable and unwilling to put aside their Spanish ties, few older exiles ever became fully reconciled to Mexican life and values. With their own emotional and psychological dilemmas unresolved, these exiles inevitably conveyed much of their uneasiness to their children, and the children grew up with roots in two distinct cultures.

[47] José Moreno Villa, "Nos trajeron las ondas," poem, in *Cuadernos Americanos* 17 (September–October, 1944):194.

8. THE EXILES AND SPAIN

A homeland is not forgotten in a single generation. And, in particular, among the Spanish Republican exiles in Mexico who so often have reminded their children of their identity, the homeland is by no means forgotten. The number of refugee organizations dedicated to aiding Franco's opponents and critics in Spain has been declining gradually, but evidence indicates that the feeling that the exiles should "do something" toward "rescuing" Spain is still quite strong. That "something" might take a variety of forms, indicating different levels of involvement: aid to political prisoners, money to opposition groups in Spain, written propaganda against Franco, refusal to visit Spain while Franco remains in power, participation in Spanish exile associations of one or another type, actual involvement in Spanish opposition movements, or simple verbal approval accorded others who are engaged in opposing Franco. Even the exiles who consider themselves entirely "Mexicanized" seem to have retained some feeling of personal involvement in the fate of Spain.[1]

PERMANENT EXILE AND RETURN TO SPAIN

It is true that most of the refugees have resigned themselves to a more or less permanent exile, and that none expect the return of a Republic in the same form as it existed in 1931 or 1936. It is also true that within the past two decades all of the associations have seen declining memberships and fewer activities.[2] Yet, if the refugees are more resigned and less active, it is not primarily because they feel less strongly their situation as Spanish political exiles or their responsibilities as Republicans. Rather it is because they feel far more helpless now than before to "do something to rescue Spain from Franco." In over thirty years of exile they have accomplished practically nothing toward this goal, and their Republic is nearly forgotten in Spain. When Franco ceases to rule, the exiles who then return to Spain will be essentially foreigners in that country.

The older refugees now in Mexico have come to expect that they too will die in exile, yet, in the first decade or so after they arrived, while there was still hope of returning, death in exile was much feared and discussed. "Death in exile in the first instance signifies the total frustration of the one pleasant thought that sustains life, returning. It is a death which precedes birth, which annuls it. What death in exile destroys is not a past but a future."[3] From the first years of exile, funerals, more than weddings or other ceremonies brought the Republicans together: "Emigration? This: showing our bald heads and burying each day's dead." So reads the caption of a Spanish exile cartoon depicting a new stone in a cemetery.[4] The author of the caption later used the funeral of a prominent exile as the theme and focal point in a novel depicting the absurdities and

[1] In all sixty-six of the interviews I was able to arrange, only one individual succeeded in stating convincingly that he no longer cared what happened in Spain. Yet he was a prominent professional who had been close to many of the Republican leaders; as such, he really could not avoid becoming involved in exile activities.

[2] See Michael Kenny's description of Spanish associations in the 1950's, in "Twentieth Century Spanish Expatriates in Mexico: An Urban Subculture," *Anthropological Quarterly* 35 (October, 1962): 169–180.

[3] Vicente Llorens Castillo, "El retorno del desterrado," *Cuadernos Americanos* 40 (July–August, 1948):216–233.

[4] Simon Otaola, *La librería de Arana*, p. 381.

the frustrations of exile life.[5] León Felipe, on the occasion of the death of his close friend and fellow poet, José Moreno Villa, complained:

> Ya no tenemos los españoles desterrados otro
> moneda para pagar nuestros deudas que la
> elegia y el lamento
>
> Todos se van
>
> .   .   .   .
>
> Muertos, seguimos caminando por el lado opuesto de la Patria.[6]

In the two decades after the Second World War the situation in Spain changed significantly. The country made economic strides which although uneven and not achieving general prosperity, were greater than the exiles had ever thought would be possible under Franco. A cultural regeneration occurred, and the Republican intellectuals no longer were the sole, nor even the major, disseminators of Spanish literature and art. Even in the political realm, a limited amount of opposition and debate came to be accepted and expected by the Franco government. The exiles always hoped that Franco would be ousted by a popular resistance movement which would look for guidance to the ranks of the old Republican leadership. Instead, none of the old parties, with the possible exception of the Communists, ever became significant elements in the anti-Franco struggle. New movements, new groups, and even new political goals have taken over. Moreover, presently active forces, instead of admiring the refugees for having left Spain, feel that they deserve no voice in Spanish affairs, because they chose to lead an easy life in exile rather than to stay in Spain and share the fate of their countrymen.

A number of refugees, particularly the prominent political figures, vowed that they would return to Spain permanently when Franco fell but would not return while he remained in power. For many of them, to have returned to Spain in the 1940's or 1950's would have been extremely dangerous. However, by the end of the

---

[5] Otaola, *El cortejo.*

[6] León Felipe [Camino Galicia], "¿Que se hizo el Rey Don Juan?" This is an elegy to José Moreno Villa, printed in José Moreno Villa, *Voz en vuelo a su cuna*, Introduction.

1950's Franco's hostility toward the Civil War refugees had abated, and since then the safety of all but a few refugees who care to visit or return to Spain has been guaranteed.[7] Given the present conditions in Spain and the attitude of the Spanish government, the exiles find themselves in a moral dilemma: Is it any longer significant, even symbolically, to deny themselves the satisfaction of seeing Spain once again? Or, on the other hand, should they feel obliged to return to Spain once Franco falls, thereby surrendering the life they have built in Mexico in order to go back to a country which scarcely remembers them? "Bitter impression; the hunger which one endured living detached in a foreign country. One ends up feeling exiled again, and in one's own land."[8]

The issue of returning to Spain poses three separate problems: whether or not the exile should return to Spain permanently; whether or not he should travel to Spain as a visitor, remaining only a limited time; and whether he should do either before or after the fall of Franco. The exiles of the Spanish Civil War no longer are political exiles. That is, they no longer are forced by political coercion to live outside their country. Nevertheless, the situation which drove them into exile in the first place, Franco's rule, remains in force. The old political resolves of the refugees often seem inappropriate to the present situation, and the problem no longer admits a single "morally correct" resolution.

The exiles who want to return and live permanently in Spain must decide whether they will await Franco's death, thereby possibly taking the risk that they will die first in exile, or whether they will return presently and live as best they can under the Franco regime. Only 10 percent of the persons interviewed in 1966–1967 were sure they would return permanently to Spain, should they

<hr/>

[7] In March of 1947 Franco officially authorized the Republicans to return to Spain if they so chose. Those who applied for visas thereafter supposedly could become beneficiaries of the new authorization, unless they were guilty of crimes against the Spanish government. Since nearly all the refugees were considered guilty of some kind of political "crime," this 1947 authorization meant little. According to refugee sources, the more friendly treatment of exiles applying for entry permits to Spain was initiated by the Franco representative in Mexico, Sr. Oños de Plandolit, appointed in 1956 or 1957. His objective, I was informed, was to win Mexican recognition for Franco by placating the hostile refugees, whose opposition has been an important factor in Mexican nonrecognition. See additional discussion on this issue, below.

[8] Llorens Castillo, "El retorno del desterrado," p. 229 (my translation).

still be alive, when Franco ceases to rule. The percentage for the emigration as a whole undoubtedly is smaller since those who so stated were primarily political leaders of the Republic. In the meantime, during the past decade since the decline of official Spanish hostility toward the exiles, a small number of refugees have been quietly returning to Spain without waiting for Franco's rule to end. These mainly have been older people, willing to "compromise with the enemy" in order to live out the remaining years of their lives in their homeland; somewhat fewer are political militants, mostly in the Communist party, who return in order to participate actively in the opposition movements against Franco.[9] The number of returnees, although small, does include some prominent figures.

Most of the refugees and their children will stay in Mexico, even if all the original reasons for their exile disappear. After thirty years in Mexico, the considerations which brought them originally are no longer the major factors which cause them to remain. The exile, once political, is now as much, or more, an economic exile. The prosperity which the exiles have achieved in Mexico, coupled with the considerably more limited opportunities for work in most fields in Spain, proves a more effective deterrent to the Republicans' return than does the Spanish government. Men who have labored long to build their professional status in Mexico would find it not only impossible to re-create their present working academic or professional environment in Spain, but they might find also that there was little or no demand for their special skills.[10]

[9] I have heard some young people, still in their twenties and early thirties, talk of wishing to go to Spain for the same reason—that the only meaningful resistance is there. For these young people, of course, to go to Spain is not to return to Spain, since they have never lived there. I have no figures as to how many in this age group have decided to live in Spain; probably very few, given the usual confusion, apathy, and resistance characteristic of the children of the exiles. As for the older persons who have returned to Spain, estimates vary. Most of the refugees in Mexico claim that very few of their number have gone back, and of these, only about a half-dozen who might be considered "prominent" members of the exile community. According to the exiles in Mexico, there are fewer who return to Spain from Mexico than from other countries of exile, because in Mexico the refugees have formed a "coherent community" of Spaniards.

[10] It is perhaps for this reason that the women with whom I spoke, who did not have any professional interests in Mexico, were more anxious than their husbands or their male relatives to return. Often, the men interviewed noted that their wives, mothers, and sisters were more tied to Spain than they. On the other

In discussing their probable reaction to Franco's death, most Spaniards who had not yet revisited Spain frankly admitted that they were not sure what they would do. Approximately one-third of those interviewed stated that they did not anticipate any kind of return to Spain as long as Franco holds power.[11] But most of these were not certain that they would go back to Spain after his death, or for how long, should they decide to return. More than one person noted wryly that Franco might be serving as a convenient justification to many for not taking up life in Spain. Should they return permanently, loyal Republicans would leave behind not only their jobs and professional practices, but also most of their friends and families. Practically none of the refugees expected that their Mexico-raised children would leave Mexico to live in Spain. Moreover, the refugees, realizing how much they themselves had changed in thirty years, frequently acknowledged their fear that they would find as much or more to have changed in Spain.[12] If one can consider the death or retirement of Franco, when it occurs, to be a moment of truth in which the former exiles decide whether they are basically Spanish or Mexican, it is likely that the overwhelming

---

hand, among those who returned, according to reports of their fellow refugees, many had been encouraged to do so because they could support a luxurious retirement in Spain with the money they had earned in exile.

[11] Again it should be stressed that the sample is heavily weighted in favor of those who have been politically active and community leaders. Most of the persons who refuse to return to Spain at all until after Franco's death are in this category. Three of those interviewed had no moral objections to the idea of the exiles' visiting Spain but felt that they themselves were so prominent that their return would profit Franco too much politically. Two others interviewed considered themselves too old to undertake the travel; six claimed that their refusal to return was an important "symbolic gesture" (from a total of twenty-two who would not go back to Spain while Franco rules).

[12] Among the more politically active exiles, a very frequent and, I feel, revealing answer to the query "Would you go back to Spain if Franco were to die or retire?" was that the individual was not sure, but that he probably would not, because his life was built around Mexico—on the other hand, he might consider returning if he could work productively in Spain, and especially if he felt he was needed there. What these exiles wish to avoid is a return to Spain that would put them in the position of being mere "tourists" or visitors instead of active citizens. Even some of the younger persons interviewed, who had no serious involvement in Spanish exile activities, stated that they would consider going to Spain after Franco's death if they could help in building the nation thereafter; however, they were reasonably certain that their help would not be requested.

majority will find that they are far too accustomed to life in Mexico to make their sentimental return to Spain.

There is a high correlation between those who do plan to live again in Spain when Franco surrenders power and those who will not return, even to visit, beforehand. The correlation in the other direction is much lower. That is, by no means all those who do not wish to visit Spain before the death of Franco intend to settle there afterward. It is interesting to note that parents who do not themselves wish to return to Spain either temporarily or permanently, are often happy to send their children there in the hope that the experience will increase the children's sense of Spanish identity.[13]

Of those interviewed who had not seen Spain since the Civil War and who did not wish to return while Franco remained in power, nearly all agreed that they would like at least to visit Spain after he fell. By the mid-1950's, however, the majority of those interviewed who were in a favorable economic position and were not deterred by Franco's continued rule had visited Spain themselves, or members of their families had. Until the late 1950's, those who visited Spain, however short a time they spent, were sanctioned by the remainder of the community and, also, risked being detained by the Franco government for some past political "crime" (which most, according to government definition, had committed).[14]

Travel to Spain in recent years has been increasing steadily, with few protests from exile groups, and few obstacles from the Spanish government, which now grants visas to all but a few of the old

[13] Interview with Manuel Aragonés, former secretary of the Republican Embassy in Mexico, March 15, 1967.

[14] The Republican refugees have to make a special application to the office of the Franco representative in Mexico in order to obtain a visa and to determine if they are or are not beneficiaries of the authorization of 1947 (see footnote 7, above). If the person is known to be one of those who left Spain in the wake of the Civil War—that is, if he is still a citizen of the Spanish Republic, holding that passport, or if he is a Mexican citizen, born in Spain and naturalized in the early 1940's—his application is sent to Spain to assure that he is not subject to arrest for any still outstanding "crimes" against the Franco government. Since the 1950's, when Franco ceased to consider virtually all Republicans guilty of political crimes, about 90 percent of those refugees who have applied for visas have obtained them. I was unable to obtain figures on the actual numbers of Republicans who do visit Spain; however, the Spanish (Franco) representative in Mexico estimated that about one thousand five hundred Mexican citizens of Spanish origin ask for visas every year. Over half of these, he thought, were Civil War exiles.

political activists. The Republican refugees resent the fact that they
have to request visas from the "Fascists" in order to visit their own
homeland, but increasingly they have been willing to submit to this
minor humiliation in order to visit familiar scenes and long separated family members.[15]

It appears that the refugees' reactions to today's Spain are not
related to their political ideals or even correlated with their age.
The nature of the effect produced by a visit to Spain depends more
often on the visitor's expectations. Exiles who expect to find conditions as deplorable as they were immediately after the war tend
to be surprised and relieved to find that neither the political nor
the economic climate make daily life in Spain intolerable, despite
the continued political repression and the persistent economic difficulties. Those who in their nostalgia and sentimentality have ideal-
ized everything about their homeland, usually return to Mexico
somewhat less idealistic. Only two generalizations can be made:
first, any exiles who have gone to Spain still believing that the
refugees have been important factors in the anti-Franco resistance
have been made aware that refugee groups never have played a
major role in this resistance; second, any who have gone expecting
to find a revolutionary atmosphere in Spain readily admit after
their visit that the revolutionary element is exceedingly small—
most Spaniards fear violence more than they wish for radical
change, and even those who are working for change rarely are
fomenting revolution.[16]

Whatever a refugee's initial motivation in traveling to Spain, his
first revisit to his native land inevitably produces a strong emotional reaction. Very often the visit will cause him to change both

[15] Of those who refused to go to Spain themselves and who had children old
enough to go, only two maintained that they hoped their children would follow
their example. The others either had sent their children already, or simply stated
that their children were not especially interested in Spain.

[16] The above impressions have been pieced together from the descriptions of
recent visits of eight persons interviewed and from the secondhand reports of
several others regarding the observations of relatives or friends. The issue is
very well portrayed in the novel *Exilio*, by Sara García Iglesias, p. 236: "Pero
la vuelta imposible se ha convertido en adorable. Muchos han regresado . . . y
vuelto. Las mujeres han emprendido la peregrinación, de cuantos pesos. Y ¿que
pasa? El retroceso aterrorizado, encontrar que después de todo no esta tan mal
aquí . . . En fin, en el fondo no existe sino una verdad: el temor de que el
paraíso soñado tan remodelado por el imaginación y la nostalgia, se convierta en
cenizas, el palparlo."

his former concepts of Spain and his ideas about the proper role of an exile. There is, however, no uniform direction of the change. Some have found themselves feeling uncomfortable and foreign in their old home town, and gladly have returned to Mexico; others have insisted that they felt more comfortable and at ease in Spain than they had felt in thirty years in Mexico. Some have reported that the Spanish people remain "uncorrupted" just as they were in 1936; others have expressed their disappointment at finding the Spanish people more concerned with material well-being than with any political or social ideals.

Because of the relatively free and open communications now existing between Spain and the Spanish refugees, the increasing international importance of Spain and the simple factor of time, the Republicans in Mexico today are far more aware of the political realities in Spain and of their own situation with regard to these realities than they were even a decade ago. Specifically, they are painfully aware that Spanish liberals and leftists rarely think about them and no longer even require their aid. So long as political repression in Spain was strong, the refugees were useful in many ways in aiding and encouraging anti-Franco activities. But, with the passing of time and the development of strong indigenous, post-Civil War political movements, there has been little left for the old Republicans to contribute. Through the 1940's and 1950's the Republican Embassy in Mexico used to sponsor, and individual refugees contributed to, invitations and support for Spaniards persecuted by the Franco regime, so that such persons could leave Spain and find work and refuge in Mexico. Now there are fewer people who need this assistance. While there still remains a need for monetary aid to political prisoners and their families, the new prisoners are likely to be young students, unknown to the refugees, rather than members of refugee-supported political groups. The refugee intellectuals, at one time, used to devote their efforts to publishing and distributing the works of Spaniards hostile to the government. Now, not only is it less frequently necessary for the Spanish opposition to publish its articles abroad, it is rather the refugees who are reading and contributing their articles to the more liberal Spanish periodicals.[17]

17 For example, such periodicals as *Revista del Occidente, Cuadernos para el Diálogo, Insula, Indice.* The information and comparisons drawn in this para-

The changing international situation has brought most of the Republicans-in-exile to the point of reevaluating their unyielding hostility toward Franco Spain. The first suggestions that the exiles ought to abandon their efforts at bringing down the regime and concentrate instead on dealing with the political realities of the country came from the periodical *Las Españas* as early as 1947.[18] The general reaction of the exile community at that time was highly negative, and, due in a large part to the political pressure subsequently brought to bear on *Las Españas*, it did not publish between 1952 and 1956. In 1956, reiterating and strengthening their former position, the editors of the periodical's second series urged exiles to "leave the trenches,"[19] and to build bridges between themselves and Spain. The editors of *Las Españas* and those who agreed with their position represented the conservative factions among the exiles;[20] political activists of all tendencies were, at that time, still vigorously opposed to what they considered a defeatist and reactionary position. Within less than four years following the 1956 editorial, however, the demand for reevaluation and for more realistic cooperation with forces in Spain had become a dominant theme. The contributors to *Las Españas*, it is fair to say, remained determinedly anti-Franco, but they assumed that the Civil War was irrevocably lost. They criticized, on the one hand, the active politicians who devoted all the energy of opposition to the simple objective of toppling Franco and, on the other hand, criticized the exiles who chose to build a new life in Mexico and to forget about Spain. Editorials spoke in terms of serving Spain and working to improve it from the basis of the realities of the contemporary situation, and of planning for the probable tomorrow.

Exiles concerned about their role in the future of Spain realized

---

graph came primarily from interviews, with Manuel Aragonés, former secretary of the embassy, March 15, 1967, and with Alfonso Ayensa, an economist and an official in the government in exile from its foundation in 1945 to 1952, July 19, 1966.

[18] See chap. 4.

[19] Editorial in *Las Españas* 1, second series (July, 1956).

[20] For example, one of those most strongly upholding the advisability of building bridges was the noted philosopher Luis Recasens Siches, who later gained the enmity of his fellow exiles not only for going back to Spain, but for publicly making peace with the Franco regime. See his article "Intelectuales españoles en México," in *Epoca* 2 (June, 1965):26–27.

by 1960 that they could participate in Spanish affairs only by uniting their efforts with those of their countrymen in Spain. Since then, the idea of trying to build bridges to the interior has been generally accepted, but there is much difference of opinion as to the most effective kind of bridges to build. Exiles in the various political parties have intensified their support for the internal opposition groups they consider closest to themselves ideologically. Politically unaffiliated leftists, especially the younger ones, have lent their support to the active opposition movements among Spanish youth, movements which include a wide range of political views. The more conservative exiles, remembering their disillusionment at the results of the violence during the Civil War, have been seeking to find a unifying principle which will bring together the diverse elements of "Popular Spain," including, by their definition, all those who are opposed to Franco and in favor of a more democratic alternative. The conservatives are no longer committed to any specific political order but stress the need for more understanding of Spain's cultural diversity as opposed to increased violence and popular resistance.[21]

So far, years of concerted efforts on behalf of the Republican cause have yielded only a few accomplishments. Thanks to Republican influence, the Franco government was barred from the United Nations for a number of years after World War II (Spain was admitted to UNESCO in 1955). The presence of so many influential exiles in Mexico undoubtedly has served to reinforce Mexico's early commitment to deny legal recognition to Franco. Finally, many individuals in Spain have been greatly aided by contributions and support extended by the exile community. Nevertheless, as nearly all readily admit, the total impact of the Republicans-in-exile on their homeland has been small, and will almost certainly be even smaller in the future.[22]

[21] See the editorial in *Diálogos de Las Españas* 3 (July, 1959):1, and an article by Pere Bosch Gimpera, "Lecciones de una larga experiencia histórica," in ibid., 4 and 5 (October, 1963):3–5.

[22] Of those interviewed, fewer than 20 percent judged that there had been some positive results from their past efforts. For the most part, they thought their most favorable influence had been in serving as the "conscience" of the major powers, reminding them that at least one Fascist government had survived World War II; for a brief time Franco was not treated with the full respect accorded "legal" governments. A few also considered themselves partly responsible for Mexico's continued policy of nonrecognition of Franco.

AGE AND IDENTITY

Older refugees have taken comfort in the belief that although they did not realize their ideals, they did what they could for the Republic and for Spain during and after the Republican defeat. The men and women who left Spain while still young or before reaching adulthood feel a greater sense of frustration. They went into exile before they could make any significant contribution to their homeland, but in many respects they continue to feel far more Spanish than Mexican. Those who were taken out of Spain as children recall their Spanish past only dimly. They know it primarily through the reminiscences of their parents or through a heightened awareness of Spanish culture gained from their education in one of the Spanish *colegios*.

Parents frequently complain that they have not been able to instill a vital sense of Spanish identity in their offspring, and there are few Spanish families, even among the most successfully acculturated, who wish the younger generation to ignore altogether its Spanish origins. In their efforts to remind young people of their identity, parents frequently send them to Spanish schools, regularly accompany them to regional centers, encourage the development of social contacts among fellow refugee families, and almost always ply them with an abundance of nostalgic conversation.[23]

The young people, in their turn, have reacted in a variety of ways. Those from the most active families often have accepted the experiences of their elders as meaningful and significant, and they have gone on to some extent to involve themselves in issues related to Spain. When they have done so, their ideas and impressions generally have evolved in different directions from those of their elders, but their involvement, nonetheless, has remained real. More often, children have rebelled against what they consider excessive emphasis on Spain on the part of the older generation. Some have chosen, instead, to become as Mexican as possible, refusing all con-

---

[23] Some young people described their parents as always having claimed, on the one hand, to be fully adapted to Mexico, but, on the other hand, as having exerted strong pressure on their children to form friendships and especially to marry within the Republican community. This seems to have been especially prevalent among Catalans and Basques, who wanted their children to marry within the regional, rather than merely the general, Castilian community.

tact with things Spanish. More of them, while considering themselves primarily Mexican, remain proud of the fact that they are Spanish and that their parents were among the Republican refugees. Few, indeed, have been active in the associations of the older exiles, but fewer would deny that they have maintained a special interest in events taking place in Spain. A surprising number of young people participated in the Movimiento '59, and many more might have responded had they believed there was something meaningful they could have contributed to Spain.[24] That most second-generation Spaniards in Mexico have done practically nothing to associate themselves with their parents' efforts has been due more to disillusionment with the results of those efforts than to absolute disinterest in Spain.[25]

The group which came to Mexico as older children or young teenagers, in many ways, has been least able to identify its proper role in exile. "Ours is a confused generation," or words to that effect, characterized responses of nearly all those in that age group interviewed. They are not, as the older groups, Spaniards who have adapted to Mexico. They do not, as the youngest of the refugees, consider themselves definitely more Mexican than Spanish. Feeling strong ties to both Mexico and Spain, they identify fully with neither. They refer to themselves as *hombres fronterizos*:

For many years . . . the young Spanish refugee in Mexico felt that he would never be able to affirm himself as an individual, that he would never reach his full maturity until he had resolved the ambiguity of

[24] See chap. 4.
[25] From conversations with about a dozen persons ranging in age from their twenties to about forty: None was active in or had any faith in the activities of the older associations. Even the few who were themselves involved in youth groups, or who had been involved at the time of the Movimiento '59, did not believe their own activities were really effective but felt a responsibility to do something. There was unanimous agreement to the effect that the older generation had overidealized Spain and the Republic, that the politics of exile had been, at best, unrealistic, since World War II, or, at worst, positively destructive, and that the younger people, in both Spain and Mexico, were far more realistic than were most older exiles with regard to Spain. All stressed that very few of the younger groups were active in any of the associations—with the possible exception of a few teenagers who participated in some of the newly formed young people's groups in the ateneo. Nevertheless, despite all, every one of those with whom I spoke admitted to a special feeling of involvement with events in Spain.

his nature, originating in the fact of being a Spaniard without real sustenance in Spain, while at the same time being Mexican, really sustained in Mexico. . . . It is certain that unconsciously he has had the idea that in order to aspire to maturity he would have to have, like everyone else, an established nationality. . . . He can renounce neither his *españolismo* nor his *mexicanidad*.[26]

The young Spanish writers and poets of this age group frequently have found an outlet for their feelings in literature. They have consistently contributed to Mexican literature, but in the early 1950's they also devoted much energy to creating a few literary periodicals of their own. The most important of these was *Presencia*, then *Clavileño*, *Segrel*, and, later, *Hoja*.[27] Although the literary quality of these journals was high, they were often criticized, even by some who contributed to them. While presenting themselves as general literary journals, they seldom included work which dealt with the problems of literature or philosophy. Nor did their contributors represent any specific literary attitude or outlook. Rather, "aggressive enthusiasm, polemics and bellicose attitudes" typified the generation of Spanish poets which came to maturity around 1950, according to Arturo Souto, who himself is one of the better known writers of that generation.[28] Souto has attempted to explain why some critics came to refer to the group as *jóvenes viejos* ("old youngsters"). They were poets who had matured artificially, who had contemplated but not lived the bitter experiences of their elders. By the mid-1950's, according to Souto, although the work of these writers had matured and increased in depth, the entire gen-

[26] Luis Rius, "Los españoles en México: Historia de una doble personalidad," *El Heraldo*, February 17, 1967, p. 6A. The term *hombres fronterizos* is his (my translation).

[27] These periodicals published essays, poetry, stories, and a variety of translations; among their editors and contributors were José M. García Ascot, Carlos Blanco, Roberto Ruiz, Ramón Xirau, Francisco Aramburo, Angel Palerm, Tomás and Rafael Segovia, Manuel Durán, Jacinto Viqueira, Luis Rius, Jorge Guillén, Víctor and Fernando Rico, Alberto Gironella, Arturo Souto, Juan Espinasa, Enrique Rivas, Francisco de la Maza, Ramón Gómez de la Serna, Celedonio Martínez Serrano; they have, for the most part, gone on to important careers as critics or writers in Mexico and in other countries (Max Aub, "Una nueva generación," *Sala de Espera* 21 [June, 1950]:12–15; Arturo Souto Alabarce, "Nueva poesía española en México," part 2, *Ideas de México* 2 [September–December, 1954]:31–37).

[28] Souto Alabarce, "Nueva poesía," *Ideas*, p. 32. (This is my own loose translation.)

eration still continued to be characterized by melancholy and frustration.[29]

Max Aub, an important writer of the older generation, criticized the young poets for their lack of realism and the entire exile community for having caused them to develop that way. For eleven years, said Aub, writing in 1950, Spanish exiles were looking backward, and during this time those who began exile at around twelve to eighteen years of age were reaching manhood.

Caught between two worlds, without firm ground beneath their feet, influenced by an irrational philosophic movement, by a secondhand Spain, they have not yet managed to open their eyes to reality. This same vague disparity has caused their political position to be unstable. They are repelled by communism. . . . Capitalism is not attractive, and the liberals who doubtless have their sympathies have been dying. Neither do the young people have their own language; at times, in the most pure of their works, as is natural, Americanisms begin to appear. . . . I see that these youths are content with little, getting along, influenced in this by their families who still dream of the Calle Alcalá [in Madrid], which to many of these boys surely would have seemed narrow and provincial. This is a terribly respectful generation which conforms to the world around it. . . . I'd give anything to see them confront life with the energy of youth and leave this romantic, existentialist dust which we got twenty-five years ago in the *Revista del Occidente*.[30]

These same young writers, in the 1960's, no longer strive to recapture for themselves a Spain that has passed. While still maintaining close ties to one another, those who formed an identifiable group of young Spanish writers in the early 1950's now write as individuals, with close relationship to Mexicans as well as to their Spanish colleagues. They have accepted and participated in Mexican life; they still, however, have ties which they can neither break nor fulfill with Spain.[31]

29 Ibid., p. 33.
30 Max Aub, "Una nueva generación," *Sala de Espera*, pp. 12–15 (my translation).
31 There was evidence of these ties at a meeting at Wesleyan University in Connecticut, April 20, 1968, where a large group of Spanish critics, writers, and teachers assembled. Those attending included many men who had spent their adult lives and in some cases almost their entire lives widely separated from one another. After the Civil War, some had remained in Spain, others

The very youngest of the exiles are more secure in their Mexican environment. Most have little to do with Spanish Republican issues or activities. While they are found in the Ateneo Español more often than are those in the group discussed above,[32] the functions which attract them are purely social and cultural and sometimes include Mexican participants.[33] The Spanish *colegios*, which many still attend, have been gradually increasing the enrollment of students from Mexican families, and, since the 1960's, the faculties have been almost entirely Mexican-trained.[34] Once generally considered the most progressive schools in Mexico in their educational methods, the *colegios* are judged by more recent students to have become somewhat conservative and rigid.[35]

This youngest group of Spaniards has received, on the whole, less pressure from parents to become involved in Spanish causes. Those who came to Mexico as older children grew up while the exiles were still actively working and hoping for the fall of Franco and their own return to Spain, but those who came as infants, or who were born shortly after their parents' arrival, know only the exile which has already acknowledged its own defeat. By the time they were old enough to understand their parents' ideals and commitments, their parents had begun to accept the fact that the Republic had died.

While the older groups usually admit that they have more Spanish than Mexican friends—or distinguish their Spanish friends

---

had lived in various countries of exile including the United States, Mexico, and other Latin American countries. Despite the vast differences in age and experience among them, they talked intensely of their shared feelings for Spain, its language, tradition, and culture, and they debated questions which concerned them all vitally as Spaniards, wherever they had lived.

[32] The somewhat older group, discussed above, has avoided the ateneo, characterized by many of them as a relic and a symbol of the past which has failed to respond to changing times. Apparently the generation of *hombres fronterizos* did at one time attend the ateneo with some frequency but found its administration too rigid.

[33] See chap. 4, on the activities of the ateneo. In some of the social clubs organized for young people, such as the dramatics clubs, Mexicans do participate with the young of Spanish families.

[34] See ibid., for a discussion of the *colegios*.

[35] Interviews, with Javier Aleja and his wife, May 3, 1967; with Julio García Coll, March 3, 1967.

as the more intimate—this is not true of the youngest group.[36] Nevertheless, these young people are conscious that, because they come from Spanish families, they are "different" from their Mexican friends and contemporaries. The being "different" often implies being "better." Frequently, although proclaiming themselves fully Mexican, subjectively and objectively, they go on to indicate the advantages of their Spanish background: they are more punctual; they are more candid than Mexicans; they are potentially better husbands or wives.[37] One quite revealing aspect of the enduring cultural pride of these young Spaniards is that, although entirely educated in Mexico, they still on occasion prefer to speak the Spanish of Spain rather than the Spanish of Mexico,[38] the speech they have heard at home or perhaps in Spanish *colegios*, instead of that of the country they consider their homeland.[39]

[36] Of the parents interviewed, more than half of those whose children were of school age when the family emigrated to Mexico or whose children were born in Mexico, said that their children had more Mexican than Spanish friends. The rest of those interviewed could be divided almost evenly among those whose children's friends were said to be more often Spanish than Mexican, those who claimed that their children's friends were as often one as the other nationality (or else represented a variety of nationalities—usually the case when the children attended French, German, or American secondary schools), and those who did not offer any information concerning their children's friends. Of the group whose children have had more Spanish than Mexican friends, half the parents interviewed came to Mexico when their children were already in their teens; in most of the remaining cases, the parents themselves were more than usually politically active. Of the younger people interviewed, those few who were active in Spanish affairs had more Spanish than Mexican friends; those who were not active had, more often than not, a majority of Mexican friends. Of those who came to Mexico as adolescents, it was frequently noted that while their oldest and closest friends were Spanish, the number of close Mexican friends had been increasing during their adult lives.

[37] The idea that Spaniards were inherently superior to Mexicans was almost never stated outright by the younger Spaniards, but there were implications in this direction in practically every interview or conversation on the subject.

[38] I heard the Castilian accent used among young people when they were in exclusively Spanish company, especially at formal meetings. Among Mexicans, these young people usually speak as Mexicans.

[39] Some scholars, such as Vicente Llorens Castillo and Juan Marichal, who are in exile in the United States, have noted that the Spanish accent neither has been fully maintained by those who came to Mexico as adults, nor has it been accurately learned by those who have been educated in Mexico. According to these scholars, older refugees have kept the Spanish pronunciation, but use it with an adopted Mexican syntax, while younger people exaggerate their Castilian sounds and use them with a totally Mexican syntax.

THE CENTERS—MORE SPANISH THAN POLITICAL

During the early years of exile the many political and cultural associations of the refugees were their primary links with Spain and served as points of dissemination for whatever information could be exchanged regarding friends and relatives still there. This has long since ceased to be the case. Many associations still exist, however, and many older people continue to participate in their activities. The exile organizations have become a means by which the old Republican community preserves its social coherence, and exiles assemble for lectures, films, debates, and formal meetings as much to renew friendships and shared interests as to discuss relevant issues. The younger people, however, have been socialized more often by means of the Spanish schools and family friendship patterns than through the formally constituted political groups in which some of their parents still participate.

Only the regional centers, especially the stronger Catalan and Basque centers, have continued to serve in an added socializing function for young as well as older Spaniards whose loyalties have been both Spanish and regional. In the building of the Orféo Catalá, for example, there are facilities for recreation, cinema, theater, and lectures, as well as an extensive library and a restaurant. The Orféo Catalá also runs sports clubs and special excursion groups.[40] In addition, large numbers of young Spaniards have been attracted to Spanish soccer teams, which are based in the various Spanish regional and social centers (Gallegos vs. Valencianos, etc.), and are not exclusively, or even mostly, of the Republican community. The largest of the Spanish soccer teams which is not of a regional group is that of the Club Mundet. It is composed primarily of sons of the *antigua colonia*, but it is open to all Spaniards. By means of such clubs, some of the Republican youth have formed cordial, if superficial, ties with contemporaries from quite different political backgrounds.[41]

The Spanish Republican community is, at present, fragmented. Each group has its small core of active members, but most refugees participate regularly in none of them. Such official gatherings as

[40] See chap. 5 for more information on the regional associations.
[41] Interviews with Julio García Coll, March 3, 1967; Javier Aleja, May 3, 1967; also, several conversations with Sergio Pich Romero.

the celebration of the founding of the Republic or homages to distinguished Spaniards or Mexicans have served to reunite the older and most important figures of the Republican community. At times of crisis in Spain, larger and more varied groups have gathered in the Ateneo to listen to information and debates. Generally, the strongest ties among the Republicans are those of long-standing friendship. This is true of persons of all ages, all professions, and all political persuasions, and it sometimes accounts for close personal relations between people who have followed quite different paths since the end of the war.

Many Republicans in exile still wish to accomplish some useful function for Spain. Even more regret that they have been able to do so little. A great many of the refugees not only have ceased to act politically, but have found that what continues to tie them to Spain and to make it difficult to adapt to Mexican life is less their political failure than the strength of their Spanish cultural background. That is, even having accepted that the Republic will not return, it is still no easier for them to accept exile in Mexico. A surprising number of Spanish refugees of almost all ages continue to speak nostalgically and sentimentally of Spain, and this sentimentality helps to explain why the regional centers continue to function actively while other political and cultural entities have dwindled. It also provides an insight into why so many Republicans have been able to establish cordial relations with their erstwhile enemies, the members of the *antigua colonia*, or, at least, why they rarely object if their children do so.[42]

Some among the Republicans even have taken steps toward association with the officials of the Franco government, both in Spain and in Mexico, although the vast majority of exiles consider that

[42] About one-third of the Republicans had something favorable to say about the members of the *antigua colonia*, or had some friends among them. There were very few instances of close friendships, and often acquaintanceships were based on a tacit agreement not to discuss politics. Practically none of the Republicans showed themselves any longer bitter toward the *antigua colonia*. The members are usually businessmen or merchants, whereas the Republicans (as in the interview sample) are more often intellectuals or professionals; hence the two groups have had little in common, and this as much as political differences has kept them from extensive interaction. Cordial relationships ("cordial" is the term by which refugees usually refer to their relationships with the Spanish colony) between individuals usually begin either in regional centers or, for young people, through the Spanish soccer leagues and sports clubs.

182 EXILES AND CITIZENS

this compromises the dignity of the Republican community and calls into question the very reason for exile. The extent to which the refugees still are self-conscious and ambivalent about their role as exiles from Franco's Spain was demonstrated by an incident in 1967 which created a crisis in the Republican community of Mexico.

One of Franco's representatives, Martínez de Mata, was sent to spend a few months in Mexico, in the hope of improving relations between the Spanish and the Mexican governments. Before the Civil War this same Martínez de Mata had been active in the liberal student movement, the FUE, to which so many of the refugees also belonged.[43] As a result, he had had personal friends among the men who later became leaders of the Republican community in Mexico. When Martínez de Mata arrived in Mexico, a small group of these Republicans agreed to meet one night in August for what they expected would be an informal dinner with him. Instead, the event proved to be a formal banquet of homage to the Franco official, and the following day the banquet was reported in the Mexican press with a list of those who had attended.[44]

The reaction was immediate. On August 20, it was announced that Antonio María Sbert and Eligio de Mateo Sousa had been ousted from the Centro Republicano—they were the only members of the centro among those who had attended the dinner. They were expelled specifically for having participated in homage to a Franco representative.[45] Mexican opinion next joined and intensified the protest. Why should Mexico continue to withhold recognition from the Franco government, asked one journalist, if the very Republicans who have been recognized in his stead no longer are *antifranquista*?[46]

Despite their protests and their insistence that they only had in-

[43] See chap. 5.
[44] See Antonio Barrilado, "Despedida a Sr. Martínez de Mata," *Novedades*, "sección social," Sunday, August 13, 1967, p. 6. The names he listed were "Lic. Cervantes, Ing. Antonio Sbert, Villa, Lic. Mariano Granados, Dr. Luis Fumagallo, Coronel Antonio Camacho, Camps Ribera, José María Izauneta, Dr. Joaquin D'Harcourt, Arq. Arturo Sáinz de la Calzada, Eligio de Mateo Sousa, and Francisco Jiménez." These men cover a fairly broad political spectrum. (D'Harcourt, in fact, had not attended.)
[45] "A los Republicanos españoles y la opinión pública," *El Día*, August 20, 1967, p. 3.
[46] "Nos deja un Heraldo franquist," *El Día*, August 22, 1967.

tended to share an informal meal with an old friend, all of the Republicans who were involved in the affair were ousted from virtually every association of the Spanish exile in Mexico. In the Ateneo Español, the expulsion of the erring members was preceded by large, long, and heated debate. Spanish exiles, who for years had not attended any meeting or lecture of any Republican association, appeared in the Ateneo in early September to pass judgment on their fellow refugees. The issue was more than a problem of individual political indiscretion, for the men involved were among the most prominent men in the emigration, and their actions reflected upon the entire community. Moreover, the public debate over the unfortunate banquet raised a more vital question: What, after all, was the proper role for Spanish Republicans in Mexico, nearly thirty years after their original exile?

The refugees no longer were refugees, since nearly all of them could return to Spain in safety if they so chose. In 1940 they had been Republicans-in-exile, but by 1967 they were simply Spanish-born residents of Mexico, with no expectations that they ever would reestablish a Spanish Republic. The leftists and radicals of the Civil War had become, for the most part, stable citizens and political moderates, thirty years later. The Spanish representative Martínez de Mata had more in common with some of the refugees than the latter had with other refugees, or with their own children. In short, to be a Spanish Republican refugee, after thirty years away from Spain, was more a symbol than a reality.

The symbol, in the end, was judged crucial. Those who defended the accused argued that, in the past, many exiles had participated in social functions with Franco sympathizers, and that, therefore, it was unfair to select one incident arbitrarily for punishment. This incident, however, had been made public, and the reputation of the entire community was seen to be at stake. Not only were men who attended the banquet ousted from the Ateneo as a result of the night's long debate, but those who formally defended them also felt obliged to leave the association.[47]

How will the former Republican refugees resolve their ambivalence in the future? Incidents like the one narrated above indicate that even after so many years it is increasingly difficult for the

[47] This represents an accumulation of accounts related to me by a variety of persons who were present at the Ateneo during the debate.

refugees to uphold their political loyalties. Present attitudes represent a kind of fusion of their abiding Republican consciousness and their Spanish nostalgia, even though the two sentiments are, to an extent, contradictory. It is clear that the balance between Spanish cultural ties and political loyalties is a matter on which there is no longer any community consensus. Thus, each individual must determine his own identity. In the meantime, since it has been neither possible nor desirable to continue in a completely "Spanish" style of life in exile, the refugees have all made at least some adjustment to life in Mexico. The nature of that adjustment, as we will see, has been no less complex and problematic than their relationship with Spain.

9. PERSPECTIVES

When the Spanish Republicans arrived, Mexico was entering a period of rapid development. The upheavals of the revolution had ceased, and Cárdenas was providing progressive, ambitious leadership. World War II had just begun, and Mexico, like other Latin American countries, soon found itself in an unusually favorable economic position due to its ability to provide the Allies with commodities in short supply. Also, by the time the refugees came to Mexico, there was, for the first time since the revolution, adequate national capital to finance industrial, economic, and cultural innovation. All that was lacking was the skilled labor to implement Mexican plans. The Spanish Republicans who sought refuge in Mexico were poor in capital but immensely rich in skills. Within a few years of their arrival, most of the refugees were successfully employed and working closely with Mexicans in a variety of fields.

The exiles who sought refuge in Mexico did not represent a cross section of Spanish society. Rather, they comprised a select and, for the most part, upwardly mobile group. Even among the nominally working-class refugees there were many who had left Spain in the first place because they had acquired positions of leadership during the war, thereby enhancing their social status but increasing their political vulnerability. In exile they worked ambitiously to continue their upward trend, and usually succeeded in attaining a social and economic position above that of the Mexicans of the same class origin. Like so many immigrant groups in rapidly developing countries, the Spanish refugees were quite successful. Not surprisingly, middle- and working-class Mexicans sometimes resented the "good fortune" of the men who came to Mexico to flee political persecution, but who seemed willing to accept wealth and position as a compensation for their political losses.[1]

Cárdenas's policy toward the Spanish Republicans, the Mexican welcome to the refugees, and the exiles' commitment to and involvement in Mexico represented the first instance since the colonial period in which Spaniards and Mexicans sought to make common cause. But the refugees and their hosts perceived each other, and judged each other, across a cultural and historical chasm. The situation was new and promising, but old misconceptions, stereotypes, and prejudices remained virtually intact. The following pages are concerned with the perceptions, attitudes, and assessments made by Spaniards and Mexicans about one another. The unbiased truth may lie—as it usually does—somewhere between, but, in describing the experience of the Spanish refugees in Mexico, the perceived truths weigh more heavily.

ASSESSMENTS OF MEXICO

Perceived Obstacles to Integration and Incorporation

From the first, the Spanish refugees were profoundly grateful to Mexico for having welcomed them and for having extended to them the rights of citizenship. Because of the government's generosity, the refugees, in turn, were able to participate in Mexico's

---

[1] Although such hostility was not often shared personally by the Mexicans of intellectual and professional eminence with whom I spoke, these same men often referred to such attitudes as part of "popular" opinion. My own experience with Mexicans in informal conversation tended to validate this.

cultural, material, and social development and, through this participation, in their view, to contribute to overall Mexican progress.[2] The refugees have frequently noted with pride that their social and economic successes have been to the benefit, not to the detriment, of Mexico as a whole. Nonetheless, many refugees believe that they have succeeded in their efforts despite obstacles inherent in the Mexican social, political, and cultural environment.[3] The obstacles most often mentioned are direct prejudicial laws and a general popular nationalism which borders on xenophobia.[4]

The Law of Professions, passed in 1944, prohibited anyone not born in Mexico from holding an administrative position in a governmental agency. The Spaniards, representing by far the largest group of naturalized citizens in Mexico, considered this law to be specifically aimed at them. Most important among government institutions in which Spanish ambitions have been forcibly limited are the national universities. The law has meant that an intellectual not born in Mexico cannot aspire to become the director, or even the assistant director, of an academic faculty, although he can be a full professor in any field.[5] The number of Spaniards serving in the

[2] For example: "The Spanish emigration of 1939, which must be the subject of more study than the recent history of Spain, is also concerned with the economic and cultural history of contemporary Mexico. . . . The Spanish emigration has been strongly involved in Mexico's development" (In Luis Rius, "Maestros españoles in la UNAM," *El Heraldo*, March 7, 1967). Rius goes on to elaborate on the contributions of the many professors of Spanish Republican origin at the University of Mexico.

[3] At least half of those interviewed stated that they had felt the existence of definite obstacles at one time or another in their careers. Others interviewed, who had encountered none personally, assumed that obstacles probably had existed for most.

[4] One of the more notorious instances of unexpected Mexican hostility was directed against the well-known Spanish musicologist Jesús Bal y Gay, early in exile. An older Mexican woman, a former singer, arose at an opera performance and denounced Bal y Gay for some criticism he had written about the opera in his regular column in the newspaper *El Universal*. She asserted that such criticism was inadmissible from one who had been a refugee, welcomed by Mexican hospitality, and that Bal y Gay had offended Mexican society. Soon thereafter, Bal y Gay lost his position as music critic on *El Universal*'s staff. This story was told to me by several people, and appears in *Crónica de una emigración*, by Carlos Martínez, pp. 46–47. The dates on which these events occurred are not given, nor did anyone seem to remember exactly when it was. Spaniards appear to consider such instances extremely important, however.

[5] I was told of only two Spaniards who acquired academic administrative posts, and both are young: one, Santiago Genovés, is an unusually talented anthropologist at the National University, whose appointment as assistant head

various Mexican universities has been so great that the restrictions placed against their moving from academic to administrative posts have been keenly felt.

The Spaniards complain that discrimination goes far beyond what has been legislated. The question of Mexican xenophobia and the extent to which it may have inhibited Spanish success is complex. It is mentioned and discussed far too frequently, however, to be dismissed simply as a reflection of the personal disappointments of a few refugees or as one of the general discomforts commonly encountered by foreign groups in almost any country:[6] Spaniards who have failed to achieve the degree of success toward which they aspired are not alone in criticizing Mexican nationalism, although they tend to do so the more strongly. Those involved in the more highly competitive professional fields are not the only ones who talk of xenophobia, although the problem affects them personally. In many cases emphasis on Mexican nationalism may represent another aspect of Spanish nationalism. That is, those who stress most strongly the undesirability of Mexican nationalism tend to be closely tied to their re-created Spanish world in Mexico. Yet, even those Spaniards whose professional lives and social interactions are substantially more Mexican than Spanish continue to consider themselves foreigners and to expect that the Mexicans always will treat them as such.

A well-known and highly respected anthropologist, who has always worked closely with his Mexican colleagues, who claims to have more Mexican than Spanish friends, and who has participated little, if at all, in Spanish Republican activities in Mexico, nonetheless noted that his own case was exceptional: "It is true, how-

---

of the anthropology faculty was criticized by some Mexicans (Interview with Juan Comas, February 7, 1967). The other is Emilio Vega, who succeeded in becoming the head of the architecture faculty at the University of Guanajuato, thanks to strong student support (Conversation with Emilio Vega, December 22, 1967). Many Mexicans agree that the Law of Professions is unfair. Lic. Antonio Martínez Báez, for one, has frequently contested it juridically as being unconstitutional, but, although he has won a few cases, the law remains on the books (Interview with Antonio Martínez Báez, April 26, 1967).

[6] Even José Gaos, who at all times advised Spaniards that there was a common identity between Spaniards and Mexicans, and who worked with Mexican intellectuals in defining the Mexican identity, warned the Mexicans against the developing trends of nationalism and racism (Gaos, *En torno a la filosofía*, p. 76).

ever, that in general it is more difficult to enter the personal circle of friends of Mexicans than of Spaniards. . . . The Spaniards are more extroverted."[7] A wealthy former judge, successful at a variety of enterprises from the time of his arrival in Mexico, and one of the few lawyers who managed to return to practice his legal profession, had little confidence in Mexico. His son, a cardiologist trained under the best doctors in Mexico, was studying in the United States, and his father hoped he would not return: "In Mexico there is always the danger that his skill will be sacrificed to political influence, and he might be denied a position in favor of some politician's son."[8] One of the best-known writers of the Spanish exile commented on those of his colleagues who had made an honest effort to become assimilated: "Even for those who are considered adapted . . . it has been very difficult for the older generations. The problem is on the Mexican side. There is no means by which Mexicans can recognize the Spaniards as Mexicans; all the laws, written and tacit, work against it, and so does the Mexican psychology. Mexicans do not easily assimilate other cultural groups."[9] And an economist expounding the duty of refugees to work for the benefit of their adopted country stressed that "we must recognize the reality of Mexico . . . Even though the Mexicans do not always sympathize, or understand us, we must make a profound effort to understand them."[10]

While there was nearly universal agreement among those interviewed that the Spanish could be proud of their contributions to Mexico, many complained that their contributions were unappreciated by, and even unknown to, the general Mexican population. The complaint was not that individual Spaniards had gone unrecognized. On the contrary, among the refugees, men in all fields have been accorded numerous honors and prizes. The interviewees insisted, however, that Mexican honors bestowed on individuals in the emigration did not constitute Mexican appreciation of the group's efforts. In other words, the exiles concluded that nationalism prevented the Mexicans from fully acknowledging the importance to their country's progress of such a foreign group as the

[7] Interview, February 7, 1967. (See statement in footnote to Preface.)
[8] Interview, September 7, 1966.
[9] Interview, August 14, 1966.
[10] Interview, February 21, 1967.

Spaniards. Two of the internationally prominent members of the exile group commented wryly that they always had been referred to and treated as Spaniards (foreigners) in Mexico before their fame was assured, but that afterward they were named among "prominent Mexicans" and the fact of their foreign birth was seldom mentioned.[11]

Race and Culture

Given the admitted failure to realize or even to agree on political aspirations with regard to Spain, the Spanish Republican community to a large extent has lost its political identity. The Republican refugees at present are distinguished from other Spaniards in Mexico mainly by history, and from the Mexicans by race and culture. Since they have become, with time, more emphatically Spanish than Republican, they resent all the more the Mexican mestizo's conscious racial pride.[12] A number of Spaniards interviewed minimized the importance of the Indian past in Mexico and stressed the extent to which Spanish culture has survived since the colonial period. Several of them suggested that one of the major contributions made by the Republican refugees was in opening the doors to more European influence in Mexico.[13]

Although expressing sympathy for and interest in the Mexican Indian, few Spanish exiles approved of official Mexican *indigenis-*

[11] Interviews, December 29, 1966, and February 7, 1967.

[12] It appears difficult for Spaniards, whatever their political stance, to understand and sympathize with the Mexican attempt to emphasize the Indian and disparage the Spanish past. The Republicans, generally, believe that Spain made positive as well as negative contributions to Mexican life, and that mestizo misrule is no more excusable than Spanish misrule. The idea that the present leadership in Mexico might identify more with its Indian forebears than with Spaniards seems absurd to most Spaniards.

[13] Whereas prominent Spaniards in Mexico liked to speak of Hispanic unity between Spain and the Americas when they first arrived, many Spanish intellectuals and professionals now insist that the only future for Spain lies in participating in the European community of nations. The Movimiento Europeista de México was formed in 1965 by political moderates, including many intellectuals; its purpose has been to study and to encourage efforts in Spain aimed at Spanish entry into the European economic community. Its founders see more hope for the development of Spanish democracy through closer ties with western Europe than through closer ties with the Spanish-speaking Americas. (See Agrupación Europeista de México, "Plan de trabajo, comisiones y ponencias" [November, 1965].) The group published a bulletin, *Intercontinentes*, four or five times a year.

mo.[14] Many criticized the Mexican government for its use of pro-Indian sentiment as a political tool, while failing to improve the lot of the Mexican Indian. A large number of refugees also viewed *indigenismo* as indicating an anti-Spanish orientation at the base of Mexican national pride.[15] Cortés, they recalled, won brilliant battles in Mexico, but has been honored nowhere in that country, whereas Cuautémoc, who lost his battle and was tortured by the Spaniards, has become a symbol of the Mexican's pride in his race and history.

Some of the refugees expressed their dislike of Mexican racial nationalism, and contrasted Mexican views to what they felt were the healthier Spanish attitudes toward race. Republicans frequently emphasized the fact that Spaniards, traditionally, have not been a racist people, that they themselves are a mixture of many races and have mixed freely with the native American peoples since the days of the Conquest. Other Republicans, in turn, pointed disapprovingly at their fellow refugees, accusing them of viewing Mexicans as racially inferior. In fact, a few have publicly maintained that the particular combination of the Spaniard and the Mexican Indian produced a race characterized by the less desirable traits of both.[16] Those who have held such opinions, naturally, discourage the marriage of members of their families with native Mexicans and generally have very little to do with them socially.

Much more often, disclaiming any intended racial overtones in their views, the Spaniards interviewed made culturally biased statements regarding Mexican characteristics: that the Mexican tends to be irresponsible or hypocritically polite; that Mexican men make poor husbands; that the Mexicans are a materialistic people.[17] As

[14] *Indigenismo* is the form of Mexican nationalism which puts emphasis on the contribution made by the original Mexican Indian and the Indian culture to contemporary Mexican nationhood (See chap. 7).

[15] In her analysis of textbooks of Mexican history, Josefina Vázquez de Knauth confirms this view, noting that during and after the Cárdenas epoch, "No siempre el indigenismo fue indigenismo, sino que a veces se convirtió en antihispanismo." When textbook writers stressed *indigenismo*, "El libro resulta más antiespañol que indigenista" (*Nacionalismo y educación en México*, pp. 165, 193).

[16] No more than three or four persons made such strong statements in interviews, but a much larger number of those interviewed reported that this was a common view held by many exiles.

[17] About half the interviewees voiced such stereotyped sentiments in response to the questions, What is your opinion about marriage between Mexicans and

might be expected, negative opinions about Mexican traits could be
correlated inversely with the amount of interaction between the
refugee interviewed and the Mexican community and were more
prevalent among the less successful Spaniards.[18] Again, Spaniards
who drew unfavorable stereotypes of Mexicans almost always excluded Mexican intellectuals from their negative generalizations.

Whatever the Spanish judgment of Mexican characteristics, almost all noted important cultural (and racial) differences between
Spaniards and Mexicans. The differences probably had appeared all
the more marked, because, when the exiles first arrived, they expected to find a culture much like their own. Among all of them,
no more than two or three persons who came to Mexico were really
well versed in the history of that country, or for that matter, about
any of the Latin American countries.[19] On the contrary, knowing
only that Mexico was a Spanish-speaking nation and shared with
Spain a common history and religious background, nearly all the
refugees thought they would find themselves in a familiar environment. Moreover, a great many of them, especially some of the intellectuals, assumed that the former colony still looked to the old
mother country for its cultural direction.[20] Only slowly did the

---

Spaniards? and, Are there any factors which make social relations between
Mexicans and Spaniards difficult? Spaniards interviewed who did not wish to
sound overly critical, qualified their negative characterizations of Mexicans by
criticizing the Spaniards as well, or by saying that the factors named were not
important to good Spanish-Mexican relations. Of those who did not make
generalizations like those described, about half refused to make any value judg-
ments at all in the interviews.

[18] Other questions asked were, In your professional life, have you worked
closely with Mexicans in your field since your arrival? Have you participated
in intellectual or professional associations with Mexicans? Have any members
of your family married Mexicans? Have you more Mexican or more Spanish
friends? Those who replied positively to my questions and who claimed many
Mexican friends were, in almost all cases, successful and satisfied in their
professional lives also. Women tended to be more critical than men.

[19] Enrique Diez-Canedo, Américo Castro, and Rafael Altamira were named as
the only intellectuals with really strong interest in and considerable knowledge
about the Americas. Their interest, of course, predated the exile by many years.
All of the Republican Spaniards interviewed admitted that they had come to
Mexico knowing practically nothing about Mexico or any other Latin American
country.

[20] See chap. 7, above, on hispanism and Hispano-America; those refugees who
came to Mexico as in a "second conquest," expecting to lead the Mexicans in
greater progress were, perhaps, the most disappointed. Mexicans have shown
considerable contempt for Spanish paternalism.

Spanish exiles come to realize the extent of their misconceptions and to accept that Mexico and Spain are more different than alike. "The origin of all this discomfort and confusion is in the racial differences. The change of norms would not have surprised us in China. But coming to Mexico and hearing a Ramírez or a González talking Spanish, we expect that he will behave like a González from there [from Spain]. It bothers us; it surprises us; the very basis of our logic is offended by his anarchic and absurd behavior."[21] Having found Mexico so different from what they had expected and distinct in so many ways from Spain, the exiles who developed an interest in their second homeland have tended to focus more on the distant past than on more contemporary issues. Only five of the sixty-six interviewees stated that their major interest lay in contemporary problems, while considerably higher interest was expressed in such subjects as colonial history, history in general, and Mexican cultural history. The specific areas of greatest exile interest, according to their stated preferences, were the pre-Columbian past and Mexican-Indian culture, that is, the areas of Mexico which are most different from Spain and with which the Spaniards have been least involved since their arrival.[22] Nearly all the exiles had strong opinions about recent Mexican political and social events, but seemed to prefer exploring the literature and artifacts of the less controversial indigenous past.

The Spaniards expressed strong opinions about contemporary Mexico among themselves, although they almost never put their opinions in print. Theories and analyses of Mexico were frequent topics of conversation in informal gatherings. Nevertheless, the evidence on which the refugees based their analyses usually was weak. Few of the refugees have traveled widely in Mexico or have lived outside of the urban center for any length of time. In general, they seemed better acquainted with Europe than with the Americas,

21 This is the explanation given by one of the characters in Sara García Iglesias's novel *Exilio* (p. 227) of why it was so hard for him to adjust to Mexico. I have heard similar remarks from many of the refugees.

22 Thirty-five respondents, over half of the interview sample, declared their major interest in Mexico to lie in the study of Mexico's indigenous or colonial past. Sixteen persons declared their major interest to be in Mexican culture, literature, and art. The rest were divided over a wide range of subjects, or else declined to express any dominant interest.

and the older refugees, as already noted, tended to have relatively few close Mexican friends.

Politics and Revolution

One aspect of contemporary Mexico, the revolution, evoked considerable admiration from Spanish Republicans. It is clear that whatever its faults, the Mexican revolution has at least partially overcome social and political forces similar to those which defeated the Spanish Republic so early in its existence. Though admitting this, only a minority of the refugees considered that the Mexican and Spanish experiences had a great deal in common in terms of goals, ideology, or existing conditions. The two movements were alike in that initially both were basically liberal and bourgeois efforts to overthrow orthodox, almost feudal structures;[23] but Spain saw few, if any, of its reforms realized, whereas Mexico not only liberated its people from the aristocracy, but went on to create a "revolutionary" government which has been growing stronger ever since.

The Spaniards have not participated directly in Mexican politics and, in private, frequently criticize the Mexican political system. The very factors of which they tend to be most critical, however, also arouse their admiration and respect. Their view of their own past experience helps explain this attitude. The Spanish Republic, in part, was an experiment of the intellectual elite; in contrast, according to the refugees, the Mexican government has included few intellectuals, and has converted most of those few into politicians. The Republicans judge the Spanish politicians to have been far more high-minded and nobly intentioned than their Mexican counterparts, and to have been more sincerely concerned for the well-being of the common people. But, they admit, the Republican politicians, largely for these very reasons, were ill-prepared to deal with the political realities of Spain. Mexican politicians, they also

[23] Members of the ideological parties—Socialists, Anarchists, and Communists —tended to stress the much stronger ideological content of the Spanish Republic as compared to Mexico, whereas members of the Republican parties and apolitical people saw similar goals in both, and often praised Mexico for having succeeded in doing more for its people than Spain had. Radicals and Communists have commented that, of the two, the Mexican revolution was much less limited by a rigid bourgeois ethic than the original Spanish Republic, although they judge that little of the original radicalism still survives in Mexico.

admit, have been quite effective in preserving the stability of the country and of their own place in it. If given another chance, many of the exiles commented, they would put the political lessons they learned in Mexico to use in Spain. The intellectuals would stay out of politics, the politicians would learn to be more pragmatic, and the enemies of democracy—the church, the military, the large landholders—would not be permitted to survive, in the name of democracy.

Of all institutions in the Mexican system, the Spanish exiles have found it most difficult to accept or understand the Partido Revolucionario Institucional (PRI), the party which, under various names, has monopolized political power in Mexico since the late 1920's. Politically oriented Republicans consider that the PRI is not a political party at all, for it seems to them to lack any ideological base. They readily admit, however, that the PRI does function successfully as a united entity, containing many factions, and does coordinate political activity. The Republicans had sought meaningful political unity, but failed to attain it, either in Spain or in exile. Not the least of the reasons for their continued disunity was that their tendency to view politics ideologically limited the flexibility of their various parties. Thus, refugees concluded that the Mexican system functioned more efficiently precisely because it is not based on ideology. This being so, they agreed, there was no place in the system for the type of politics to which they were accustomed. Therefore, even if the refugees had wished to participate in Mexican politics, and even if the Mexicans had been willing to allow them to do so, it would have been extremely difficult for men reared in the political tradition of Spain to have worked effectively in the Mexican framework.

None of the Spanish political parties have had any ties with the Mexican parties, save the Anarchists, who have worked, on occasion, with the few remaining Mexican Anarchists.[24] There is no European-type Socialist party in Mexico with which Spanish Socialists could identify, and, naturally, there are no equivalents in

[24] A special issue of the Anarchist CNT periodical, *Tierra y Libertad* (October, 1963), was dedicated to the Mexican revolution. It included articles by a few Mexican intellectuals and articles about nearly all the major figures of the revolution. The Anarchists have a special admiration for Ricardo Flores Magón; see chap. 6, above.

Mexico of the Spanish Republican or the regional political parties. Although both the Mexican and Spanish Communist parties operate on the same international directives, the groups are and always have been entirely separate. Spanish Communists, like all the Spanish refugee groups, have avoided intervening in any Mexican issues.[25] Because the Spaniards have not intervened, the Mexicans of all political affiliations, in turn, have allowed the refugees to operate politically, free of Mexican interference.[26] Some of the exiles who have remained active in the Spanish parties, although admitting the futility of such activity, claimed that they would have preferred a greater involvement in Mexican affairs. This proved impossible and they, being "inherently political animals," had to devote their energies to Spanish politics instead.

Variations in Perspectives

General attitudes and opinions about Mexico vary not only according to individual temperaments and personal experiences, but to some extent can be correlated with age, profession, and political view. Older refugees, naturally, are more aware of the similarities in and the differences between the Spanish Republic and the Mexican revolution. Exiles holding strong political ideologies (Socialists, Anarchists, Communists) tend to have less understanding of or respect for the PRI than do the more politically pragmatic Republicans. The better-educated and more widely traveled refugees have usually developed more interest in and sympathy for Mexican cul-

[25] All the Spanish Communists interviewed insisted on this point. Some have friends among the Mexican Communists, but relations have been purely social and usually superficial. Wenceslao Roces, a prominent Communist intellectual, Marxist theorist, and professor in the National University, said that he had always made an effort to identify himself with leftist student movements at the university, but did not otherwise participate in Mexican politics. See chap. 6.

[26] The exiles have made a point of avoiding all acts that might result in Mexican criticism being directed against them. There have been a few exceptions to what the Spaniards regard as their good record: one was the financial failure of the Sociedad Mexicana de Crédito Industrial, managed by Spanish financier José Sacristán Colas in the early 1940's. This was the last private credit agency in Mexico. Another was the arrest of Víctor Rico Galán, accused of conspiracy in 1966. In this case, Spaniards strongly resented the fact that the Mexican press stressed his Spanish origin, for he had come to Mexico as an orphaned baby and had been raised there.

tural differences than have Spaniards who know little of Mexico beyond the capital.

Such factors as age and profession have been especially important as indicators of refugee attitudes and responses on the issue of Mexican nationalism. In general, however, the more the exiles behave as Spaniards, the more intensely they feel Mexican hostility toward them. The more they regard themselves as the victims of Mexican dislike, the more they are apt to laud Spanish characteristics. It is obvious that the expectations the older refugees had for Mexico have been quite different from those of their Spanish-born, but Mexican-educated children. Even in the case of the latter, however, so many have grown up in self-consciously Spanish families and have gone to Spanish schools that they cannot be considered fully incorporated into Mexican life.

Above all, those exiles who most often profess their complete satisfaction with Mexico and the treatment they have received from Mexicans are the few, carefully selected intellectuals invited to the Casa de España in 1938.[27] Because they came at a mature age, they never expected to become "Mexicanized" and asked only to be given the opportunity to live among colleagues in a sympathetic environment where they could work productively. The Mexicans offered this environment, and more. Prominent Spanish intellectuals have enjoyed the cooperation and respect of their Mexican counterparts, the attention of the finest students in the country, and open communications with the outside world, all of which were denied to those intellectuals who remained in Spain.[28]

In terms of age groups, those who have complained most of discrimination in their professional pursuits are the refugees who came with professional experience but were too young to have earned an important reputation. Younger men, who had just com-

[27] Most of these men were either in the oldest age group, or among the older members of the second age group. They were all well established and prominent in their fields.

[28] Those few intellectuals who accepted the invitations of such other countries as Chile and Argentina had similar advantages, but they did not have extensive contact with so many other Spanish refugee intellectuals as did those in Mexico. Intellectuals who stayed in France or went to the United States or Great Britain were offered professional advantages but suffered at first from the language barrier; for the most part, they were employed in American, British, and French universities, teaching the Spanish language and Spanish literature.

pleted their education and training in Spain, frequently found it difficult to find work in the fields for which they had been prepared and had to seek opportunities in other areas. Unlike those of their countrymen who had been invited to Mexico on the basis of their special skills, less prominent intellectuals—doctors, lawyers, engineers, journalists, and so on—competed directly with Mexican nationals and, according to many of them, at times advanced more slowly than less competent nationals.

Both Mexicans and Spaniards expected that the exiles' children would adapt more easily than their parents, and would be integrated into Mexican life. To this day, many parents describe their children—now young men and women in their thirties and forties—as almost entirely Mexicanized, whereas the latter insist nearly as often that, in fact, they feel uncomfortable and somewhat alien in Mexico. The younger refugees, educated at least in part in Mexico, have seldom complained of professional discrimination, but they did stress that they felt discriminated against socially and culturally. Nearly all the Spaniards noted that close social ties were more difficult to establish than professional relations, but the problem has been more acute and complex for the younger than for the older groups. The majority of the former, it would seem, do not fully identify themselves as Mexicans. On the other hand, since their knowledge of Spain is mostly secondhand, they cannot compensate for their discomfort—as do their parents—by feeling more Spanish.

Among working intellectuals, whatever their age, social and professional relations between Spaniards and Mexicans generally are easy and intimate. Spanish intellectuals may praise or criticize Mexicans as a whole, but they tend to exclude Mexican intellectuals from their characterizations. The academicians, scholars, writers, and critics of the emigration seem to view themselves primarily as intellectuals and then as Spanish intellectuals. Therefore, they consider their Mexican counterparts as colleagues, enjoying the same advantages and confronting the same obstacles as they. While they sometimes complain that Mexico is not an intellectually oriented country, that intellectual efforts are poorly remunerated, or even that in some areas there is not complete freedom of opinion, they usually claim to be describing problems common to all serious intellectuals in Mexico, regardless of nationality.

The Second Conquest?

During Cárdenas's presidency, both the cultural and the political elite in Mexico leaned farther to the left than at any other time in Mexican history. Mexican intellectual and political leadership, as a whole, strongly supported the Spanish Republicans, and the Catholics and conservatives who were pro-Franco had little influence in official circles. Rumors of "reds" and radicals supposedly ruling the Spanish Republic did not overly distress the Mexican elite.[29] On the contrary, some pro-Republican Mexican intellectuals were later disappointed to find that the most prominent of their Spanish counterparts were not radicals at all, but political moderates—classical liberals.[30] However, whether or not the Mexican leftists felt that the Republic was revolutionary, or potentially so, they did see a common bond between themselves and the Republican leadership, and they warmly welcomed the exiles—especially the intellectuals.

Once the initial hostility toward the refugees had declined in the public at large, Mexicans began to wonder whether the newcomers could, in fact, become absorbed into the national context. Most approved the fact that the exiles had no interest in Mexican politics and no intention of becoming involved in them. Only those who had hoped to integrate the Spanish refugees into Mexican life were displeased to find that many of the exiles were so involved in Spanish affairs that they seemed to verge on ignoring that they were in Mexico.

The sudden appearance of a new, large, and active Spanish community in Mexico City was somewhat disconcerting to many Mexicans. There were far too many refugees to go unnoticed by the Mexican population, much less to be absorbed into it. Although speaking the language of their host country, the Spanish newcomers could easily be distinguished from native Mexicans by their ac-

[29] All of the Mexicans interviewed who recalled the arrival of the Spanish refugees agreed on this point. As described in chapter 3, the general public was less favorably disposed toward the refugees than were the intellectuals or the political leaders.

[30] Jesús Silva Herzog (Interview May 4, 1967) emphasized that, while the Mexican intellectuals at the time of Cárdenas were considerably more radical than the Spanish Republican intellectual elite, this was not the case in relation to the Republican emigration as a whole.

cents, behavior, and life style. Moreover, so quickly did the
Republican exiles achieve economic success that they seemed increasingly to resemble the older Spanish colony—the *gachupines*.
After 1939, Mexicans were very much aware of the presence of an
expanded, active Spanish population and, it would seem, were more
aware of this group as "Spaniards" than as political refugees from
Spain. "In the solarium of the YMCA, groups of Spaniards show off
their hairy bodies, ignoring by their shouting, the signs which urge
SILENCE to the retiring natives whom they outnumber and with
whom they do not mix. They fill the cafés downtown, wander in
picturesque groups along the Paseo de la Reforma: they exclaim in
high voices, they appear resigned to the irreconcilability of their
character with the silent, gloomy, discreet character of the fellow
countrymen of a Ruiz de Alarcón, who cannot tolerate that of a
prolific Lope, or vice versa."[31]

Spaniards in Mexico: Some Problems

"The history of Mexico is the history of a man seeking his par-
entage," said Octavio Paz, depicting his country as an orphan,
estranged from both its Indian and its Spanish heritage.[32] The
presence of the Spanish Republicans placed the Mexican problem
of identity in an interesting if confusing perspective. Politically,
the Republicans embodied the liberal and democratic principles for
which Mexico initially befriended them. Moreover, they fled their
homeland and came to Mexico in order to seek independence from
an oppressive Spanish government, motives similar to those of the
Mexicans who more than a hundred years previously had revolted
against the Spanish Crown. Nonetheless, in the century since independence the Mexicans had built their own separate national identity, and the Republicans, however liberal they may have been,
were viewed as belonging to the Spanish past. Their race, culture,
and European orientation prevented them from being fully assimilated into the American context and from being fully accepted by
their Mexican hosts.

The refugees' well-intentioned declarations of having come to
Mexico in a "second conquest" which would undo some of the

[31] Salvador Novo, *La vida en México en el periódo presidencial de Lázaro
Cárdenas*, pp. 479–480.
[32] Octavio Paz, *The Labyrinth of Solitude*, p. 20.

wrongs of the first conquest, seemed to reveal an underlying assumption that Mexico was Spain's client state, at least in culture and technology. Mexican nationalists did not want reminders—good or bad—of Spain, nor did they wish to acknowledge the contributions of Spanish culture, for their concern was to realize themselves more fully as Mexicans, and, like Jorge Cuesta, to reiterate their belief "that Mexico has re-created itself in opposition to its past, repudiating the inert, parochial, caste-conscious nature of its Indian and Spanish inheritance. The true Mexican tradition does not carry on the colonial tradition; on the contrary, it denies it."[33]

The early emphasis of the refugee writers upon a liberal Hispanic ideal which would include the Spanish-speaking countries of America and Europe in a linguistic and cultural union, never found much response even among sympathetic Mexicans.[34] The latter welcomed the Republicans in a spirit of brotherhood and recognized them as sharing in a common Hispanic intellectual heritage and value system.[35] Nevertheless, the Mexican commitment had been made simply to aid the Spanish Republic and, afterward, to welcome its political refugees to Mexico. This action demonstrated the Mexican respect for the Spanish Republican ideals, but it did not entail any fundamental reevaluation of Spain. The Mexicans did consider the refugees to represent the "best of Spain," and believed that their presence would be positive in effect and beneficial to Mexico. The "Hispanic tradition," however, had always implied the dominance of Spain, whereas the Mexicans believed in the predominance of America.[36] Finally, the very fact that the Spanish Republic had failed, while the Mexican revolution seemed to have worked and was vital, reassured most Mexicans that they had little to learn from the Spanish experience.

[33] Ibid., p. 161; see also Samuel Ramos, *El perfil del hombre y de la cultura en México*. Ramos also deals with the Mexican search for identity and the ambiguous role of Spain as a factor in that search.

[34] See chap. 7.

[35] See, for example, Alfonso Reyes, "América y los *Cuadernos Americanos*" (*Cuadernos Americanos* 2 [March–April, 1942]: 9–10).

[36] In Sara García Iglesias's novel, *Exilio* (p. 160), a Mexican explains to a Spanish friend that, although the concept of Hispanic unity is an attractive idea, it is unacceptable to Mexicans because, in Mexican opinion, the Spaniards will always treat it with implications of imperialism. "There cannot be Hispanoamericanism so long as Spain claims that it is Hispanism and does not descend from her anachronistic pedestal to listen to the voice of America."

The liberals of the Spanish Republic wished, initially, to convince the Mexicans that the Hispanic heritage represented cultural ties which united Spanish-speaking peoples and that, under a liberal government, Spain would share the same aspirations toward independence and justice as the American republics. Mexicans, however, preferred to stress what differentiated them from their former mother country, rather than to reexamine the ties which had bound them to her in the past. Whether intended sincerely or paternalistically, Republican efforts to revitalize Spanish traditions in Mexico were viewed unsympathetically by most Mexicans.

In Sara García Iglesias's novel, a Mexican student, Héctor, working in a medical laboratory, silently criticizes his eminent Spanish professor: "How could he tell him that since he arrived in Mexico, he had done everything wrong? All of Mendoza's early acts had been breaches of etiquette. Ignorance of his surroundings, the absurd idea of similarity with Spain, had made him make many mistakes. The good faith with which they were made did not make them any less unpardonable." Despite the Spaniards' gratitude for Mexican aid, Hector mused, men like Mendoza viewed "New Spain" as the "younger daughter of the old country [who was] a little backwards and provincial," but whom they were prepared to serve—returning the favor extended to them: "They believed that their names and their achievements were as well known as Mexican figures were unknown and obscure. Nonetheless, many were able to find a helpful environment, where they quickly noticed the differences and had time to adapt. The others, like Mendoza, only found a syrupy courtesy that puzzled them by its inconsistency, tolerant attention, and complete disdain."[37]

Differences of Degree

While disagreements have persisted among those judging the role the exiles have played in Mexican progress, controversy has been least intense over assessments of the worth and importance of the prominent Spanish intellectuals. This is, perhaps, because, before the Civil War, major Mexican scholars had frequently spent a year or more studying in Madrid and had developed close personal ties

---

[37] Ibid., p. 128.

with Spanish students and professors;[38] or, perhaps, because Mexican intellectuals in general had long respected the accomplishments of the Spanish cultural elite, and they felt both personal warmth and scholarly respect for their Spanish counterparts.[39] The two Mexicans who were most involved in inviting the Spanish intellectuals to the Casa de España, Alfonso Reyes and Daniel Cosío Villegas, had both spent considerable time in Spain and were partially motivated by the wish to aid their personal friends. Others, among them Manuel and Antonio Martínez Báez and Jesús Silva Herzog, who had also had some firsthand Spanish experiences, encouraged the Mexican intervention in Spain and the invitation to the refugees.[40] Given the prestige and influence of these persons and the international reputation of some of the Republicans, it is no wonder that, in general, Mexican intellectuals were glad of the opportunity to welcome and work with the Spanish refugees.

Relationships within the universities and in scholarly circles were surprisingly trouble free from the first, and Mexicans who worked with the Spaniards expressed their relief at the extent to which the Republican intellectuals behaved with tact, respect, and understanding.[41] José Gaos, in particular, was praised frequently by Mexican colleagues and students for having aided them in arriving at a greater understanding of their own identity. Octavio Paz writes, "Mexico owes a debt of gratitude to the Spanish philosopher José Gaos, the teacher of the young intelligentsia. . . . Our new

[38] Alfonso Reyes, "América y los *Cuadernos Americanos*," p. 9; Dr. Manuel Martínez Báez described his visits to Spain as having altered the initially unfavorable impressions he had acquired during his schooling in Mexico (Interview, April 27, 1967). He eventually married a Spanish woman and has been one of the Republican exiles' most loyal friends. The Spanish poet José Moreno Villa, in his autobiography, *Vida en claro*, frequently mentions his own friendship in Madrid with Alfonso Reyes and other Mexicans.

[39] The influence of José Ortega y Gasset and Miguel de Unamuno was nearly as strong in Mexico as in Spain itself. The works of the writers and scientists of the so-called Generation of '98, and those of many of the scholars and scientists who followed, were well-known and widely distributed in Mexico. (See Patrick Romanell, *Making of the Mexican Mind: A Study in Recent Mexican Thought*, pp. 144–145; John Phelan, "México y lo mexicano," pp. 309–318.)

[40] Interviews with Dr. Manuel Martínez Báez; Antonio Martínez Báez, April 26, 1967; Jesús Silva Herzog, May 4, 1967.

[41] Interviews, with Daniel Cosío Villegas, Jesús Silva Herzog, Arturo Arnaiz y Freg, and Dr. Manuel Martínez Báez.

teachers do not offer the young a ready-made philosophy, but rather the opportunity and means to create one."[42] It would seem that their Spanish nationality was not an obstacle to cooperation with Mexican professors or in teaching relationships with students. Spanish teachers introduced new techniques and approaches to Mexico's academic life, and, even when the teacher was not particularly inventive, his European training allowed him to provide at least a somewhat different perspective from that of a Mexican professor. In serving as teachers of Mexican university students who would become the nation's elite, the Republican intellectuals became an important presence in Mexico.[43]

No matter how great the Mexican respect for the Spanish intellectuals, however, the Mexicans do not credit the Spaniards with having modified or changed Mexican intellectual thought. Individual scholars readily acknowledge the influence that certain Spaniards in specific fields have had on them, but there is no apparent evidence to support the widespread contention of the exiles that their presence has significantly affected the philosophical and spiritual development of Mexican intellectual thought. Both within and outside of intellectual circles, the Mexicans considered the refugees as valuable assets, but not innovators, of Mexican development. Few Mexicans have failed to stress that however useful Spanish skills may have been, they were only catalysts to the process of growth. Improvements in Mexican education, industry, publishing, medicine, or whatever, did coincide with the application of Spanish efforts in these fields. However, so far as Mexicans were concerned, these were improvements which would have occurred, albeit more slowly, had the Spaniards never appeared.[44]

[42] Paz, *Labyrinth of Solitude*, p. 163.

[43] Mexican acknowledgment and appreciation of the impact of Spanish intellectuals can be found in Antonio Alatorre, *Literature de la emigración republicana*, p. 7; and in Vázquez de Knauth, *Nacionalismo y educación en México*, p. 161.

[44] Mexicans are both amused and annoyed by Spanish pride in listing their contributions, and by their claims to have been responsible for the improved quality of certain teaching facilities and of the publishing industry, or for the expansion of medical services. Even those Mexicans who do express gratitude for the Spanish contributions, and who have admired the work which the refugees have accomplished in exile, give the refugees credit for having been

Further, most Mexicans do not agree that the Spanish Republicans have had to feel inhibited about criticizing aspects of Mexican life. While the Spaniards frequently have complained that Mexicans will not accept criticism, the Mexicans, in turn, just as often have characterized the Spaniards as hypercritical—finding fault not only with Mexicans, but with all groups, including fellow Spanish exiles. Therefore, even though Mexicans frequently acknowledge that there are obstacles to serious political or social criticism in Mexico, they also have concluded that no amount of freedom of speech would be adequate to satisfy the Spaniards' urge to criticize.[45] Since the Mexican press has been totally open to participation of Spanish writers, their opinions have been frequently and widely disseminated.[46] At times, in the Mexican view, the Spaniards have shown themselves almost paranoid in assuming that their opinions are unwanted, and in exaggerating Mexican xenophobia. For example, when the literary periodical *Letras de México* announced that hitherto its major responsibility was to be the representation of Mexican popular opinion, Spanish poet Juan Rejano wrote asking that the periodical not close its columns to foreign contributions. The editor, Ermilo Abreu Gómez, answered with surprise that not only were contributions from all free intellectuals living in Mexico still welcome, but that Spanish intellectuals were regarded with special honor and were not really considered foreigners: "They do not need another express invitation, because this is their home."[47]

---

important catalysts in Mexican development, but not for being the sole innovators in that development. See for example, Daniel Cosío Villegas's comments on the Mexican and Spanish publishing industries, "España contra América en la industria editorial," in his *Extremos de América*, pp. 308–310.

[45] Since the Mexicans in the interview sample were usually sympathetic in their views on the exiles, I can only assume that if most of them judged the Spaniards to be hypercritical in this way, their opinion must be shared by the broader Mexican populace which is less well disposed toward the Spaniards.

[46] Although, at the time the refugees arrived, the Mexican press was for the most part hostile toward them, eventually there were Spanish journalists working on nearly every major newspaper and periodical; for example, *Novedades, Excelsior, El Día, Siempre, Política, Sucesos, Tiempo, Hoy, Revista de Revistas, Revista de América*, and others.

[47] Ermilo Abreu Gómez, "Repuesta a Juan Rejano," *Letras de México*, August 15, 1946, p. 313.

Integration and Involvement

In the eyes of the Mexicans, the real measure of the Spanish Republicans' success lies as much in their degree of identification with Mexico as in their concrete contributions and accomplishments. Naturally, not all Mexicans agree on the quantity or intensity of Spanish integration in Mexico or on the impact of the Spanish Republicans as a whole. While Mexicans have expressed respect, appreciation, and even love for many Spanish refugees as individuals, they have felt less generously toward the structure of the Spanish Republican community. Its numerous political, cultural, and social associations—all serving to remind the exiles of their homeland—are viewed by Mexicans as major deterrents to Spanish involvement in Mexico.

It was expected that, during the first few years of exile, the Spaniards would think of making a temporary home in Mexico, only until they could regain their homeland. Yet the extent to which the refugees maintained their dedication to Spain and to the re-creation of Spanish life in Mexico—even after they lost hope of returning—seemed to constitute a rejection of Mexican hospitality and a slight upon the Mexican citizenship which so many of the refugees adopted. The "jokes" which have been lightly exchanged in the Spanish community, such as, "The refugees still sleep with a packed suitcase under the bed so they will be ready to return to Spain at a moment's notice," have been taken quite seriously by Mexicans in some quarters. It is not that the Mexicans actually believe that the refugees will return to Spain, but they do consider such humor to reflect the exiles' fundamental refusal to accept life in Mexico.[48]

The refugees' initial determination to avoid participation in Mexican politics mollified most of the Mexicans who had at first opposed the Republicans on the grounds of their supposed political

[48] One of the most important indices of absorption and assimilation of Spanish exiles is the choice of a marriage partner. More than three-quarters of the interview sample reported that at least one child or close relative had married a Mexican, but in almost all cases one or more family members had married other Spaniards or the children of other foreigners. From the interview data, it would seem that Spanish men frequently marry Mexican women, but Spanish women rarely choose Mexican men; close to half of the interviewees, in fact, stated that they considered Mexican men to be unsatisfactory as husbands.

radicalism. Decades later, however, some Mexicans began to feel that the political abstention had gone too far. Not only were the refugees themselves not involved in politics, but their Spanish-born, Mexican-educated children rarely participated. Even the young people who were born in Mexico, having full Mexican citizenship, infrequently joined the PRI or took part in any political action which involved only Mexicans.[49] The Spanish refusal to participate in Mexican politics seems to carry with it a lack of real interest in contemporary Mexico. Professionally, it is clear that a large number of refugees have become intensely involved in certain aspects of the Mexican environment. But, in the judgment of a majority of Mexicans, the Spanish Republicans lack a general interest and involvement in Mexican affairs.

Mexican intellectuals and those in the higher professional categories agreed, to an extent, that the political and social system discourages the active involvement of foreign groups. But, they considered this fact to have been used mainly as an excuse for Spanish alienation, and did not accept fully the Spanish view that Mexican nationalism and xenophobia had discouraged the refugees' involvement in Mexican matters. The Mexicans also criticized the Spanish exiles for behaving hypocritically and inconsistently. Since the Spanish Republicans failed in their own political experiment and subsequently refused to take a position or to become involved in Mexico's problems, it does not seem to Mexican observers that the refugees should be so ready to criticize whatever in Mexico displeases them.

A small matter, but one of nearly universal annoyance to Mexicans who know the refugees, is that of language, or, more precisely, accent. Spaniards, including many younger ones, continue, more or less, to speak with the accent of Madrid, Barcelona, Valencia, Seville, or wherever they originated and among some refugee intellectual groups there is a high value placed on the closeness of one's accent to that of scholars in Spain. Among the Mexicans, on the other hand, the Castilian accent implies affectation and snobbish-

---

[49] Informants in the National University, or recent graduates from it, described the Spanish students (sons and daughters of Spanish parents) as participating in student activity primarily in the "international" set—student groups oriented more toward the outside than toward Mexico. The indications are that this situation is changing with the Mexican students' increasing radicalism and anti-government feeling. This will be discussed more fully in the following chapter.

208 EXILES AND CITIZENS

ness, and Mexicans fail to understand why the exiles would want to put so much effort into maintaining it. Not only do Mexicans resent the fact that so many of the exiles have refused to adapt linguistically and that they sound scarcely more Mexican in the 1960's than they did upon their arrival, nearly thirty years ago, but Mexicans also consider the Castilian Spanish ugly and linguistically inferior to the Spanish spoken in Mexico.[50]

The Mexicans recognized the Spanish Republicans as part of a liberal tradition which had flowered in Mexico for generations. It was for this reason, among others, that they welcomed the refugees from the Spanish Civil War. Although the initial distinctions between Republicans and *gachupines*, between political refugees and unsympathetic, financially ambitious immigrants have been clouded over, Mexicans remain proud of the fact that Mexico did accept the exiles and incorporated them into the national life; few Mexicans oppose the government's recognition of the Spanish Republican government instead of Franco, and very few—if any at all—really regret that the Republican refugees are living and will remain in Mexico.

[50] See chap. 8.

10. A WORTHY LEGACY

Even in a world which takes international mobility for granted and which has become accustomed to political exiles, the Spanish Republican emigration to Mexico stands out as unusual. Little of what has been learned about immigrant groups and the problems of adaptation applies more than marginally to the Spanish case. Most of the world's immigrants have been drawn from economically disadvantaged people of working-class or rural backgrounds. In such countries as the United States, Australia, Israel, and Argentina, economic development has been profoundly affected by the presence of large numbers of foreign born, and, in general, as the immigrants gradually have worked their way from low social and economic status to material success, they have sparked reactions of nativism and antiforeign nationalism, particularly among the working and lower middle classes of the host countries.

In most countries which have received large immigrant groups, the newcomers have settled either in rural areas away from the population centers or in separate districts within the major cities. Arriving relatively gradually, the immigrants have been able to find neighborhoods or communities of their own people, in which many aspects of their original culture have been preserved. The existence of these separate communities has been an important factor in easing some of the immediate tensions of acculturation for groups which are likely to be linguistically, culturally, and sometimes racially dissimilar to the native population. On the other hand, physical and cultural separation, coupled with the very low social status accorded to the working-class immigrant population in most countries, has delayed, sometimes permanently, the natural process of cultural and racial mixing. For example, although cultural similarities were strong among the late nineteenth- and early twentieth-century Italian and Spanish immigrants in Latin American countries, new groups remained separate and unaccepted by the native populations for more than a generation.

The Spanish Republican refugees in Mexico contrast dramatically with the more typical groups described above. They arrived in Mexico virtually all at once and were at no time either physically separated or culturally isolated from the mainstream of national life. More important, among the exiles, well-educated, skilled, and professionally trained elements predominated over working-class people. Therefore, they interacted more with the Mexican elite than with the lower classes and, as a result, have played a very different role in national development than immigrants usually play.

In looking for groups with which to compare and contrast the Spanish Republicans, the emigration of European intellectuals to the United States in the 1930's and 1940's at once comes to mind. The impact of these prominent scientists, scholars, and artists has only recently been analyzed,[1] although as a whole their international reputations outweigh those of the Republican Spaniards in

[1] Two recent books on the subject are *Illustrious Immigrants: The Intellectual Migration from Europe, 1930–1941*, by Laura Fermi, and *The Intellectual Migration: Europe and America 1930–1960*, edited by Donald Fleming and Bernard Bailyn.

Mexico.[2] Like the Spanish refugees, the Germans, Austrians, Hungarians, and others fled the rise of fascism in their homelands. Like the Spanish intellectuals, they arrived in such large numbers that their very presence and need for work stimulated the expansion of existing academic, scientific, artistic, and musical facilities in the host country. As the Casa de España was created to accommodate the refugees in Mexico, so too the New School for Social Research and the Museum of Modern Art served as havens for the European refugees in New York.[3] Most important, the intellectuals of Europe had an enormous impact on higher education in America. In the social sciences and in psychoanalysis, in the natural and atomic sciences, and in the arts and music, America became the international center for many fields which had previously been weak or nonexistent there. Furthermore, all the traditional academic areas were revitalized as a result of the influx of new ideas, concepts, and theories, and by the interaction of intellectuals previously oceans apart.

Yet, for all the similarities between the Spaniards in Mexico and other European refugees from fascism in the United States, their experiences differed in important ways. In the first place, in contrast to the Republicans, the other European refugees had not been, as a rule, politically active, or interested in politics, prior to exile.[4] Once in the United States many of them sought to combat Nazi propaganda, but, after the defeat of the Fascist regimes of Europe in the Second World War, whatever tendencies had existed toward involvement in exile politics declined. After the war they could choose whether they would remain in the United States or return to Europe, but they were not faced with the dilemma of the postwar Spanish refugees, whose homeland continued to be dominated by Franco.[5] Although New York was the major refuge for the European intellectuals, they were eventually scattered in academic centers throughout the country, again in contrast to the Spaniards,

---

[2] A substantial number of Spanish intellectuals settled in the United States. Nearly all of them, however, have taught Spanish language and literature in U.S. universities, and their influence has largely been limited to these fields.

[3] Fermi, *Illustrious Immigrants*, pp. 95ff.

[4] Ibid., p. 34.

[5] Among the large number of Jewish intellectuals and eastern Europeans, however, very few chose to return.

who were concentrated increasingly in Mexico City and made that city their cultural center. Finally, the size, the complexity, and the level of development in North American academic and cultural life provided greater flexibility and diversity for European refugees than the Spaniards found in Mexico's less developed, more nationalistic cultural and academic institutions.

To return now to the case at hand: The special nature of the Spanish experience in Mexico was conditioned by four characteristics. First, the Spanish exiles were politically motivated, hence unusually committed, politically, culturally, and emotionally, to their homeland. Unlike previous Spanish emigrés, the Republicans almost certainly would have remained in Spain, had not their country become involved in a disastrous civil war. Moreover, once in Mexico, a satisfactory economic position was not, in and of itself, a sufficient condition for their contentment. Arriving in Mexico en masse and constituting a highly politicized, on the whole well-educated group, the Spaniards were able to maintain a sense of solidarity as a community with a shared experience and mission. And they were able, more successfully than most immigrant groups, to pass on their sentiments and values to their children, thereby making it less likely that the latter would adapt fully to Mexico.

Though they had chosen to live in Mexico and to accept their political defeat, many of the refugees persisted in identifying themselves culturally with Spain. Their cultural ties with Spain, in turn, have served to support the continued existence in exile of active regional entities, Spanish-oriented groups, clubs, and associations of all kinds, and a substantial flow of Spanish periodical and other literature. Most important of all, the effort to preserve ties with Spain resulted in the availability of a fundamentally Spanish primary and secondary education for their sons and daughters.

The second factor which must be considered is the special relationship between Spain and Mexico, a relationship long characterized by tensions and mutual distrust. Because of the colonial domination of Mexico by Spain, the two countries shared a common language and religious background, and a similar culture. Yet the new arrivals frequently overestimated the likenesses in Spain and Mexico and failed to appreciate the fullness and depth of Mexico's special personality. The shared colonial past gave the Mexicans more reason to be wary of the intentions of the exiles than it gave them cause to trust them. The effect of the common language and partly shared culture was to facilitate the early adjustment of Spaniards to their new home and to make it easier at first for Mexicans to work with them. However, the effect of the misconceptions, the historical distrust, and the hostility between the two nations was to make it more difficult later on for the refugees to adapt fully or to be accepted by the Mexicans. Where relations were best, among intellectuals, there were always latent suspicions of Spanish cultural imperialism, or of Mexican supernationalism. Where relations were most sensitive, on issues of Mexican politics, the Spaniards could not possibly act correctly. In choosing the less objectionable of the two courses open to them and not participating at all in Mexican politics, they thereby left themselves open to the charge of indifference.

A third important factor was the unusually high caliber of the Spanish refugees, which qualified them for positions of status and importance in Mexico.[6] Their subsequent prominence in Mexican life inevitably resulted in a degree of resentment and controversy. It was impossible for the Spaniards to rise to positions of importance and influence without arousing Mexican sensitivity to cultural and economic imperialism. The exiles were not always innocent of assuming their own superiority over their hosts, nor were the Mexicans at all times tolerant of the social and cultural characteristics of their guests.

Some relationships, of course, caused fewer problems than others, and, on the whole, those between intellectually and socially prominent Mexicans and Republicans were least difficult. The Mexicans who comprised the small intellectual, social, and economic elite considered themselves the equals, or nearly so, of the Spanish Republican elite—whatever the accomplishments of the latter—and there were no serious problems of competition. Among persons of lower status the situation was distinctly different, and feelings of discomfort and hostility have been common among people, both

[6] Because of the nature of the Mexican and Spanish selection processes, and because of the high cost of reaching Mexico, the proportion of Spanish Republican intellectuals and professionals in Mexico was higher than in the emigration as a whole. See chap. 2.

Mexican and Spanish, whose ambitions have not been fully realized.

Finally, if the Spanish Republicans can be singled out as a somewhat special case among immigrant groups, Mexico is no less distinctive as a host country. Although sometimes welcoming individuals and groups who may have been politically unwelcome in their own country, Mexico's citizenship policies and informal practices have not encouraged foreign settlement. Unlike such countries as the United States or Argentina, Mexico has no long tradition of assimilating immigrants. Although there has always been a trickle of new arrivals, especially from Spain, there was no large-scale immigration at all until the period of the Second World War, and foreign groups today, even when they are second or third generation, are still identifiable and considered separate from the native population, whether they are Spanish-speaking people with whom the Mexicans have much in common or not.[7]

The Mexican government's treatment of the Spanish refugees and its policy with regard to the Spanish Republic have remained consistently favorable. The Spanish exiles, alone of all immigrant groups, were offered virtually automatic citizenship, which most of them accepted. At the same time, Mexican presidents have steadfastly refused to recognize the Franco government in place of the Republic, even though Franco's representatives in Mexico have been performing all the administrative functions of a recognized diplomatic mission.

Thus the Republicans have long enjoyed the position, officially, as Mexico's most welcome foreign group. Outside of official, leftist, and intellectual circles, however, it is doubtful that they have ever been perceived as different or in any way favored over other foreigners. Spaniards, and Mexicans as well, often conclude that the xenophobia and nationalism of which the Republicans have considered themselves the specific victims merely indicate Mexican dislike of all foreigners and the belief that the Republicans are no less foreign than any other outsiders. While it is clear that a non-

---

[7] Where a tradition for absorbing immigrants does exist, one may assume that it is easier for the newcomers to integrate gradually, without having to surrender their own national identity altogether or all at once. In Mexico, the distinction between Mexican and foreigner is quite sharply drawn, and the process of "Mexicanization" almost always takes more than a single generation.

Hispanic group never could have incorporated itself so intimately into Mexican society, it is also clear that hispanic culture alone is not sufficient to overcome strong feelings of nationalism and suspicions of outsiders.

On Spanish History and Mexican Development

The refugees, particularly the more prominent and better trained among them, faced exile with a high level of expectation and idealism. They realized that, as a result both of the large-scale departure of scientists, scholars, and artists from Spain, and of the repressive policies of the Franco regime, intellectual and cultural life in Spain had come to a virtual standstill after the war. Therefore they considered it their most important duty in exile to preserve and perpetuate the highest traditions of their homeland, even though they were politically divorced from it. At the same time, the refugees felt a strong responsibility to work for the benefit of Mexico so that that country would never regret its hospitality. Through their individual accomplishments and their active role in teaching, training, and collaborating with Mexicans, they hoped to enlarge Mexico's importance in the mainstream of international culture. Sincere in their goodwill and commitment, few if any of the exiles saw, initially, a contradiction in working so that the world would remember Republican Spain and in working simultaneously for the growth and development of Mexico. In some Mexican circles, however, these Spanish goals were considered contradictory and even somewhat hypocritical. Among the refugees themselves, over the past few decades, feelings of ineffectiveness and self-doubt have increased. In seeking a balanced appraisal of what was accomplished, we turn first to consider the exiles' importance to Spain, and then to assess their overall impact on Mexico.

A Spaniard writing a history of twentieth-century Spanish intellectual and cultural life would not hesitate to include the exiled intellectuals in that history. In this respect, the Republican refugees did succeed in their goal of advancing and preserving Spanish culture. During the dark days of Franco's dictatorship and censorship, in the 1940's and 1950's, the exiles were virtually the only Spanish voices still heard—speaking, writing, trying to plead the cause of a free Spain through their works. Because of the exiles, Spain was remembered in Europe and in the Americas, but, inside Spain, the exiled Republicans were for all purposes forgotten. From the end of the war, in 1939, until approximately 1959, no news about them could be publicly circulated, and few (if any) of their published works were available. A generation of young Spaniards grew up virtually ignorant of internationally known writers, poets, scientists, and philosophers among their countrymen.

In the 1960's there was a thaw, and communications reopened between the exiled intellectuals of the Republic and some of their former colleagues and students who had remained in Spain. Exile publications were allowed to be circulated more freely, and Spanish journals began to accept articles written by intellectuals living outside the country. The older intellectuals of the Republic gradually were able to rebuild a limited audience in Spain, mainly in liberal and leftist academic circles where opposition to the politics of the Franco regime had been strong. It would be inaccurate, however, to suppose that the Republican exiles have become well known in Spain. Only a few of the most prominent names are familiar, and virtually none of the exiles' published works have been widely read.[8] Moreover, while the older intellectual groups, formed before the Civil War, are still considered part of Spain's cultural community, the same cannot be said for the younger people who received all or part of their education abroad. They remain relatively unknown in the land of their birth.

Perhaps the greatest source of frustration for the exiles has been the fact that, after having devoted so much energy to the Spanish cause, they presently find themselves neither loved nor hated in

---

[8] Describing a luxurious dinner in Madrid to which he had been invited in 1969 by a group of Spanish intellectuals, presumably opposed to the Franco regime, writer Max Aub expressed his dismay at their lack of courage and their ignorance. They avoided political subjects even in friendly conversation; Aub found them not only uninformed and slightly hostile toward the Republican intellectuals in general, but also unaware of major books written by exiles in their own fields, although these books were readily available in Madrid. "Nobody asked me anything about anything," he said ("Una cena en Madrid en 1969," p. 224, *Cuadernos Americanos* 1 [January–February, 1971]:214–232). On the other hand, there have been an increasing number of books and articles published in Spain about prominent Republicans, including two on the influence and works of Max Aub (José Monleón, *El teatro de Max Aub*, and Max Aub, *Teatro* [texts and commentaries]). Writers contributing to both books regret Aub's limited audience in Spain and regret, as well, the overall lack of communication and familiarity between Spanish intellectuals inside Spain and those who left.

their homeland—merely irrelevant. Except for those Spaniards who have traveled in Europe and the Americas and have had personal contact with the exiles, interest in the Republicans has not been great. In Spanish intellectual circles, in the centers of opposition to the Franco regime, and by the public at large, they are considered, at best, well-meaning but ineffectual, incapable of comprehending Spanish events at such a distance.

The refugees have acknowledged their political ineffectiveness. Despite their early determination to play a part in the future of Spain, they found that they could have little or no influence on Spanish reality, for the simple reason that they were not physically present in it. Eventually it became sadly apparent that, in leaving their country, they had surrendered any role they might have played. Had conditions in Spain changed, enabling them to return quickly, they might have been important in their country's subsequent history, but, as the refugees realized, they could not have created the changes themselves. In the final analysis, the functions of the Spanish exiles vis-à-vis their mother country have been limited to upholding the dignity of Spanish culture, welcoming and aiding newer exiles among their countrymen, and lending moral and financial support to people in Spain who have been persecuted by the government.

The impact of the refugees on Mexico has already been discussed at some length. They arrived at a time of cultural productivity and increased national self-awareness, and many of them participated with Mexican intellectuals in a wide variety of scientific and scholarly endeavors which ultimately served to enhance Mexico's prestige and national self-image. Yet, because of the high proportion of Spaniards in intellectual and professional fields, so heavily concentrated in Mexico City, the cultural and social impact of the refugees geographically has been limited. The most fruitful interactions have been among members of the Spanish and Mexican educated elite, and the refugees have always been most comfortable living and working with cosmopolitan, outward-looking, and urban middle-class Mexicans, or with other foreigners.[9]

[9] The refugees often have identified with other non-Mexicans in Mexico, sometimes counting more friends among other foreign residents than among Mexicans. Spaniards who have chosen not to send their children to one of the Spanish *colegios* usually have enrolled them in a French, German, or American

It is instructive, again, to compare the Republican exile experience with that of the European refugees who came to the United States in the 1930's and 1940's and who were so important in the expansion of American universities. Although the Europeans brought skills and perspectives which were often lacking among scholars in the United States, Americans rarely expressed fear that the newcomers would counter "American" culture with German (Austrian, Italian, Hungarian) culture. The scholarly community and the university structure in the United States in the 1940's were too well established and secure for a serious threat to the national culture to arise from the presence of a few hundred foreign intellectuals. In Mexico, that was not the case. Not only were universities, medical facilities, publishing houses, and so on, underdeveloped when the Spaniards arrived, but Mexico was undergoing a period of cultural self-confrontation. Indian and Spanish elements of the Mexican culture were seemingly at war inside all Mexicans, especially writers, artists, and educators. The refugees, rightly or wrongly, were seen as representing the Hispanic traditions which all but the most conservative Mexicans hoped to reduce or wanted to reject.

The exile intellectuals in fact tended to identify themselves with the more modern European trends rather than with the traditional Hispanic orientation which had dominated Mexican universities in the past.[10] Nevertheless, they brought from Spain educational concepts which were more elitist than democratic and which conflicted with the views of a growing number of Mexican students and radical intellectuals. Because the Republicans continued to think of themselves, and to be considered by others, as part of Spanish intellectual life, they could not become fully "Mexicanized." Because the Mexicans were involved in searching and defining their own

---

school. A considerable number of young exiles have married outside Spanish or Mexican circles. It is not uncommon for Spanish exiles to identify themselves as neither Mexican nor Spanish, but "cosmopolitan."

[10] "The National University carries its Spanish past like a ball and chain," and, for years, especially in the 1920's and 1930's, the best minds in Mexico kept their distance from it, according to Rafael Segovia ("Mexican Politics and the University Crisis," in *Political Power in Latin America: Seven Confrontations*, edited by Richard R. Fagen and Wayne A. Cornelius, pp. 306–307). Twentieth-century Spanish intellectuals had already abandoned the traditional Hispanic approach, for the most part. Mexico moved more slowly in this respect.

separate identity, they were not particularly open to the impact of outsiders. Therefore, while Spanish and Mexican intellectuals worked well together, and while the exiles were actively engaged in a wide range of Mexican endeavors, both groups remained relatively nationalistic and resistant to each other's influence.

Although the Spaniards participated in Mexico's educational and cultural life at the highest levels, they were only minimally involved in the long-standing Mexican efforts to spread the national culture to the popular classes. Particularly during the important years—the late 1930's through the 1950's—the primary thrust of Mexican nationalism was more toward the provinces than toward Mexico City, and the most important efforts were being made in the primary and secondary schools rather than in the universities.[11] Mexican nationalists in that period paid tribute to the isolated Indians and the rural villagers, insisting that these people, and not the urbanized middle classes, represented the real Mexico. The *indigenista* movement, which was at its peak when the Spaniards arrived, had the double goal of incorporating the "disinherited" peoples into the national context through rural schools, health facilities, and national services, and, at the same time, teaching all Mexicans about the importance of their cultural roots in the Indian past. Spanish intellectuals could have contributed little to this movement even had they chosen to do so.

Turning from the realm of direct cultural impact to areas of service, Spanish accomplishments loom larger: The exiles did more than merely provide the manpower for expanded medical facilities, they opened new fields of care and research, and they helped make Mexico City into an internationally known medical center. Spanish refugees provided the greater part of the skills and personnel

[11] Rural education was a major goal of the revolution. As early as 1921 José Vasconcelos left his post as head of the National University to become head of Obregon's ministry of education. Believing strongly in the government's responsibility to educate all the people, he led what amounted to a messianic mission aimed at bringing primary education to the rural poor, and at introducing the Mexican Indian to western civilization. Vasconcelos's dream of introducing the literary classics of Europe and the Americas into rural Mexico proved impractical and ineffective, but the goal of expanded rural education persisted. Ultimately more emphasis went to making village schools into centers of useful knowledge. The messianic spirit of education declined somewhat during the 1930's and then revived again dramatically under Cárdenas's presidency in the form of *indigenismo*.

for the Mexican publishing industry, which was created virtually from scratch after their arrival.[12] And if one considers university-level education a service, leaving aside the issue of the direct cultural impact of the Spanish intellectuals, then the importance of the refugee professors cannot be denied. Once the exclusive domain of the upper classes, Mexican universities have expanded over the past thirty years, to offer advanced training for the rapidly burgeoning middle sectors. It is doubtful that the necessary expansion could have been accomplished without the Spanish professors who supplemented the teaching staffs in all the universities and helped to prepare a new generation of Mexican professionals and scholars.

Were the Spanish Republican exiles innovators in these fields, as they often have claimed, or were they merely catalysts, as Mexican critics generally insist? The question posed in these terms defies definitive answer. To state that in some areas Mexico, without the refugees, could not have attained the present level of achievement is not to undermine the crucial role of Mexican dedication, energy, and skills in all aspects of national development. It is probably true that Mexico would have been in the vanguard of Latin America economically, culturally, and artistically, even without the Spanish contributions, and that Mexicans were psychologically, economically, and politically prepared to "take off" in the very areas in which Spanish efforts were most intense. Nevertheless, it was crucially important to Mexican development that, in the moment of need, the highly skilled and motivated Spanish refugees came to share fully in the national effort.

It is paradoxical that, in the political arena, the domain in which the Republican refugees were least involved, their Mexican-born children have begun to make their presence felt. As discussed previously, the Spanish refugees did not try to influence their host country politically. They avoided controversial issues from the time they arrived, mainly because it was made abundantly clear that their political participation was unwelcome, and also because they remained so long oriented toward Spain. Nevertheless, despite their apparent willingness to live on the margin of Mexican politics and controversy, avoiding interference, their impact in these realms may yet prove meaningful.

[12] Mexico and Argentina presently dominate the publishing industry for all of Latin America.

The refugees, after all, have been living and working in Mexico for over thirty years, and they have brought up children and sometimes grandchildren in that country. Politically concerned and active parents raise politically aware children. The parents or grandparents may have been Socialists, Communists, Republicans, or Anarchists in Spain; the children often inherited their parents' ideological perspectives, although they could not share in their parents' Spanish cause. The children who were Spanish-born and Mexican-educated faced a most difficult dilemma, for they were too far removed physically and culturally from Spain to become involved in Spanish affairs, and at the same time, they, like their parents, usually avoided Mexican politics, largely, from fear of Mexican criticism were they to become meaningfully engaged in controversial issues. The result was a widespread apathy, born from their feeling that while they were not Spanish, neither were they "really Mexican."

By the mid-1960's, however, a generation of Mexican-born children of refugees had reached maturity, and with them, the long-accepted norm of avoiding political participation apparently has ended. These young people do not have the problem—or the possibility—of choosing between Mexican and Spanish identity. Mexico is their only fatherland. When and if they wish to become involved in national movements urging social and political changes, they are likely to ally themselves with other Mexican citizens of like mind. There is already evidence that they have begun to do so and that some Mexicans have noticed their new involvement.

During the student demonstrations and strikes of June-October, 1968, which culminated in a bloody confrontation in the Plaza of the Three Cultures at Tlatelolco, the sons and daughters of Spanish refugees were found not only participating in the ranks of the protesters, but serving in leadership positions as well.[13] The young peo-

[13] The crisis began as a result of protests over Mexican preparations to host the expensive Olympic Games, in 1968, and was brought to a head by the determination of authorities to maintain peace and order at all costs before and during the games. Fights between high school students were met by what was widely considered excessive police brutality. Students from the National University and the Polytechnical University and from various leftist groups organized protests, which were supported by substantial numbers of faculty members, workers, and government employees. The government and the police, for their part, occupied the universities and arrested hundreds of people. On October 2, 1968, there was a massive confrontation at the Plaza of the Three Cultures,

ple involved in these demonstrations apparently felt themselves to be as thoroughly Mexican as any of their fellow students, hence justified in protesting the actions of the Mexican government. Moreover, because they were joining with Mexican youth to challenge the government and the Establishment, they were impervious to criticism from older Mexicans who sought to blame Mexico's difficulties on the influence of foreign radicals, and who counted the refugees' children among these. Roberto Blanco Moheno wrote: "The refugees' children, some of whose parents were revolutionaries and who today are almost all wealthy . . . thanks to Cárdenas . . . these 'muchachitos criollitos' will have to understand that they have no cause to 'complete the work of their fathers.' And if they cannot understand this for simple reasons of gratitude, then let them realize that this work does not have to be done in Mexico."[14] There were undoubtedly Spanish parents who, upon reading this, turned to their university-age children with the proverbial See! I told you so! and urged them to cease engaging in such unacceptable behavior.

The Spanish youth, however, were not the only group to be breaking traditional behavior patterns. The Mexicans whom they joined were breaking even stronger traditions. In coming together, refusing to be reconciled by political maneuvers of the government or the PRI, in taking to the streets en masse to confront the nation's leadership, the Mexican students created the largest and most serious urban outburst since the revolution. It was convenient and probably comforting for older officials and critics to see foreign influence in the incidents, and to blame foreign ideas for the explosion. Accusing the youthful protesters of being un-Mexican, alien,

---

which terminated in a bloodbath. A detailed description of the events can be found in *Mexican Democracy: A Critical View*, by Kenneth F. Johnson, pp. 148–164.

[14] Roberto Blanco Moheno, "Lo que hay detras de todo esto," *Siempre*, October 23, 1968, pp. 28–29. In this article Blanco Moheno accused five specific groups of responsibility for the massacre at the Plaza de los Tres Culturas: the CIA, the Communists, certain teachers, certain politicians, and the children of the Spanish refugees. In an earlier *Siempre* article, "Los estudiantes a sus aulas y los gorilas a sus jaulas" (August 14, 1968, pp. 28–29, 70), he blamed foreign Communist agitation for the difficulties. Blanco Moheno's articles on the issue appear together in a book, *Tlatelolco: Historia de una infamia*, and the quotation above is on p. 265. Mexican officials claimed to find many people of foreign origin among the student rebels.

unconcerned with the national well-being, the government and the police released all the force at hand to defeat them. Briefly, Mexico City resembled a battlefield: On one side, in the main, were young people, who had overcome ideological and class differences to stand together; on the other side were the forces of authority and the status quo, with more than enough power to restore order.[15]

In this clash there was no question on which side the Mexico-born youth of the Spanish Republican exiles would be. Nor was there any question of excluding them, on the basis of their emigrant parents, from whatever role they might choose to play. With the violent battle of generations in 1968, young people of Spanish origin made a public debut into Mexican politics. It is inconceivable that the Spanish Republic's children in the future will be a separate entity in Mexican life.

[15] Johnson, *Mexican Democracy*, pp. 149, 162–163.

Appendix

Data for the first six chapters of this study were derived primarily from written materials, including published monographs, contemporary Mexican newspapers and journals, and the many political and cultural publications of the various exile groups. Additional commentary, anecdotal information, and clarification of issues came from conversations with individuals who at one time or another participated in the events and associations most directly affecting the exiles. The material in the last part of the book was based primarily on personal interviews and to a lesser extent upon literature and literary criticism.

Substantial interview data was especially necessary for preparation of the second part, because the printed sources, where they exist, are by themselves inadequate to define changing attitudes and orientations. A few Spanish journals at times have discussed the subject of the refugees' role in Spain, but frequently in tones of sentimentality, nostalgia, and wishful thinking, rather than in concrete terms. It is considerably more difficult to find written discussions of the Spaniards'

views on Mexico; very little has been printed concerning the sentiments of the exiles toward their adopted homeland outside of official
statements, which are always laudatory. Criticism of any kind directed
toward Mexico has not been considered appropriate for public discussion. In exploring and attempting to define the relationships among
exiles and their attitudes toward Spain and Mexico, I relied heavily
on interview information from persons in formal and informal positions of leadership in the Spanish community, as well as on discussions
with a large number of Spanish Republican intellectuals. The former
assisted me in tracing development and changes in the various sectors
of the community, and the latter provided me with helpful interpreta-
tions of the motives of the community as a whole and with descriptions
of their own experiences of exile.

The persons selected for interview were chosen to cover the widest
possible range in age, political affiliation, regional origin, and economic activity.[1] Because of the manner in which the group was selected, however, there are certain characteristics of the interview sample
which would not be typical of a group more randomly selected. For
example, less than half of the persons interviewed in the four older
age groups had gone through the usual channels of emigration to Mexico, which included internment in a French camp, followed by transport to Mexico in one of the ships chartered by the two major refugee-
aid organizations. Among those who were not obliged to reach Mexico
by this unpleasant route, about half managed through their own efforts
and with the aid of friends to acquire the needed funds and the appropriate visas. Most of the others were brought by the Mexican government to the Casa de España or were aided and cared for by the Junta
de Cultura. These refugees seldom were considered for the representative quotas from which the passengers of the refugee ships chartered by
the Republican organizations were chosen. Moreover, these more privi-
leged refugees, once they arrived in Mexico, were not subject to the

---

[1] Before leaving for Mexico I consulted Professor Juan Marichal, chairman of
the Department of Romance Languages at Harvard University, a Spanish refugee who spent many years in Mexico. He referred me to a few of the older
men of prestige in the Republican community, whom I later contacted. Through
Mexican friends I met some of the younger refugees of various political views.
Since many of my early contacts were very cooperative, I was able to snowball
my interview sample in both number and variety. Having been introduced into
the major refugee associations, I attended meetings, talked to people informally,
and arranged for formal interviews. Among those who took an interest in my
project and who were acquainted with broad sectors of the emigration were
Sergio Pich Romero, Enrique Angulo, Alfonso Ayensa, José Puche, Enrique
López Sevilla, Ricardo Mestre, and Jan Somolinos. They were extremely helpful
in introducing me to the various social and political exile circles.

residence requirements initially placed upon refugees on "official" lists. Therefore, they generally came directly to Mexico City without first spending time in the provinces.

Given the above-average socioeconomic position of the overall interview sample, the group was more heavily weighted toward political moderates than the emigration as a whole. On the other hand, because so many had held positions of relative importance during the Republic, those in the group interviewed were more reluctant and slow than the emigrants in general to give up their political affiliations and activities in exile. The group chosen for this study not only was higher than the norm in professional-academic level, but also was much higher in terms of the level of activity it represented in the Spanish Republican community.

In most cases, I asked that the informants themselves generalize about the exile community, where they could, and, although I accepted their analyses with reservations, I found them useful as guides to further investigation. The extent of the sophistication of the sample was indicated by the fact that the majority were university trained and many had lived or studied in countries other than Spain and Mexico. Cosmopolitan in outlook and international in the scope of their interests, many could view their own situation in a broader perspective than that which might be expected of refugees with more limited experience. The interviewees, especially the intellectuals, were not in any sense naïve. The questions put to them were questions they had often debated among themselves, and therefore their answers tended to be analytical as well as informational.

The Republicans' official position has been that they are well-adjusted to life in Mexico, and, in fact, have become nearly "Mexicanized," that their children have become totally Mexicanized, that there is no serious criticism among Spaniards of Mexico's political or social structure, and that the exiles have remained uniformly hostile toward the Franco regime. For most refugees these statements coincide, at least in part, with their own feelings, but there were few of those interviewed who agreed fully with so uncritical a posture. The more complete interviews offered a wide range of opinion and diverged from more than they converged with the official position. Sometimes interviews began with "standard" descriptions of contentment and harmony but concluded with statements highly critical of both Spaniards and Mexicans, frequently bitter in tone.

Age proved the most important factor in determining the refugees' attitudes toward Mexico, Spain, and their own situation. Old men and young children became refugees at the same moment but thereafter faced entirely different problems of adjustment.

The total emigration may be divided into three general divisions by age, each division representing a different set of experiences and situations. In the first group are the older refugees, those who attracted most of the attention at the time of their arrival. Among them were the intellectuals, the professionally skilled men and women, and the military officers who had been the backbone of the Republic. Many of those who came to Mexico were really too advanced in age to adapt professionally or psychologically to the new environment, but the majority were able and anxious to work in their particular fields or areas of competence. In the second group were the younger people, who came to Mexico before they were established professionally, and who were obliged in many cases to interrupt their formal education because of the war and exile. While a number of those in the first group were individuals whose work was known and valued in Mexico before they came, the younger people in almost all cases had to start afresh. Fully or only partly trained for a career in Spain, they had to turn their training to account in Mexico in a far more competitive situation than that encountered by the well-established members of the older group.[2] The third group consisted of the children of the refugees, who, at the time of their parents' arrival, ranged from infancy to school age. Only a few in this group could remember Spain at all, and the recollections of those who could were, at best, vague. By and large, this group learned about the Spanish Republic and the Civil War through family stories and schoolbooks.

In all, sixty-six persons in the sample were interviewed formally.[3] The length, depth, and extensiveness of the interviews varied considerably, depending upon the willingness of the refugee to answer the questions posed and on the time available for conversation.

In terms of age, political affiliation, professional pursuits, and social and regional background, the distribution of the interviewees was as follows: Thirty-five of those interviewed were in the first age division, sixteen in the second, and fifteen in the third. There were fourteen

[2] There seems to be an uneven distribution of ages among the refugees, in that those of the age which I classified as the second group are underrepresented in exile. Apparently many young men serving in the Republican military could not leave when most of the others did, before the war. Younger people, moreover, probably felt that, because of their youth and inexperience, they would not be held as enemies of the Franco state, and, therefore, it was not worth making the apparent sacrifice of exile. On the other hand, young people who were politically active were frequently arrested as soon as possible by Franco's armies and hence were unable to escape.

[3] The interviews referred to here do not include the several conversations held with refugees regarding specific information about a political, social, or cultural group or association.

Catalans in the sample, seven Basques, five Andalusians, and five from the Valencia region. The remainder claimed places of origin sprinkled throughout other provinces, but, for the most part, they had lived in, if they had not been born in, Madrid. Except for the Catalans and Basques, the vast majority of the interviewees had spent a year or more living in the capital. By profession, fourteen persons were working in literature or the arts (including architecture), five in the humanities, ten in the social sciences, eight in science and medicine, six in the professions (law, engineering), twelve in business or commerce, and nine in the publishing industry or journalism. A large number of those who found employment in business, commerce, or some technical occupation also devoted considerable spare time to writing and literature, and counted most of their friends among the "intellectuals." For the most part, the refugees not accounted for above were retired, were housewives, or were too young to have committed themselves professionally. Of those who identified themselves politically, there were twelve Republicans, ten Socialists (two of whom in exile had split from the main party to form a separate faction), five Communists, five Anarchists, three members of regional Catalonian groups, and five persons who claimed their only political affiliation to have been their membership in the Juventud Socialista Unificado (JSU), an association of Socialist, Communist, and radical youth during the Civil War. Even among those who stated their political affiliation, the majority had long since ceased to be politically active. Many of the refugees claimed to have had no political affiliation, although three of them did profess loyalty to Negrín, and three more were alleged by their colleagues to have been members of the Communist party in Spain.

For the Mexicans, as for the Spaniards, positive or negative assessments of relations between the two groups have been influenced by the factors of profession, age, and the amount of interaction and experience which has occurred. Mexican intellectuals in general, and older intellectuals in particular, tended to judge the exiles most generously, while others, regardless of age or profession, whose prestige and security were less strong, resented more than they respected the contributions of this large group of foreigners. Those who had not had extensive contact with the Spanish Republicans tended to judge them in line with their attitudes toward Spaniards in general, and these attitudes were seldom very favorable.

The Mexican interview sample was weighted on the side of persons friendly and sympathetic to the Spanish Republicans, and also was heavily weighted in the older age groups. Only twelve interviews were actually completed. This was virtually unavoidable because Mexicans on the whole no longer have a great deal of knowledge of or interest in the Spanish refugees. It was possible to hold numerous conversations with a wide variety of Mexicans, but most of these conversations went only as far as the exchange of impressions and generalizations regarding characteristics alleged to be common among Spanish exiles. The persons who were best informed about the refugees, and who could discuss their impact on Mexican life and their particular problems in the Mexican context, were usually the persons who had been involved in bringing them to Mexico in the first place, or who had worked closely with them since that time. Because they were sympathetic, they retained their interest and were the most willing to discuss the matter in an interview. Younger Mexicans, who had only a few friends among the exiles, or who had known them solely in their professional or academic capacities, were understandably hesitant to generalize about the larger Spanish Republican community. Individuals who were unfriendly toward the refugees, were, on the whole, unwilling to discuss the reasons for their feelings.

In the case of both the Spanish and the Mexican interview sample, written questionnaires were given to the interviewees. These questionnaires were intended primarily as conversational guides. Little attempt was made to restrict the interview to specific questions posed in writing, although as often as possible all of these questions were discussed.

LIST OF INTERVIEWEES

Spanish Republican Exiles in Mexico in 1966–1967

Alvaro de Albornoz
Javier Aleja
Manuel Andújar
Enrique Angulo
Manuel Aragonés
Max Aub
Alfonso Ayensa
Pere Bosch Gimpera
Blas Cabrera Sánchez
Félix Candela
Mada Carreña
Anselmo Carretero
María Chopitea
Juan Comas
Alvaro Custodio
José Luis de la Loma

Joaquín D'Harcourt
Angel Díaz
Rafael Fernández T.
Luis Fumagallo
José Gaos
Julio García Coll
Bernardo Giner de los Ríos
Francisco Giner de los Ríos
Manolo Giner de los Ríos
Francisco Giral
Alfonso Gorostiza
Mariano Granados
Vicente Guarner V.
Rodolfo Halffter
Enrique López Sevilla
Francisco Lurueña

Guillermo Marín
Fernanda Masip
Lola Masip de García
Ricardo and Silvia Mestre
José Miranda
Fidel Miró
Juan Montserrat
Eliseo Muñoz
Ernesto Navarro
Simon Otaola
Isabel Palencia
Angel Palerm
Sergio Pich Romero
H. Plaja
José Puche Alvarez
José Puche Planas
Máximo Regueiro

Juan Rejano
Enrique de Ribas
Luis Rius
Wenceslao Roces
Antonio Rodríguez Luna
Víctor Salazar
Manuel Sánchez Sarto
Adolfo Sánchez Vásquez
Antonio María Sbert
Jacinto Segovia
Rafael Segovia
Jan Somolinos
Germán Somolinos d'Ardois
Arturo Souto
Daniel Tapia
Ignacio Villarias
Ramón Xirau

Mexican Informants 1966–1967

Manuel Alvarado
Arturo Arnaiz y Freg
Raúl Avila
Daniel Cosío Villegas
Adrián Lajous
Antonio Martínez Báez
Manuel Martínez Báez

Luis Muro Arias
Mario Ojeda Gómez
Jesús Silva Herzog
Victor Urquidi
Eduardo Villaseñor
Arminda Yáñez Perez

Other Interviewees

José Luis Aranguren
Victoria Kent
Juan Linz

Vicente Llorens Castillo
Juan Marichal

Works Cited

Manuscripts

Comité Técnico de Ayuda a los Españoles en México. "Spanish Professors and Artists in the Emigration." Mexico, n.d.

Fería Mexicana del Libro, VIII. "España en América: La aportación de la emigración republicana española a la cultura continental." Mexico: November 20 to December 15, 1960. (Bibliography.)

Kenny, Michael. "The Integration of Spanish Expatriates in Ibero-America and Their Influence on Their Communities of Origin."

Prieto, Indalecio, and Juan Negrín. "Epistolario." Correspondence between Indalecio Prieto and Juan Negrín, May–July, 1939. Paris, 1939.

Taylor, Philip B. "The Spanish Intellectuals in Mexico, 1936–1955."

Books, Articles, Pamphlets

Abreu Gómez, Ermilo. "Repuesta a Juan Rejano." *Letras de México,* August 15, 1946, p. 313.

Acción Republicana Española. *Homenaje a don José Giral.* (Pamphlet.) Mexico City, 1963.

"Acercamiento al problema indígena." Editorial. *Romance,* April 15, 1940, p. 7.

Agrupación Europeista de México. "Plan de trabajo, comisiones y ponencias." Mexico City, November, 1965.

Alatorre, Antonio. *Literatura de la emigración republicana española en México.* (Pamphlet.) Reprinted from *Comparative Literature: Proceedings of the ICCA Congress in Chapel Hill, North Carolina.* Mexico City: El Colegio de México, 1959.

Albornoz, Alvaro de. *El gobierno de la República española en el destierro a los gobiernos y a la opinión pública de todos los paises democráticos.* (Pamphlet.) Mexico City: Izquierda Republicana en México, Ateneo Salmerón, 1950.

⸻. *Izquierda Republicana en la Junta Española de Liberación.* Speech given on February 24, 1944. (Pamphlet.) Mexico City: Izquierda Republicana en México, Ateneo Salmerón, 1944.

Alvarez del Vayo, Julio. *Freedom's Battle.* Translated by Eileen E. Brooke. New York: Viking Press, 1940.

A.nieva, Celso. "Los fusiles de México." Poem, in *El paraíso incendido, 1936–1939.* (A collection of Amieva's poems, edited by Alejandro Finesterre.) Mexico City: Ecuador 0°0'0", 1967.

Amo, Julián, and Charmion Shelby. *La obra impresa de los intelectuales españoles en América, 1936–1945.* Stanford, California: Hispanic Foundation of the Library of Congress, 1950.

Aranguren, José Luis L. *Crítica y meditación.* Madrid: Taurus Ediciones, 1955.

Aub, Max. "Una cena en Madrid en 1969." *Cuadernos Americanos* año 7 (January–February, 1971):214–232.

⸻. "Una nueva generación." *Sala de Espera* 21 (June, 1950):12–15.

⸻. *Teatro.* Madrid: Ediciones Taurus #15, 1971.

⸻. *La verdadera historia de Francisco Franco y otros cuentos.* Mexico City: Libro-Mex, 1960.

Ayala, Francisco. *El escritor en la sociedad de masas.* Mexico City: Obregón, 1956.

Azaña, Manuel. *Obras completas.* Vol. I. Edited by Juan Marichal. Mexico City: Ediciones Oasis, 1966.

Blanco Moheno, Roberto. "Los estudiantes a sus aulas y los gorilas a sus jaulas." *Siempre,* August 14, 1968, pp. 28–29, 70.

⸻. "Lo que hay detras de todo esto." *Siempre,* October 23, 1968, pp. 28–29.

———. *Tlatelolco: Historia de una infamia*. Mexico City: Editorial Diana, 1969.

Bosch Gimpera, Pere. "Lecciones de una larga experiencia histórica." *Diálogos de Las Españas* 4 and 5 (October, 1963):3–5.

Brandenberg, Frank. *The Making of Modern Mexico*. Englewood Cliffs, N.J.: Prentice-Hall, 1964.

Brenan, Gerald. *The Spanish Labyrinth: An Account of the Social and Political Background of the Civil War*. Cambridge: University Press, 1943.

Camino Galicia, León Felipe. *Antología y homenaje*. Mexico City: Alejandro Finesterre, 1966.

———. *El español del éxodo y del llanto, doctrina, elegías y canciones*. Mexico City: La Casa de España, 1939.

———. *¿Que se hizo el Rey Don Juan?* Mexico City: Ecuador, 1962.

Carmona Nenclares, F. "Hispanismo e hispanidad." *Cuadernos Americanos* año 1 (May–June, 1942): 43–55.

Carr, Raymond. *Spain, 1808–1939*. Oxford: Clarendon Press, 1966.

Carretero y Jiménez, Anselmo. *Notas sobre "Las Españas."* (Pamphlet.) Mexico City, March, 1967.

———. "La personalidad de Castilla en el conjunto de los pueblos hispánicos." In *Diálogo sobre "Las Españas."* Mexico City: Ediciones de Las Españas, 1960.

Cattell, David T. *Communism and the Spanish Civil War*. University of California Publications in International Relations, vol. IV. Berkeley, 1955.

———. *Soviet Diplomacy and the Spanish Civil War*. University of California Publications in International Relations, vol. V. Berkeley, 1957.

Chase, Gilbert. "The Artist." In *Continuity and Change in Latin America*, edited by John J. Johnson, pp. 101–135. Stanford: Stanford University Press, 1964.

Chomsky, Noam. *American Power and the New Mandarins*. New York: Random House, 1967.

Climent, Juan Bautista. *El Pacto para restaurar la República española*. Mexico City: Ediciones de América, 1944.

Cosío Villegas, Daniel. *Extremos de América*. Mexico City: Tezontle, 1949.

Cultural Creations of the Comité Técnico de Ayuda a los Españoles en México [Technical Committee of Help to Spaniards in Mexico]. (Pamphlet.) Mexico City, 1940.

"Doce de octubre, fiesta del Nuevo Mundo." Editorial. *España Peregrina*, October 12, 1940, pp. 51–54.

Domingo, Marcelino. *El mundo ante España: México ejemplo.* Paris: La Technique du livre, 1938.

Everyman's United Nations: A Basic History of the Organization, 1945–1964. New York: United Nations Department of Public Information, 1964.

Fabela, Isidro. *Cartas al Presidente Cárdenas.* Mexico City, 1947.

Fermi, Laura. *Illustrious Immigrants: The Intellectual Migration from Europe, 1930–1941.* Chicago: University of Chicago Press, 1968.

Fleming, Donald, and Bernard Bailyn, eds. *The Intellectual Migration: Europe and America, 1930–1960.* Cambridge, Mass.: Harvard University Press, 1969.

Foix, Pere. *Cárdenas.* 2d ed. Mexico City: Editora Latino-Americana, 1956.

Fondo de Cultura Económica. *Catálogo general, 1934–1964.* Mexico City.

Fondo de Cultura Económica. *Catálogo general, 1955.* Mexico City.

Foulkes, Vera. *Los "Niños de Morelia" y la escuela "España-México": Consideraciones analíticas sobre un experimento social.* Mexico City: Universidad Nacional Autónoma de México, facultad de derecho y ciencias sociales, 1953.

Frente Universitario Español. *Coincidencia de propósitos.* (Pamphlet.) Mexico City: Ateneo Español de México, 1956.

Fresco, Mauricio. *La emigración republicana española: Una victoria de México.* Mexico City: Editores Asociadas, 1950.

Gaos, José. "La adaptación de un español a la sociedad hispanoamericana." *Revista de Occidente* 4 (May, 1966):168–178.

———. *Confesiones profesionales.* Mexico City: Fondo de Cultura Económica, Tezontle, 1958.

———. *En torno a la filosofía mexicana.* Vol. II. Mexico City: Porrua y Obregón, 1953.

García Iglesias, Sara. *Exilio.* Letras mexicanas #33. Mexico City: Fondo de Cultura Económica, 1957.

Garfias, Pedro. "Entre México y España." Poem, in *España Peregrina* 1 (June, 1940):230.

Giner de los Ríos, Francisco. "España viva." Poem, in *España Peregrina* 1 (August, 1940):7–8.

Granados, Mariano. *Una solución española. Informe adoptado por la Asamblea General de Unión Republicano celebrada en México el 12 de octubre de 1947.* (Pamphlet.) Mexico City, 1947.

Hills, George. *Franco: The Man and His Nation.* New York: Macmillan, 1967.

Hobsbawm, E. J. *Primitive Rebels: Studies in Forms of Social Move-*

ments in the Nineteenth and Twentieth Centuries. New York: W. W. Norton, 1959.

Iduarte, Andrés. "Cortes y Cuauhtémoc: Hispanismo y indigenismo." In *Pláticas hispanoamericanas,* pp. 9–18. Mexico City: Fondo de Cultura Económica, Tezontle, 1951.

Jackson, Gabriel. *The Spanish Republic and the Civil War, 1931–1939.* Princeton: Princeton University Press, 1965.

Johnson, Kenneth F. *Mexican Democracy: A Critical View.* Boston: Allyn and Bacon, 1971.

Junco, Alfonso. *El difícil paraíso.* Mexico City: Editorial Helios, 1940.

Junta de Auxilio a los Refugiados en el Exilio (JARE). *Acuerdo adoptado por la Diputación Permanente de los Cortes, reunida en Paris el 31 de julio de 1939.* (Pamphlet.) Mexico City, December, 1940.

La Junta Española de Liberación ante la Conferencia de San Francisco de California. Statement by founders (pamphlet). Mexico City, April, 1945.

Kenny, Michael. "Twentieth Century Spanish Expatriates in Mexico: An Urban Subculture." *Anthropological Quarterly* 35 (October, 1962):169–180.

Larrea, Juan. "Nuestra alba de oro." *Cuadernos Americanos* 1 (January–February, 1942):51–72.

Linz, Juan J. "The Party System of Spain, Past and Future." In *Party Systems and Voter Alignments: Cross National Perspectives,* edited by Seymour M. Lipset and Stein Rokkan, pp. 197–282. New York: The Free Press, 1967.

Llorens Castillo, Vicente. "El retorno del desterrado." *Cuadernos Americanos* 40 (July–August, 1948):216–233.

Madariaga, Salvador de. *Spain: A Modern History.* New York: Frederick A. Praeger, 1958.

Marichal, Juan. "Manuel Azaña and the Generation of 1914." *Ibérica* 9 (March, 1961):3–7.

———. *El nuevo pensamiento político español.* Mexico City: Alejandro Finesterre, 1966.

Marra-López, José R. *Narrativa española fuera de España 1939–1961.* Madrid: Colección Guadarrama de Crítica y Ensayo #39, 1963.

Martínez, Carlos. *Crónica de una emigración: la de los Republicanos españoles en 1939.* Mexico City: Libro-Mex, 1959.

Martínez Barrio, Diego. *Informe político en la asamblea celebrada por Unión Republicana en el exilio.* (Pamphlet.) Mexico City, June 18, 1944.

Martínez Legorreta, Omar. *Actuación de México en la Liga de las Naciones: El caso de España.* Mexico City: Universidad Nacional Autónoma de México, Escuela Nacional de Ciencias Políticas y Sociales, 1962.

Masip, Paulino. *Cartas a un emigrado español.* (Paperback.) Mexico City: Publicaciones de la Junta de Cultura Española, June, 1939.

———. *El diario de Hamlet García.* Mexico City: Imp. M. L. Sánchez, 1944.

Medina Echavarría, José. "Cuerpo de destino." *Cuadernos Americanos* 1 (January–February, 1942):38–42.

———. *Responsabilidad de la inteligencia: Estudios sobre nuestro tiempo.* Mexico City: Fondo de Cultura Económica, 1943.

México: 50 años de revolución. Vol. IV. *La cultura.* Mexico City: Fondo de Cultura Económica, 1962.

Michaels, Albert L. "El nacionalismo conservador mexicano desde la Revolución hasta 1940." *Historia Mexicana* 16, no. 2 (October–December, 1966):213–238.

Miranda, José. "La Casa de España." *Historia Mexicana* 18, no. 1 (July–September, 1968):1–10.

Miró, Fidel. "Las prácticas totalitarias y el dogmatismo significan la muerte." *Comunidad Ibérica* 4 (May–August, 1966).

———. *¿Y España cuando? El fracaso político de una emigración.* Mexico City: Libro-Mex, 1959.

Mistral, Silvia. *Exodo: Diario de una refugiada española.* Mexico City: Ediciones Minerva, 1940.

Monleón, José. *El teatro de Max Aub.* Cuadernos Taurus #104. Madrid: Taurus Ediciones, 1971.

Mora, Constancia de la. *In Place of Splendor: The Autobiography of a Spanish Woman.* New York: Harcourt, Brace, 1939.

Moreno Villa, José. *Cornucopia de México.* Mexico City: Fondo de Cultura Económica, 1940.

———. "De la tierra y de la patria." *Romance,* March 1, 1940, p. 3.

———. "Nos trajeron las ondas." Poem, in *Cuadernos Americanos* 17 (September–October, 1944): 194.

———. *Vida en claro: Autobiografía de José Moreno Villa.* Mexico City: El Colegio de México, 1944.

———. *Voz en vuelo a su cuña.* Mexico City: Ecuador 0°0'0", November, 1961.

Movimiento Español 1959: Hojas de información. (Pamphlet.) Mexico City, January, 1961.

Muñoz, Máximo. *Grandeza y tragedia de la emigración republicana española.* Speech delivered February 22, 1958. (Pamphlet.) Printed by the Ateneo Español de México.

Negrín López, Juan. *Un discurso.* (Pamphlet.) Mexico City: Ediciones Unión Democrática española, 1942.

Novo, Salvador. *La vida en México en el periódo presidencial de Lázaro Cárdenas.* Mexico City: Empresas Editoriales, 1964.

Otaola, Simón. *El cortejo.* Mexico City: Joaquín Mortiz, 1963.

————. *La librería de Arana.* Mexico City: Colección Aquelarre, 1952.

Ortega y Gasset, José. *Rectificación de la república.* Madrid: Revista de Occidente, 1931.

Orwell, George. *Homage to Catalonia.* Boston: Beacon Press, 1952.

Palavicini, Félix Fulgencio. *México: Historia de su evolución constructiva.* 4 vols. Mexico City: Distribuidora Editorial "Libro S. de R.L.," 1945.

Palencia, Ceferino de. *México inspirador.* Mexico City: Libro-Mex, 1962.

Palencia, Isabel O. de. *Smouldering Freedom: The Story of the Spanish Republicans in Exile.* London: Victor Gollancz, 1946.

Payne, Stanley G. *Franco's Spain.* New York: Thomas Y. Crowell, 1967.

Paz, Octavio. *The Labyrinth of Solitude.* Translated by Lysander Kemp. New York: Grove Press, 1961.

Phelan, John Leddy. "México y lo mexicano." *Hispanic American Historical Review* 36 (August, 1956):309–318.

Por un movimiento de reconstrucción nacional. (Pamphlet.) Mexico City: Las Españas, October, 1949.

"El primer congreso indigenista americano." *España Peregrina,* April, 1940, p. 20.

El problema de España ante el mundo internacional, resolución aprobada por la Asamblea General de las Naciones Unidas, texto y discusión de la misma. (Pamphlet.) Mexico City: República Española, 1946.

Quintanilla, Patricio. "Comité Técnico de Ayuda a los Españoles en México, Memoria." N.d., n.p. [Official records of the SERE.]

Ramos, Samuel. *El perfil del hombre y de la cultura en México.* Mexico City: Universidad Nacional Autónoma de México, 1963.

Ramos Oliveira, Antonio. *Historia de España.* 3 vols. Mexico City: Companía General de Ediciones, 1952.

Recasens Siches, Luis. "Intelectuales españoles en México." *Epoca* 2 (June, 1965):26–27.

Rejano, Juan. "Deberes de los intelectuales españoles en la hora actual." *Nuestro Tiempo,* September 1, 1950, pp. 16–24.

————. *La esfinge mestiza: Crónica menor de México.* Mexico City: Editorial Leyenda, 1945.

Relaciones internacionales de México, 1935–1956 a través de los mensajes presidenciales. Secretaría de Relaciones Exteriores, Mexico, 1957.

Reyes, Alfonso. "América y los *Cuadernos Americanos.*" *Cuadernos Americanos* 2 (March–April, 1942):7–10.

———. *Marginalia.* 1st ser., 1946–1951. Mexico City: Tezontle, 1952.

Ridruejo, Dionisio. *Escrito en España.* Buenos Aires: Editorial Losada, 1962.

Rivas-Cherif, Cipriano de. *Retrato de un desconocido: Vida de Manuel Azaña.* Mexico City: Ediciones Oasis, 1961.

Roces, Wenceslao. *La cultura de nuestro tiempo.* Mexico City: Ediciones España Popular, 1948.

Romanell, Patrick. *Making of the Mexican Mind: A Study in Recent Mexican Thought.* Lincoln: University of Nebraska Press, 1952.

Salcedo, Ovidio. *Posiciones y orientaciones de la Juventudes Socialistas.* Lecture delivered February 19, 1944 at a meeting of Juventud Socialista. (Pamphlet.) Mexico City, 1944.

Segovia, Rafael. "Mexican Politics and the University Crisis." In *Political Power in Latin America: Seven Confrontations,* edited by Richard R. Fagen and Wayne A. Cornelius, pp. 306–315. Englewood Cliffs, N.J.: Prentice-Hall, 1970.

Silva Herzog, Jesús. "Veinte años al servicio del mundo nuevo." *Cuadernos Americanos* 119 (November–December, 1961): 7–18.

Smith, Lois Elwyn. *Mexico and the Spanish Republicans.* Berkeley: University of California Press, 1955.

"Sobre la unidad espiritual de los pueblos de América." *Romance,* March 15, 1940, p. 7.

Sommers, Joseph. *After the Storm: Landmarks of the Modern Mexican Novel.* Albuquerque: University of New Mexico Press, 1968.

Somolinos d'Ardois, Germán. *25 años de medicina española en México.* (Pamphlet.) Mexico City: Ateneo Español de México, 1966.

Souto Alabarce, Arturo. "Nueva poesía española en México." *Ideas de México* Part 2, vol. 7 (September–December, 1954):31–37.

Spanish Junta of Liberation. *Press Conference.* (Pamphlet.) Mexico City, March 3, 1945.

Tapia, Daniel. "La generación del '29 y los heterodoxos en el exilio." *Las Españas* 2d ser., 26–28 (July, 1956):42.

———. "La otra mujer de Lot." *Las Españas* 3 (July, 1948):11.

Taylor, Philip B. "Myth and Reality: How Red Were the Spanish 'Reds'?" *Michigan Alumnus Quarterly Review* 62 (February, 1956): 117–125.

Thomas, Hugh. *The Spanish Civil War.* New York: Harper & Row, 1961.

"Unión de intelectuales españoles en México, constitución, mensaje de saludo a todos los intelectuales españoles antifranquistas de España." In *Las Españas* 2 (September, 1947):12.

Unión de Profesores Universitarios Españoles Emigrados. *Libro de la primera reunión de Profesores Universitarios*, Report of meeting. (Pamphlet.) Havana, 1944.

Vázquez de Knauth, Josefina. *Nacionalismo y educación en México*. Mexico City: El Colegio de México, 1970.

Vernant, Jacques. *The Refugees in the Post-War World*. New Haven: Yale University Press, 1953.

Vicéns, Juan. "La bibliografía hispánica." *España Peregrina* 1 (August, 1940):17–21.

Whetten, Nathan L. *Rural Mexico*. Chicago: University of Chicago Press, 1948.

Whitaker, Arthur. *Spain and the Defense of the West*. Council on Foreign Relations. New York: Harper & Row, 1961.

Witney, Fred. *Labor Policy and Practices in Spain: A Study of Employer-Employee Relations under the Franco Regime*. New York: Frederick A. Praeger, 1965.

Newspapers, Periodicals, Bulletins

Adelante (Socialist), Mexico City, 1943–1959.

Ateneo Español de México (bulletin), 1963–1964.

Ateneo Español de México: Memoria (annual reports), Mexico City, 1950–1966.

Ayuda: Boletín del Comité de Ayuda al Pueblo Español, Mexico City, 1966.

Boletín, Corporación de Antiguos Alumnos de la "Institución Libre de Enseñanza," del "Instituto-Escuela" y de la "Residencia de Estudiantes" de Madrid, Mexico City, 1966–1967.

Boletín al Servicio de la Emigración Española (Negrinist), Mexico City, 1939–1940.

Boletín de Información, Unión de Intelectuales Españoles, Mexico City, 1956–1957.

Boletín Informativo de la Unión de Profesores Universitarias Españoles en el Extranjero, Mexico City, 1943–1944.

Comunidad Ibérica, Mexico City, 1962–1966.

Cuadernos Americanos, Mexico City, 1942–1962.

Diálogos de "Las Españas," Mexico City, 1956–1966.

España Peregrina, Mexico City, 1940–1941.

España Popular (Communist), Mexico City, 1940, 1954–1956.

Estaciones: Revista Literaria de México, Mexico City, 1956–1960.

Excelsior (Mexico City daily), Mexico City, 1939–1944.

El Hijo Pródigo: Revista Literaria, Mexico City, 1943–1946.

Ideas de México, Mexico City, 1953–1956.

Intercontinentes: Organo de la Agrupación Europeista de México, Mexico City, 1966–1967.

Las Españas: Revista Literaria, Mexico City, 1946–1954.

Litoral, Cuadernos de Poesía, Mexico City, 1940–1941, 1944.

Nuestro Tiempo: Revista Española de Cultura, Mexico City, 1949–1953.

El Popular (Mexican labor daily), Mexico City, 1939–1940.

Presencia, Mexico City, 1949–1950.

República Española (Negrinist), Mexico City, 1942–1946.

Romance: Revista Popular Hispanoamericana, Mexico City, 1940–1941.

Rueca, Mexico City, 1941–1948.

Siempre, Mexico City, 1966–1968.

El Socialista (Negrinist-Socialist), Mexico City, 2d ser., 1942–1952.

Solidaridad Obrera (Anarchist), Mexico City, 1942–1946.

Taller, Poesía y Crítica, Mexico City, 1939–1941.

Tierra Nueva: Revista de Letras, Mexico City, 1940–1942.

Tierra y Libertad: Revista Anarquista, Mexico City, 1963–1966.

El Universal (Mexico City daily), Mexico City, 1939–1940.

Index

Centro Vasco: welcomes refugee Basques, 93–94

"Children of Morelia": 26–27, 41

Chile: receives Spanish exiles, 39

Christian Democrats: and Spanish workers, 139

Church, the: in Spain, and Second Spanish Republic, 4, 6, 8–9

Ciencia: achieves importance, 79

Círculo Cultural Jaime Vera: created, 120–121; seeks broader support, 121–122; and Giral government, 122

Civil War (1936–1939), the: ends Second Spanish Republic, 4–6; outbreak of, 12–13; internationalized, 13–14, 22–23; outcome of, forces activists into exile, 20, 21; affects publishing industry, 75

Clavileño: 176

Climent, Enrique: effect of exile on art of, 67

Club España: rejects refugees, 94

Club Mundet: 180

CNT. See Confederación Nacional de Trabajo

colegios: opening of, 84–85; as agent of Spanish acculturation, 85–87; increasing Mexican influence on, 87–88

Comas, Juan: researches Mexican subjects, 65

Comité de Ayuda a los Presos Españoles: work of, 132–133

Comité Técnico de Ayuda a los Españoles en México: evacuates refugees from France, 37–38; finances of, 48; figures of, on refugee distribution, 52–53; founds special schools, 84–85

Communists: and the Spanish Civil War, 5–6; influence of, in Spain, 14–15; and popular militias, 15–16; and *Las Españas*, 98; and the Ateneo Español, 101, 103; political views of, 108, 110; and Popular Front, 109; and Junta Española de Liberación, 111; in exile government, 115; and other organizations, 122, 123; and Republicans, 129–130; involved in Spanish opposition movements, 130–132; and non-Communist intellectuals, 133–135; and Anarchists, 136–137; and youth groups, 141, 142, 143; maintain separate Mexican and Spanish parties, 196. See also *Negrinistas*

Comunidad Ibérica: created, 140

Confederación de Trabajadores Mexicanos (CTM): split in, over refugee question, 44

Confederación Nacional de Trabajo (CNT): during Civil War, 10, 13; Communist suppression of, 16; excluded from Junta Española de Liberación, 111; and cooperation with anti-Franco groups, 135, 137; philosophy of, 136; strategy of, 138–140; split in, 140–141. See also Anarchists; syndicalists

Congreso Indigenista Interamericano: considers pro-Indian legislation, 156

Cornucopia de México: 158

Cortes, Spanish: and 1931 election, 6

Cosío Villegas, Daniel: and founding and establishment of Casa de España, 28–31, 203

Costa-Amic: created, 76

CTM. See Confederación de Trabajadores Mexicanos

Cuadernos Americanos: created, 78; purpose of, 159, 160

Cuba: receives Spanish exiles, 39

Cuba, the: transports Spanish refugees, 38

Cuesta, Jorge: on Mexican identity, 201

Cultura Gallega: 94

De Grasse, the: transports Spanish refugees, 38; arrival of, 50

Díaz, Porfirio: as symbol of reaction, 149

doctors: emigrate to Mexico, 70–71; placement of, in Mexican society, 71–73

Dominican Republic: receives Spanish exiles, 39

EDIAPSA: created, 76

Ediciones Libro-Mex: created, 76

educational reform: and the Spanish Republicans, 8

Eisenhower, Dwight: protest against, 142

El Colegio de México. See Casa de España

El Hijo Pródigo: 78, 159, 160, 176

El mexicano y lo mexicano: 65

El Popular: pro-Republican sympathies of, 44

El Socialista: on the UDE, 121

El Universal: on Spanish politicians, 52